Symbiosis

Symbiosis: Popular Culture and Other Fields

Edited by
Ray B. Browne
and
Marshall W. Fishwick

Bowling Green State University Popular Press
Bowling Green, Ohio 43403

Contents

Preface

Ray B. Browne

The study of popular culture—or perhaps we should say of popular culture*s*, with the singular *culture* signifying the generic summation of all the popular cultures in a society—has become an integral part of academia. The estimate in 1988 is that over a million and a half American students take a course, under one name or another, in the United States every year. And the number is growing rapidly. The study of popular culture is growing also, though at a somewhat less accelerated rate, in countries around the world, especially in England, France, Italy, West Germany, behind the Iron Curtain, in Australia, Japan, and Mexico, as well as in Latin American countries. In 1988 there are Popular Culture Associations in Japan and Mexico, and the number of these academic organizations is growing, though slowly.

The study of popular culture is mushrooming partially because by nature popular culture is protean and thus provides everybody interested in any aspect of culture, and especially of the humanities and social sciences, means by which to investigate new and important aspects of learning which in the past have been generally ignored. There is no doubt that popular culture permeates all aspects of life around us today as it has in the past. There is no doubt, either, that as the world moves, slowly or rapidly, toward some kind of control by the people—either through democracy or through the manipulation of the people by single individuals or totalitarian political systems—the cultures of those people become more and more important. People equal culture(s). A nation—and a world—is the sum of its cultures, and those cultures are the popular culture in its multifarious manifestations.

There is no need in this Preface to define popular culture because most of the essays in this book provide ample definitions as parts of their discussion. Let us just say that popular culture is the vernacular, everyday culture of the people, as opposed to the narrow elitist culture which artificially constitutes some ten percent of a nation's lifestyle. Some people in fact quite properly argue that the elite culture is also a part of the popular culture, since it constitutes a part of the total lifestyle of a people and remains close to the general trends no matter how much the elitists protest against inclusion and insist that their way of living is different from and superior to that of the general lifestyle of the nation.

i

ii   Symbiosis

The new thrust in popular culture studies is some twenty-five years old. As academics we need to try at this point to see where the rapid development of these studies over this quarter-century has brought us and where it is leading us. There is no doubt that these studies have led us into the direct and thorough investigation of most of the humanities and social sciences and is rapidly spreading into the natural sciences as well. What then are the implications of this great groundswell of interest in this particular aspect of academia?

For years many of us in popular culture studies wondered if the proper application of this concept should be the introduction of the approach, the popular culture point of view, into the many disciplines that constitute the humanities and social sciences in academia. Thus we suggested that a literary study of best-selling fiction, a sociological study of sports, a home-economics approach to fashion, a sociological/historical study of popular music, and the like across the board, could unearth many valid observations. The approach was indeed fruitful.

In literature, for example, the early work of Howard Vincent in such studies of Herman Melville's works as *The Trying-Out* of Moby-Dick (1947) and *The Tailoring of* White-Jacket, Henry Nash Smith's study of how the elitist Henry James learned to write by studying popular fiction, and researches into how James Joyce used popular culture in novels like *Ulysses* were fruitful but elementary. More sophisticated studies similar in approach have grown out of the earlier literary investigations. A current example is David S. Reynolds' *Beneath the American Renaissance: The Subversive Imagination in the Age of Emerson and Melville* (1988). In this book Reynolds thoroughly investigates the literary popular culture during the so-called American Renaissance and its effects on the leading literary figures of the time. Such probings are helpful but the approach and attitude used by Reynolds are skewed and condescending, thus to some extent invalidating the conclusions. Reynolds demonstrates how the literary figures Poe, Emerson, Thoreau, Hawthorne, Melville and Emily Dickinson took the popular material around them and "improved" it into "great" literature. He concludes:

Hawthorne and the other authors discussed in this book fully assimilated their popular culture only to transcend it through the affirmation of the suggestive and the subtly human. They struggled mightily with what James called the journalistic monster— the sprawling mass of nineteenth-century subliterature, much of it in newspaper or pamphlet form—and they learned much from the struggle. In particular, their deep engagement with the popular subversive themes and idioms supplied them with literary material. But they refused to sacrifice their artistic powers in the fight. Instead, they victoriously created literary works in which the monster of popular culture suddenly took on human aspect and lasting appeal. In different ways, they memorably reconstructed the popular subversive imagination.

Such a conclusion demonstrates that Reynolds and this school of literary commentators are looking into the popular culture for the wrong things and are abusing their findings, as far as the popular culture potentialities are concerned. Popular culture scholars—especially Leslie Fiedler—have been maintaining for years that popular culture is subversive, and is the building blocks which others use in their literary efforts. Reynolds and his point of view represent one attitude; popular culture scholars reflect another. It all depends on one's point of view. Reynolds is concerned with the "weakness," the "evil" in popular culture which must be "reconstructed"; the popular culture scholar generally is more concerned with the real vitality, the strength and importance of his material, not its putative crudeness and weakness.

So popular culture scholars are no longer content to leave their field of study in the hands of the conventional scholars no matter how massively they bring their research to bear. We are afraid of the bias, the point of view, the need of regular scholars to justify their fields of research and their careers. We are convinced that popular culture studies have their own theories and methodologies and that these should be carried into and be made integral parts of the investigations of the humanities and sciences. In other words, it is not sufficient to think of the various allied disciplines—say, history, literature, anthropology, sociology, music, home economics, law, philosophy, etc.—as needing to have their popular culture elements and dimensions recognized and studied. Rather it is imperative to have the basic theories and methodologies of popular culture studies made an integral part of the study of each of those particular disciplines, for popular culture is more integral than superficial. We need, thus, the popular culture approach to the study of literature rather than the literary study of popular literature; the popular culture-sociological study of sports rather than the sociological-popular culture approach to sports; the popular culture approach to various aspects of history rather than merely a historical study of what historian David Grimsted calls "neglected" aspects of history; the popular culture approach to the icons, rituals, taboos of present-day fundamentalistic religion rather than the investigation of fundamentalist religion. And so on. Most aspects of popular culture—and thus of life—have been "neglected" in the past. The appropriate way to study popular culture aspects of civilization is to encompass and include *all* aspects, not just those which now are recognized as having been "neglected" in the past. Popular culture is more than the sum of all "neglected" aspects of civilization.

The present collection of 21 essays is an effort to show the relationship of some 19 academic disciplines to popular culture. In the first three essays I try to show how popular culture is basically what the humanities have become or should be recognized as having become, how popular culture can and should easily be used as an incentive and a means for alleviating print illiteracy, and how popular culture studies in popular books need to be understood and promoted.

In the fourth essay, George Dove uses one genre in popular fiction—crime fiction—to work out a new theory and approach to that particular genre. In the next essay, Gary Edgerton discusses the popular culture method in film studies. And in the next essay, Paul Loukides discusses the stock elements of American feature films.

In the following essay, historian Carlton Jackson discusses historians' two possible approaches to their subject matter and suggests that the use of popular culture will be fruitful. Following that essay, James Combs demonstrates the uses of popular culture in political science studies, as does George H. Lewis in the following essay, switching to the field of sociology, in his paper entitled "Dramatic Conversations: The Relationship Between Sociology and Popular Culture.

In the following paper, Arthur Neal and Theodore Groat demonstrate how demography and popular culture studies are related. In the next Diane Raymond discusses the dependence of thorough studies in philosophy on popular culture, as does Peter Homans of the dependence of psychology on popular culture in his paper, "Psychology and Popular Culture: Psychological Reflections on *M*A*S*H*." This line of thought is continued in the two essays by Marshall Fishwick—"Communication and Popular Culture"—and Linda K. Fuller—"Systems-Theoretical Aspects of Popular Culture and Mass Communication."

Two areas that obviously tie in closely with popular culture and need more exploration follow: "Marxism and Popular Culture: The Cutting Edge of Cultural Criticism," by Michael Real; and "Post-Structuralism and Popular Culture," by David R. Shumway.

Three areas which might not immediately seem close to popular culture are investigated next: "Material Culture in a Popular Vein: Perspectives on Studying Artifacts of Mass Culture," by Beverly Gordon; "Where Architecture and Popular Culture Diverge," by Dennis Alan Mann; and "On Teaching Law and Popular Culture," by Anthony Chase. Their closeness to popular culture is amply demonstrated.

There is no doubt that popular culture properly studied must be international as well as inter-and multidisciplinary. Unfortunately not many scholars are at this time dedicated to the international study of popular culture. Many, indeed, study the popular culture of foreign countries. But they do not investigate the international and comparative aspects of cultures. That is an area that definitely needs immediate investigation. Toward that end, Bruce Daniels' essay, "International Approaches to Popular Culture: Possibilities, Problems, and an American/Canadian Example," casts a great deal of light.

Finally, so protean is the study of popular culture that many people are not content with definitions that have been forthcoming. In the last essay in the volume, Harold E. Hinds, Jr. suggests that "popularity," that is large numbers of users, is the bottom line in definitions of popular culture.

We have in these 21 essays demonstrations of the importance of popular culture studies in some 19 different areas, and how these areas rely on and can benefit from the interlinking with popular culture studies. Obviously, there are many fields in the humanities, social sciences—and even natural sciences—which are not covered. The most conspicuous ones are, of course, American Studies and folklore. But we have always felt that American Studies and folklore are so similar to the study of popular culture—broad and interdisciplinary—that the generalities valid for popular culture are equally valid for them. This collection of essays tells us much more.

What should become apparent is that popular culture studies are more than the sum of their parts. In other words, adding twenty-one examples of how popular culture can be used in various disciplines is not what this collection tells us.

Then what does the collection tell us? Does it give us some kind of hitherto unsuspected super popular culture theory and methodology? Something that covers all and is more inclusive and permeating than we suspected? No. What in effect it demonstrates is that our original theory about the nature and importance of popular culture studies still holds. But within that outer parameter there are sub-cultures. The number is almost too large to attempt to itemize: race, gender, games, ethnicity, music, architecture, art, fads, fashions, cartoons, finance, museums, sports, automobiles, "strips," humor, literature, drinks, dances, and on and on and on. Though diverse in nature and action all are manifestations of popular culture. Each can be studied from or by various disciplines. But each discipline generally stops well within the bounds of its training; most do not extrapolate into the beyond, what should be the implications and possible reaches of the studies.

That extrapolation—the implications—should be the subject and concern of popular culture studies. Ideally, at least, popular culture studies should be the common denominator that all these areas and methods of approaching and theorizing have. The popular culture is the symbiosis of all the fields, and therefore the most effective overall tool for analyzing and understanding a culture. Restriction of analysis to one "school" or "method" on theory twists, distorts and limits true reality.

For example, India is a very complex land of 750-950 languages and dialects and therefore cultures, depending on who is doing the counting. The people of that sub-continent are "Indian" at least in nationality. But all groups have strikingly different ways of living, of looking at the phenomena of life, of the things they have to look at. What they all have in common is their popular culture. That popular culture, so one Indian scholar asserts, is the one common theme that makes all of the peoples "Indian." It is the "Indianness" that the inhabitants of the Indian sub-continent possess. It is the "Indianness" of the people, of the nation, of the civilization. It rides above and through all the other manifestations of the "Indianness" that the nation possesses. It is the result of all the other attributes of the citizens, the core of their being. It is largely—if not only—through their popular culture that the Indians and their Nation can be understood. What obtains for India holds true to one degree or another, for all nations.

Although graphics are overly simplistic and generally inadequate, perhaps we can make one which will demonstrate the dynamics of popular culture. Our best symbol is a giant revolving wheel. At the center of the wheel lies human nature and expression. Radiating out from that hub are all the manifestations of that human nature and expression: art, architecture, literature, sports, games, gender differences, fads, fashions, music, dances, finances, rituals, heroes, religious practices, circuses, travel, etc. On the inside of the rim of the wheel are the various conventional academic areas and disciplines which have developed their own theories and methodologies for interpreting the various manifestations of life and culture: anthropology, art, literature, music, political science, sociology, philosophy, etc. As the wheel turns, the various interpretations achieved by these various disciplines are thrown out to the edge. During the turning of the wheel, the various areas of culture on the spokes slop over from their discrete areas and become mixed with all the others. As they are filtered through the various academic disciplines these cultural manifestations and their interpretations get further mixed.

Popular culture studies should constitute the outer realm of the revolving wheel, that portion where all the mixtures from the hub finally end up. Ideally, popular culture studies, careful of the mixture of all phenomena, should try through being a symbiosis of all cultures to achieve some understanding of the phenomena. Not that popular culture studies are going to be a court of last appeal, a superior order which will necessarily find "truth" in the various phenomena.

But popular culture studies, simply because they are the largest mixture of all the ways of looking at phenomena might arrive at more "reality" in these phenomena than the more discrete areas have. The popular culture approach is the omni and humanistic approach. The popular culture scholar and critic realizes that the most valid results of his/her investigation can be achieved if the critic mixes all the theories and methodologies of other disciplines using as much or as little as needed to see the phenomena from all sides and through all dimensions. This having been done, the omni theory develops naturally into what can best be seen as the "humanistic" approach. Since the sum total of all human motivation and action impinges somehow on the human experience, it stands to reason that the investigation which probes into that impingement tends to develop into the most comprehensive and revealing analysis. The most nearly comprehensive analysis, then, is that omni-humanistic investigation that is as broad as possible.

This popular culture approach to understanding and revealing the meaning of the human experience takes some of the confusion out of the spinning wheel of life because it is best able to see the streaks as they extend in the spinning circle, and make some sense out of them. At least such is the hope.

The spinning wheel continues to revolve and to move on, mixing in ever greater confusions the fluids of life. The task of the popular culture scholar is to photograph the swirl and then interpret the mixture. The task is not small. If it were there would be no real motivation for the human being to devote so much time to its resolution. But the accomplishment is bound to be more comprehensive and more insightful than that of the elitists, who despite every sign to the contrary continue bullheadedly to insist that the narrow elitist culture of developed countries is all important. So those people continue to tour the world in their carriages, believing that what they do and think really is significant and at the slightest sound of attack they draw those carriages into a defensive circle and walk in the inside while the world spins on outside the circle at 1000 miles an hour. The world and the outcome of the human experiment is too important to leave in the hands of such people. Reality demands more. Though scholars interested in popular culture studies might not have all the answers they at least have most of the questions. Their probings will be more than worthwhile and will continue to expand the realm of reality in their search for the full human experience.

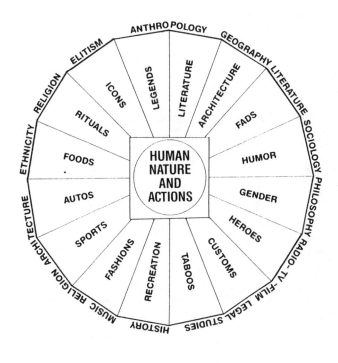

Popular Culture as the New Humanities

Ray B. Browne

The winds of change that swept across America during the Sixties finally breezed through academia and blew the dust off some of the concepts of what constitutes the ideal educational curriculum, and in so doing demonstrated the importance of the study of popular culture for both the academic and the non-academic worlds. This discovery was needed because now perhaps for the first time on so large a scale both groups are coming to realize that, like it or not, the popular culture of America is the force that has overwhelming impact on shaping our lives. The so-called "elite" or "minority" culture may have some influence according to the degree it is brought to the people and made applicable to their everyday lives. But the popular culture is already *with* the people, a part of their everyday lives, speaking their language. It is therefore irresistibly influential. What it is, the way it works and its relation to the other humanities need to be understood if we are to appreciate its overwhelming influence in our lives.

By the term "popular culture" we generally mean all aspects of the world we inhabit: the way of life we inherit, practice and pass on to our descendants; what we do while we are awake, the dreams we dream while asleep. It is the everyday world around us: the mass media, entertainments, diversions, heroes, icons, rituals, psychology, religion—our total life picture. Although it need not necessarily be, it is generally disseminated by the mass media, particularly since the middle of the nineteenth century.

Most important, the popular culture of a country is the voice of the people— their likes and dislikes, the lifeblood of daily existence, their way of life. In America presumably popular culture is the voice of democracy—what makes America the country she is. The culture may be manipulated in our day by the media barons—who may react too slowly to the voice of democracy (as revealed in the peculiar showings of the Nielsen ratings)—or by the society which may demand too much for the people who create their culture for them. Like it or not, every American owes it to himself and his society to make a great effort, through formal or informal study and analysis, to understand the culture around him or her. Often the student will discover, if he can rid himself or herself of blind prejudice, that much of the popular culture is to be appreciated.

Reprinted from *Journal of Popular Culture*, Spring 1984, Vol. 17, No. 4. Reprinted with permission.

1

Actually, of course, there is nothing new in studying popular culture, that is, the culture of the times. As the editors of the *Literary History of the United States* asserted: "Each generation must define the past [as well as the present] in its own terms." And if there is opposition to the new way of looking at the phenomena of life, that is only natural, as John G. Cawelti (in *The Six-Gun Mystique*) quite properly observed: "Whenever criticism feels the impact of an expanded sensibility [which often is tied in with a political thrust] it becomes shot through with ideological dispute."

The political thrust is particularly sensitive at this time. The humanities as the football of political bias and self-interest generally continue to get redefined according to the political attitude running the show. Apparently not knowing or caring about real or objective definitions, the National Endowment for the Humanities, for example, the one institution in the United States that has a vital role in the humanities, has always bent its definition to fit that of the chairman and the politician in charge of the White House. Three administrations ago, Ronald Berman, as Chairman, was an avowed snob despite the fact that he had been the speech writer for Spiro Agnew, who made much political hay railing against the effete elitists of the East Coast; Berman obviously pleased president Nixon, again in a strange way since Nixon was so strongly against the Eastern elite group. The next Chairman, Joseph Duffy, reflecting the political attitude of Jimmy Carter, tried to redefine the humanities in a somewhat different way. As a graduate of Yale University he had been trained into foreswearing his West Virginia coal-mining background, but he finally learned that there is no reason to find his childhood antithetical to a true meaning of the humanities. In his speech before the Congress at his nomination, Duffy said that he felt "There need be no issue of a separated elite as against popular participation" in the humanities. "The work of the humanistic conversation should by its nature be spread into every part and region of the country."

The present Chairman, William J. Bennett, however, has swung decidedly back to the elitist side. Mr. Bennett is either confused about proper definitions or depends entirely upon his own interpretations. For example, in a speech last year to the National Federation of State Humanities councils, he laid down four commandments. He allowed that "in pursuing the goal of fostering a better understanding of the humanities on the part of the public, there are boundaries that may not be crossed, no matter how imaginatively." Two of the commandments are paradoxical:

1. "You may not ignore the humanities.
2. "You may not trivialize the humanities."

To call efforts to broaden and modernize the humanities movements to trivialize them is a peculiar attitude that only an intellectual could take. These two commandments are mutually contradictory and they lead to negative and far-reaching results. For example, now in 1984 the National Endowment for the Humanities is calling upon the academic community to study the

Constitution and America in a Bicentennial Celebration. One would think that this interest in the impact of the Constitution upon American life would include all levels. But apparently not. The NEH Bicentennial Commission told one person who applied for a grant to hold a convention on the impact of the Constitution on American Popular Culture that this kind of material was not worthy of support; the people in Washington interested in the Constitution and this Bicentennial Celebration are Constitutional lawyers and serious historians, and they are not interested in the America of common people.

The fifty local state humanities councils which have been created to bring the Humanities to the state level vary sharply among themselves in the matter of definitions and projects they encourage and support. Though confused by the signals that come from Washington they tend to be a little less elitist than the national office. All, however, both the Washington headquarters and the state offices are more elitist than the National Endowment for the Arts, though uninformed logic would tend to suggest that the NEA should be far more elitist than the NEH. Perhaps the political manipulations of the humanities, since the humanities are hard to define, are understandable, something we have to live with.

It is more difficult, however, to understand the attitudes of some academics in well-established disciplines and areas of study who at least profess interest in forming the cutting edge of thinking and innovation. Ideologically based and apparently thoroughly rationalized, the academic groups when off the mark can be mischievous. They often masquerade as "friends" to re-evaluated and relevant definitions when in fact they are antagonists and adhere to old, elitist and questionable definitions and attitudes that do the humanities much harm.

This attitude takes all kinds of turns in different directions, sometimes aided and abetted by the NEH and other foundations. For example the summer NEH seminars for "Humanities in the Schools: Programs for Teachers and Administrators" for 1984 contain disturbing aspects. The announcement—and remember this is for public school teachers—is pretentiously presented with the cover elaborately displaying quotations from Plato—*in Greek*—Cicero—*in Latin*— and Thomas Jefferson. Roughly translated Plato's dictum says, "Knowledge depends on what you study," or perhaps more accurately, "If you don't understand what has gone before in context you remain uneducated." Cicero's statement says something like "Understand in context what happened before your time if you do not want to remain naive." Jefferson's quotation is the often-used, "If a nation expects to be ignorant and free, in a state of civilization, it expects what never was and never will be." No one would disagree with the aptness of the quotations, though Plato, we should remember, was the elitist who referred to the common people of his time as "oxen," and the Greek and Latin phrases are pretentious for most public school teachers; they would surely have been more effective in English. But apparently the purpose of the humanities, at least as seen by the NEH, is to mystify and impress more than to enlighten and lead. And undoubtedly there have been people since the Romans, other than Jefferson, who had apt things to say about the humanities.

Further, some of us might well disagree with the NEH's definition of the humanities relevant for American school teachers and through them children of the 1980s as revealed in the seminars that are to be held in 1984. Some of the subjects are "The English Heritage from Chaucer to Pope," "Shakespeare: The State of the Art," "Shakespeare in Production" and "An Institute on Homer's *Odyssey*." I would suggest that anybody outlining these courses as the most appropriate in the humanities for our public schools in this decade is going to have a hard time steering our humanities programs between the Scylla and Charybdis of elitism and conservatism and will, deliberately or not lose us, as Odysseus was lost, in the eastern Mediterranean of old and dead ideas.

That there are stirrings of discontent and questioning can be seen in various statements by directors of the state NEH groups. One of the more cogent is that of Alan J. Shusterman, who writing an essay called "Plain Folks and Fancy Reading" in College English pointed out the damage done by authors of so-called "signature" art in their willful effort to write away from its general public. His hesitant conclusion leans toward an enlightened attitude about the new humanities: "Provided that a popular test is not made into an object for categorization or scorn, a skillful and unassuring teacher can use it to move to analysis of culture, dramatic method, historical analogues, or sometimes critical techniques." Such an attitude is surely a suggestion in the right direction.

As an antidote to such poison many critics of today, on the bases of some commonsense observations and assumptions, are modifying their attitudes toward the arts and culture. Susan Sontag, for example, in an often-quoted statement observed in *Against Interpretation*, "One cheats oneself as a human being if one has respect only for the style [and the content, presumably] of high culture." Roger Rollin, writing in the *Journal of Popular Culture*, argued against any form of evaluation. To him the only real authority about beauty and excellence is not the critic but the people, especially in the popular arts. In literature, he points out, the rule is "one person—one vote." Popular culture represents the triumph of the democratic esthetic. Mark Twain, Rollin might have reminded us, was proud of the fact that whereas Henry James wrote for the select few, he, Mark Twain, wrote for the millions.

All works of art—from the least pretentious to the grandest "elite"—differ not in kind but in degree. All exist on a continuum that can perhaps be best described as a flattened ellipsis somewhat like the CBS logo. On the right end is folk art, on the left end (both politically and creatively) is the so-called "signature" art. Between the two—occupying perhaps 80% of the scale—is popular art. Between the three types there are no clear lines of distinctions, only grey areas overlapping each other, one growing out of and merging into another. In all areas along this continuum, there is a vertical scale of esthetic accomplishment. Some folk creations are strong and effective, some are weak. In "elite" there are some strong statements and some weak.

Undoubtedly the largest range of strengths and weaknesses lies in the popular area, because there are far more attempts here by people with widely varying ranges of talent. But it is a grave mistake to assume that all creators of the popular arts achieve no worthwhile standards. Many do indeed. Stephen Foster's songs, for example, to a large majority of Americans are more nearly immortal than are those of Frederic Chopin. Huck Finn's path in life will always be of much greater significance than Lambert Strether's, *Uncle Tom's Cabin* a more moving statement about the downtrodden than William Dean Howells' *Annie Kilburn* is or ever was.

Students of popular culture and the popular arts keep constantly in mind the function of the democratic arts, a point which sometimes disturbs "elite" critics. The popular arts are almost always pragmatic and functional. Alan Gowans, in *The Unchanging Arts*, perhaps says it most succinctly: "To know what art is, you must define what it *does*. You can define art only in terms of function. High art historically grew out of low art, and the functions of low art have remained unchanged throughout history." The function is to get something done—to convert the sinner, to explicate the human form, to say something about human experience—yes, to sell soap. Debating about esthetic accomplishments without keeping these purposes and functions in mind is to center on only part of the object's purpose and accomplishment.

The popular arts are more and more being equated with the humanities, or what could more properly be called "The New Humanities," as the realization grows that the conventional humanities have probably not succeeded in their function, and because acceptance of popular culture as the "New Humanities" arises from the ever-widening belief that in a democracy the democratic institutions, as well as the ordinary people, should be a main focus of attention and study. The humanities must include the arts. Historically, many academics—as well as non-academics—have looked upon the humanities and the study of a whole culture from an elite point of view. They have insisted that the humanities teach us how to live life most fully but have treated the humanities as though they were designed exclusively for the educationally and financially privileged and were to be denied to the ordinary taxpayer.

The "New Humanists" believe that this traditional elitist point of view is tunnel-visioned and myopic, and that it is misleading to study artistic creations as though the creators lived in a vacuum, oblivious to and unaffected by the society around them.

These "New Humanists" are or ought to be all-inclusive in their interests, then, because popular culture by definition has wide parameters and multiple purposes, and can comment on virtually every aspect of life. Russel Nye, for example, states, in *The Unembarrassed Muse*, a major study of the popular arts in America: "The study of popular culture, done seriously and with proper purpose and methodology, can open up new areas of evidence which can contribute greatly to what we know about the attitudes, ideas and values of a society at a given place or time; in so doing, we find a broader and deeper understanding of our society."

In studying and trying to understand a culture—drawing forth its humanities—the act of comprehending the precise and literal details in which the creator worked tends to clothes and enrich the object, giving it in the real sense of the word the humanistic truth that it could not otherwise have. Many of the works of popular culture may not be esthetically pleasing, to be sure. Neither are many elite works, especially until age and custom and elite persuasion have made them familiar and valuable. But in cultural studies esthetic value is irrelevant, beside the point. Esthetic value must be looked upon as a pleasing bonus if it is present, but by no means necessary. In fact, sometimes esthetic value can be the cause of much danger. D.G. Griffith's *The Birth of a Nation* (1915), for example, became a dangerous movie, with overwhelming aftereffects of racism, because it was esthetically pleasing. Contemporary so-called Plantation Novels, in the tradition of *Mandingo*, have no esthetic qualities, to most people at least, yet apparently they satisfy some deep-felt need of many present-day readers, which though it might be repugnant to most of us, is obviously of value to them, and we need to be aware of that appeal. The fact is that both so-called "signature" and popular artists are, each in his or her own way, merely trying to pin their names to the bulletin boards of history. They are striving not to be forgotten after death. The question of the esthetic value is then the total effect of the item itself—and its value involves far more than its esthetic quotient.

The Popular Humanities do most of the job of perpetuating a culture, as T.S. Eliot recognized years ago in crying out against popular books: "I incline to come to the alarming conclusion," he wrote in *Essays Ancient and Modern*, "that it is just the literature that we read for 'amusement' or 'purely for pleasure' that may have the greatest...least suspected...earliest...influence upon us. Hence it is that the influence of popular novelists, and of popular plays of contemporary life, require to be scrutinized." It is both ironic, and somehow appealing, that, like Shakespeare in the electronic age, Eliot has come to be known and appreciated most widely by the people he feared and despised in the stage production of his work *Cats*. Richard Hoggart, one of today's leading English social observers, comments, in a typical British understatement, "Literature at all levels has the unique capacity to increase our understanding of a culture." It is an attitude increasingly recognized by people of all esthetic bias. For example, Thomas Hoving, former executive director of the New York Metropolitan Museum of art and chief editor of *Connoisseur* magazine, told Nancy Shulins, an AP Newsfeature Writer, in an article dated March 11, 1984, "There's a role for it [popular culture], no question. It's not the culture I care much about. But if we had examples of it from Pericles' Athens, we'd certainly be better off."

The so-called works of amusement and pleasure, as Eliot referred to them, exert their overwhelming influence because all of us come unavoidably into contact with them daily. They present in simple and therefore usable ways the ideas of the time. Often the ideas are oversimplified and may be relatively unimportant singly and individually. We therefore are inclined to look down upon them, despite the fact that we all at least pay lip service to the hypothesis that in order to live most fully we need to include as much of life as possible. Yet we frequently concentrate on—or claim to be interested in—only what we call or have been told is the important. As A.O. Lovejoy remarked in his book *The Great Chain of Being*, many of us are not interested in ideas unless they come to us dressed in full warpaint, when in fact it is the small ideas or the accumulation of them that is important.

Actually in the seeming gap between what might be called "elite" and "popular" humanities there is no break whatsoever, as Robert Coles, psychologist and Pulitzer Prize winner, recognizes: "The humanities," he says, "belong to no one kind of person; they are part of the lives of ordinary people, who have their own various ways of struggling for coherence, for a compelling faith, for social vision, for an ethical position, for a sense of historical perspective," for a meaning—a *raison d'etre* in life.

Richard Hoggart, speaking in a larger context, said essentially the same thing: "The closer study of mass society may make us have sad hearts at the supermarket, but at the same time it may produce an enhanced and tempered sense of humanity and humility, instead of the sense of superiority and separateness that our traditional training is likely to have encouraged."

Leslie Fiedler perhaps pushes this reasoning to its logical conclusion because he believes that popular culture can achieve man's greatest challenge, that of bringing us all together again. The popular culture—or popular humanities—then, given their way, can unite us into a community which existed before people became separated by class, education, interests and desires. This function might be especially appropriate for television, with its completely democratic audience, which tends to relegate Gutenberg obsolete and to promote visual culture, the oldest kind, and with it an oral community which is broader and more democratic than the world of print, with its few but real limitations. In this world John Ball's lines in his speech at Blackheath to the men in Wat Tyler's rebellion have a ringing pertinence: "When Adam delved and Eve span / Who was then a gentleman?"

A late voice to speak out on the need for a new look at education and for the humanities—and generalists—was Ernest L. Boyer, former U.S. Commissioner of Education, in "Toward a New Core Curriculum" (published in the *NEA Advocate*, April/May 1978). He addresses the point that Hoggart was discussing, coming down hard on those educationists who speak about "liberal versus vocational" education to the disparagement of the latter. "Education," he insists, "has always been a blend of inspiration and utility, but because of tradition, lethargy, ignorance and snobbery, mindless distinctions are made between what is vocationally legitimate and illegitimate." In a reversion to what must seem to many a dangerous respect of Ben Franklinism, Boyer insists that the work ethic should play a strong role in the true meaning of liberal education. His remarks obviously parallel and attack the assumed distinctions between "elite" and popular humanities.

With or without Boyer's emphasis on the work ethic, no one in the New Humanities would suggest that investigation of popular culture replace the traditional humanities where those can be demonstrated to be valuable, where they can prove their worth. Or that the study of popular phenomena and culture be blind in celebration rather than keen analysis. Such studies must deserve the same care and precision as any other area in the humanities. Any other attitude would be non-intellectual and bound to defeat the purpose of education.

But, on the other hand, there is no question that it is imperative that the old concepts be tested and modified to incorporate new approaches, new definitions and new areas of subject matter. Otherwise the Humanities—in all their ramifications—will be proved misguided and generally inadequate to present-day needs and possibilities. Maybe it will be found that the "eternal truths" that the Humanities are supposed to reveal will be found to have more effective spokespersons in sources that have not been recognized in the past.

This means that there should be no sacred domains among the old humanities. They must periodically be asked to revalidate themselves, and if they cannot they must be retired until rejuvenated. Doubtless many of the workhorses should be given sabbaticals. The present-day classroom—and research desk—is the one place that cannot afford to become a museum of dead ideas and concepts. None of us ought to be willing to go "back to basics" in anything, as the blind cry of conservatives is today, or *back* to anything, especially to the humanities. At least we should insist on going *"forward"* to new basics. *Basics* to any kind of life move irreversibly forward.

Such a statement need not get anybody's back up. It is not a condemnation of what we have done in the past, it does not invalidate anybody's life's work, anybody's literary or artistic loves, even anybody's evaluations of esthetically commendable or contemptible materials. Rather it is a call for intellectuals and other people interested in studying and understanding American life and culture, in its broadest and richest sense, to become broader-viewed, more openminded and less exclusive. Nobody says one has to approve or like all the "great" works of the arts of the past or of the present; we have our personal Nielson-like ratings evaluating them from 1-10. Only people in the humanities or the arts act under the assumption that we must like what we work on and work on only those things we like; the scientists, to our betterment, do not restrict their interests to the "good" things in life. It is foolish for us to pull an ostrich-like hiding of the head and be unaware of the winds that sweep our bodies while the thinking part is in the sand. Such an attitude is not only self-defeating; it is dangerous to one's own and the culture's well-being, because in truth American culture continues to grow and develop in its own way pretty much irrespective of intellectuals' approval or disapproval, though sometimes the progress is in spite of the disapproval. Intellectuals may long for the return of the train as a romantic way to travel, and the typewriter as the perfect machine to write on, but the satellite if flying well and the word processor is on many kids' desks.

The academic's tendency is to be rather open-minded while he doesn't know much and doesn't have much to defend. But as he or she gets more and more specialized he tends more and more to be proprietary and protective over what he knows, apparently in developing such an attitude fulfilling a deep-felt need within himself to justify what he is doing. Often we turn off our listening button and on our broadcast button too soon. We learn to "profess" exclusively while we should still be learning while professing. Such a one-way activity is indeed dangerous, for it is self-defeating. We should remember that Josh Billings, one of our insightful humorists of the 19th century reminded us: "It ain't the things we don't know that makes such fools of us, but a whole lot of things that we know that ain't so." We should always keep an open mind about the valuable things we know and the worthwhile attitudes we hold. Otherwise we insult our intelligence and jeopardize the natural and peaceful development of culture and mankind.

To paraphrase Lincoln, the Elitists can fool some of the people all of the time and all of the people some of the time, but they cannot fool all the people all the time. As they try to fool society in general, the only ones they really fool are themselves. They are like the emperor who struts around making people think that his clothes are superior when in fact he is not wearing any. Although Elitists through time continually change their statements about their clothes, history always recognizes the fraud and convicts them of indecent exposure.

The regrettable aspect of the process is that history moves slowly and is mainly accurate in retrospect only. The preachments of the elitist should be recognized contemporaneously for what they are. We cannot wait for the future to inscribe what we already know—that the elitists were pushing points of view out of self-interest and that these points of view represented generally only what they believed or pretended to believe; such nonsense surely did not represent a consensus.

A society that reads its present and future exclusively or mainly by looking backwards through a mirror needs to re-examine its orientation. Instead a society needs to look around at the various aspects and trusts in their contemporary world. For academics a proper examination is the numerous other fields of inquiry going on around them. There is a symbiotic relationship between popular culture and these many other fields of investigation. It is the obligation and opportunity of all fields to discover the potential richness to be found in this symbiotic relationship and to exploit it.

Popular Culture:
Medicine for Illiteracy
and Associated Educational Ills

Ray B. Browne

Statistics on the rising tide in functional illiteracy in the United States are staggering. Some reports indicate 13% of Americans are not literate. Other figures state more precise numbers: 20-27 million Americans are "seriously illiterate," 40 million are "marginally illiterate" and 4 million adults are studying to learn to read and write. Even if all these figures are too high, on a personal level, illiteracy is crushing. Young people as well as older persons are intimidated by their illiteracy and the fact that the literate condescend to them. Sometimes the reaction is violent. Young people fight and kill when insulted about their illiteracy. British crime-writer Ruth Rendell centered one of her novels on a housekeeper who was illiterate and flashed out and murdered her employers because they kept leaving her notes that she could not read. Society, as well as the individual, is deeply and seriously wounded by the illiteracy of its citizens. Thomas Jefferson quite properly felt that a country cannot have a democracy if its citizens are not literate.

In a world of such mischief created by illiteracy, it is time that educators turned to radical cures for this disease and its fellow-horsemen of a potential apocalypse, school drop-outs, indifference to education and under-education (fade-outs) if they can be found. As many of us have been pointing out for years, such a radical cure is available in the educational value to be found in popular culture.

Popular culture is the practical—pragmatic—Humanities. So it can be used as a tool to assist us in education. It can be utilized in many ways to overcome illiteracy, to keep people in school, to encourage life-long learning and to energize our educational system and the materials we teach.

As a healthy preamble it can be used to counter the hocus-pocus of academia that presents literacy—and education in general—as a magic that one can achieve only after a long and arduous investment of time and labor. This pretentiousness quite understandably puts many people off. The current, 1987, business of celebrating the Bicentennial of the U.S. Constitution is an excellent case in point. In one effort, the Commission on the Bicentennial Educational Grant Program has recently solicited grant applications for "the development of instructional materials on the Constitution and Bill of Rights" for use in elementary and secondary schools because there is a "lack of citizen knowledge

Reprinted from *Journal of Popular Culture*, Winter 1987, Vol. 21, No. 3. Reprinted with permission.

about the Constitution and American history." To correct this lack of knowledge, the Commission proposes funding institutes where thirty or more social science teachers will be taught by "two Constitutional scholars" giving a series of lectures and being aided by two "master teachers." Note the language: "two Constitutional scholars" and two "master teachers." Now everybody knows that words and labels are cheap and meaningless. But a great deal of harm can be done when a government agency is so pretentious that they set about teaching tax-paying citizens—not to mention public school teachers—about *our* governing document in such phony language. Paternalism does indeed die hard. Apparently the educators in Washington still do not want the people in this country to understand the Constitution on their own. It must be spoon-fed by Constitutional scholars and Constitutional historians. Perhaps it might be threatening to have people understand the Constitution rationally in the light and language of 1987. Undoubtedly the Constitution, like education in general, could profit by a little less pretentiousness surrounding it. That is, it should be viewed in its popular culture setting, in the setting of the people whose life it guides and controls.

Popular culture is the everyday lifeblood of the experiences and thinking of all of us: the daily, vernacular, common cultural environment around us all, the culture we inherit from our forebears, use throughout our lives and then pass on to our descendants. Popular culture is the television we watch, the movies we see, the fast food, or slow food, we eat, the clothes we wear, the music we sing and hear, the things we spend our money for, our attitude toward life. It is the whole society we live in, that which may or may not be distributed by the mass media. It is virtually our whole world.

Though popular culture is to many people the monster that has caused the problems of functional illiteracy and lack of interest in solid education in the first place, it is really—viewed disinterestedly—merely an environment, a force, a background and foreground and a means of communication and entertainment. It can and should be used as a key to open the possibilities of proficiency in the use of conventional language, especially by those whose use of the language of the media—the main disseminating force of popular culture—is very high but whose utilization of the printed word is generally weak and undeveloped.

The principle I am proposing is that pragmatically one begins with the known and proceeds to the unknown, that one uses what he/she already knows in order to learn something unknown. I propose that educators, recognizing this principle, use it in getting people of all degrees of proficiency and unproficiency in the printed word to expand their capabilities.

That the popular culture around us is known, that it occupies most of the time of nearly all of us and that therefore properly channelled it can be the single most powerful force to encourage and drive people toward a goal seems to go without saying. The sticking point will be in getting interested people on all levels of education to accept popular culture as a worthwhile and effective tool in teaching instead of as a distracting and weakening diversion, and in motivating them to act on this knowledge. In education, as elsewhere, we all need scapegoats to lay the blame on for faults we see in society and what we might secretly admit is our own failings to accomplish the jobs we would like to achieve. To paraphrase Lincoln, if we would make some progress in a task, we must first recognize the means by which the progress might be made, and then we should persevere in our goals. I suggest that we know that experience has taught us that in the teaching business we proceed from the known to the unknown, that we use every device we can in that teaching process, that the popular culture around us is well known, and that therefore we should use it as educational devices in promoting literacy and love of education and learning.

Popular culture is in fact being used successfully in many areas, especially among pre- and early-schoolers in the highly useful *Sesame Street* and *Mr. Rogers' Neighborhood*, and in numerous computer and non-computer children's games which are teaching children vocabulary and simple sentences. It is also being used in the continued education of senior citizens. What is involved is basically the rudiments of communication. Once the basics have been established, the same principles should be used to build more vocabulary, more complicated sentences and more sophisticated communication. In other words, the popular culture can be used to establish the basics of communication and, as I shall argue later on, in the continued growth of literacy, sophisticated communication and to lure people into a love of learning and education. In other words, I am suggesting that popular culture can be a kind of textbook for beginners in all fields of learning. It can begin at the beginning. It can develop into all kinds of sophistication, and it can spur interest in every aspect of life and learning known to man and woman.

The beauty of using the popular culture is the motivation it provides if it is used as a spur to learning instead of an end in itself. Sometimes the tendency is to use the popular culture as a goal, as entertainment, but it is very easy to switch from entertainment to instruction, from passive acceptance of communication to participatory communication, if educators merely make the effort.

Some people in the television medium recognize this potential and are willing to put their money where their mouth is. Bill Moyers, for example, in 1987 gave up a lucrative position with CBS and settled with PBS for one-tenth his CBS salary because he wanted to do more "think" pieces for television. As reported by the Associated Press, April 26, 1987, Moyers said, "Television is a wonderful medium for teaching, as Mister Rogers has proved, as MacNeil-Lehrer has proved, as any carefully crafted documentary proves. It's a wonderful medium for teaching." Moyers essentially summed up the educator's opinion when he said: "The world is endlessly fascinating, and journalists are beachcombers permitted on the shores of other people's ideas and experiences, and they're all around you."

The lure of popular culture to people is constantly brought to our attention. Children spend more time watching television than they do in the classroom. Add to this all the extra time they spend absorbing popular music, eating, dressing, going to the movies, talking about all these activities, and you have most of every day of most people's lives. That is, popular culture is a constant classroom in which education can take place virtually eighteen hours a day. The trick is to make passing the time of our lives, of entertainment, into an educational exercise. All people like to be entertained. The literate and sophisticated want to be entertained, the illiterate want to be entertained. The entertainment of the literate does not differ much in kind from that of the illiterate, only in degree. Both kinds of people want desperately to communicate, and the communication of both does not differ in kind, only in "sophistication." Generally speaking, both have the same experiences in our everyday culture. They go to the same movies, watch the same television, sing the same songs, share the eating and dressing experiences. We are all locked in the America of our day. It seems logical therefore that the literate and the illiterate use the experiences they share, the motivations they have in common, to bring both groups together in communication and shared American life.

We have always prided ourselves on being a practical people. America has always been the land of the tinkerer, the craftsman, the people who can do things, build tall buildings, develop faster means of communication. People have always developed skills because they have seen those skills as being practical and useful. The much-vaunted high literacy rate of the nineteenth century in America developed because people needed to communicate, wanted to develop a sense of community, longed to rise in the social and financial world, and realized that the proper way to accomplish those goals was through the leading communication medium of the time—the printed word.

Despite what may at times seem to be the contrary, Americans still want to communicate; they yearn to develop a sense of community, and they surely lust after social and fiscal upward mobility. Communication among people is more desperately needed today than it has ever been before. In a world which seems forever fragmenting into more and more islands of interest and abilities, people simply are yearning to find the ties that bind them together. Everybody is searching for bonding with other people.

Few people in the United States today are not able to understand and communicate in some of the various media of popular culture. Some cannot handle the printed word but can easily understand and use the various other symbols promulgated by the media. Since literacy is a term which applies only to an old-fashioned technology, we should expand the term to include the ability to understand and use the vocabularies and structures of other media, the symbols of communication such as television, radio, movies, popular music, rapping, jiving, fashions, vernacular architecture, fast foods, etc. That is, *literacy* should include *mediacy*.

One becomes proficient in the communication symbols because one needs to. So it has always been. In the folk community, people learned to communicate because it was necessary. They learned the visual media—home and community activities, farming, everyday needs and means—because they realized that the visual media contained elements that they needed to understand in order to get along.

It is likewise easily demonstrable to the populace at large today that they need to understand and be able to communicate the symbols used in everyday communication in media other than those in which the communication occurs. In our compartmentalized world, the media tend to create islands of in-groups which can understand and communicate in a specific language without being able to communicate outside that particular group. Such people are *mediate*—that is, can understand the language of a particular medium—but may not be able to handle other languages and specifically not the printed word, the one language common to them all. Thus several "languages" may be requisite for communication.

The lure to be held out for people learning other languages of communication can be entirely pragmatic, selfish and self-serving. One gets along better and more easily in life, one gets farther ahead, one becomes happier if he/she understands and uses the dominant symbols of communication, which at this time happen to be the written word.

An excellent case in point was the ability of Americans to use the dominant means of communication in the middle of the nineteenth century. Although only 60% of adult Britons were literate in 1851, over 90% of America's white population was. There were many forces driving Americans toward literacy—the need for family cohesion, the church, schools, etc—but the main ones were, of course, private: ambition, loneliness, hunger for knowledge and self-improvement. People did not learn to read and write primarily because they were told to. They learned because it was demonstrated to be for their personal benefit.

But for the past fifty years or so, it has not been demonstrable that the only—even the preferred—way of getting ahead in America is through the print medium. Technology has invented new means of one's surviving—even flourishing—and has provided people with choices. They could become literate or remain illiterate in the conventional medium yet still get ahead.

Many people have chosen illiteracy because the road to literacy in the conventional medium has seemed too difficult to accomplish. The seeming difficulty of achieving literacy in the printed word is, of course, an illusion, often created by people who for one reason or another thought and taught that it was difficult, in other words promulgated by people who themselves had an entirely false notion of what literacy is and does.

Literacy is a democratic tool available to and usable by all. It develops in and is expanded by the latest tools of democracy, that is the latest gadgets of technology. The printed word was, after all, printed by technology. Now there are other technological tools developed which promote different kinds of literacy, in other words *mediacy*. No longer is the printed word the key to survival. Television, movies, music, and all the other manifestations of the culture around us, are reestablishing an oral and visual culture in which literacy in the printed word is not absolutely necessary. Naturally the clash between the old and the new is traumatic.

What we have is one technology pushing out another and older technology, with the practitioners of the old clinging to it because they have not worked out a way to manage and manipulate the new. Practitioners of print literacy have reason to recognize the force of the new technology. The cost in emotional and financial terms to change from print technology to electronic technology will be staggering. It is hard to imagine a world that is visually and symbolically, and numbers, oriented, pretty much devoid of conventional printed words, depending on a different kind of mediacy. We can hardly imagine and cope with a world that uses the standard means of communication flashed on the computer screen. How can we even contemplate a world that virtually ignores the old forms of literacy? The answer is of course that the clash is made to seem more dangerous than it really is. There are around us several worlds of communication and all are compatible, all can be interfaced, can speak to one another. Scientists and mathematicians, musicians and medical doctors, operate in the worlds of symbols peculiar to their trade while at the same time living in the world of the printed word. But the mutual incomprehensibility among the several jargons creates areas of expertise, and one that suffers most is the area of composition-literacy.

It is a peculiar fallacy that has become almost a truism that says that educators in composition-literacy are the ones who are responsible for developing that competency because effective composition equals literacy, or that literacy comes only with artful composition. So other educational departments that use literacy as a tool in their communication often opt out of the teaching of literacy because they were not formally trained and therefore feel themselves not competent to teach and develop composition-literacy, a feeling of inadequacy historically promoted by composition teachers. Such teachers, having installed themselves as sovereign in the teaching of literacy, have pretty much shamed members of other literate groups into withholding their assistance. Professors of history, sociology, technology, dance, education, etc., may not be able to write sentences which please their colleagues in English departments, but they communicate. Responsibility for keeping English as the coin of the realm is theirs also. After all, their sons and daughters need to communicate. On Spaceship Earth we all communicate or we fly off course. But when the English departments try to enlist the assistance of their colleagues in other departments, often they are met with shrugs of the shoulders: Literacy is somebody else's problem.

To a real degree, the English departments have caused their own trouble. Historically, teachers of composition-literacy have worked under the assumption that they are out to train people to craft well-turned, grammatically correct and graceful sentences, paragraphs and essays. This attitude was built on the assumption that in order to recognize and appreciate great literature, one must be able to write "great" compositions. In other words one writes like the "masters," imitating them in style as well as thought.

Such reasoning is flawed from the beginning. In the first place there may be some correlation between the ability to write the well-crafted sentence and essay and the appreciation of "great" literature, but the relationship is vague and tenuous. The refutation is glaringly and embarrassingly self-evident; most literary scholars, who probe most deeply into the meanings of literature, write anything but the well-crafted and graceful sentence and paragraph. They manage to communicate, but not much more.

Secondly, it is a misassumption to believe that literacy equals grace and charm in expression. Literacy-communication equals only the ability to string together a group of words that convey meaning. Teachers who do not admit this definition are doing themselves, their students and literacy a great disservice.

The purpose of all media is communication. Electronic media communicate very well. As a medium of communication, television is not a "vast wasteland" not a "boob tube," nor a "glass teat," as people have variously called it. Nor is the medium of rock music pornographic. Other manifestations of popular culture are not evil forces trying to destroy civilization merely for the riches of unprincipled people. Some people may use them for devious and dangerous purposes. But like computers, television and music, and other media, are merely means of communication that demand "literacy," that are perhaps more important than, and surely just as natural as, the printed word, and—worse yet to some people—will ultimately replace the printed word. In other words, the *mediacy* of the new media of communication will eventually replace that of the old. The guardians of the old-style "literacy" can go with the flow or be washed over by it.

Washed over by it they will be, provided the keepers of the conventional literacy do not realize the threat and adjust to it. There seem to be two choices: keepers of the conventional literacy can use the communication capabilities of the other media and in so doing maintain literacy for all people in the conventional printed word; or ignore and despise the more advanced electronic media and in so doing guarantee the continued erosion of conventional literacy in the present forms and eventually its disappearance or anachronistic status as a minority practice. It is conceivable that a hundred years from now—or even less—conventional literacy in language will have disappeared because it is no longer useful to the general public.

That is not to say, however, that users of the conventional literacy must capitulate to the new, even before it has arrived. On the contrary. But it should be to our interests to realize that the finest tool in the retention of the old form of literacy is in fact the very electronic media that might eventually replace it. That is, the best way to retain the old literacy is to use the popular media and the popular culturing they disseminate as a means of teaching it.

People interested in promoting written literacy should understand that experiencing anything gives a basis for communicating. Communication is analogical. One experiences something in one medium, becomes interested, and wishes to have similar experiences in other media. One "reads" something in television and turns to the medium of print in order to supplement his knowledge, excitement and enjoyment. Unfortunately, of course, one who is excited by television or some other electronic medium frequently is denied access to the treasures of the printed word because he does not understand it.

Here is where the promoter of written communication can take advantage of the media. All forms of communication in the modern vernacular world can be springboards for conventional literacy. The key is getting people to realize that the printed word is the common language—the *lingua franca*—that they all need.

The electronic media provide access to and enrich the print medium. They open up myriads of opportunities to stimulate the mind and capabilities of students which then can be translated into the print medium. Students respond to the stimuli provided by rock music, by questions of youth behavior as catalogued in the media, by questions of morality, ethics, teenage and adult behavior, by the symbolism in such American phenomena as the fast-food industry, shopping malls, rituals, icons and fetishes. Some of the most exciting and useful courses taught in high school and college level composition courses have been sports-oriented: the literature of sports, sports in American culture, the history of sports. The media fairly bulge every day with subjects that excite and invite the thoughtful student and teacher: the commercialization of Christmas, sex-education in public schools, combatting the spread of AIDS, abortion, televangelism, the role of the elderly in society pet therapy, the positive and negative images of such television shows as "Dallas" and "Dynasty." The Popular Culture Department of Bowling Green State University recently ran a successful state-wide writing contest among eleventh-grade high-school students on "Should Rock Lyrics be Censored?" Uncountable instructors in composition classes have always used current events and other popular culture subjects as topics for compositions. The range of stimulating topics is boundless.

One medium foolishly ignored is the comic book. Everyone knows that in Mexico, Central and South America, the People's Republic of China, and elsewhere, comics are used to teach reading and writing as well as political ideology. In Japan, according to a recent AP article, children, women and business executives read comics all the time. According to one expert, comics exert as much influence over school kids as school itself does. Increasingly comic books are being used to simplify and augment textbooks. How-to comic books are becoming more and more popular, covering all kinds of education and activities. Japan, like America, is a very visual-oriented society. With a claimed 100% literacy rate, does Japan know something about teaching literacy that we refuse to accept? It seems so. Let me give you an example.

At Bowling Green State University we have created the Popular Culture Library and are archiving as much popular culture as we can. One of the largest collections is our comic book archive. Years ago when we were just getting started, a man from Toledo called one day and said that he would like to contribute his collection of comic books to our archives. He brought down several thousand comics—a station wagon full. Six months later he brought down another thousand comics—a station wagon full. Six months later he brought down another thousand, and sometime later another large collection. Being curious about where he was getting his books, I asked him where he got them and why. His answer was very poignant—touching—and significant. He said that he worked for Toledo Edison as a lineman, and he simply liked to read. So he bought as many comic books as he could. Now I would suggest that in that man's simple statement lies the whole kernel of an American educational system: a person so desiring to read that he would spend all available cash for the opportunity. There lies the seed for education, and one of the media.

Providing access to literacy through these various media does not mean that anybody who teaches composition through the popular culture must undergo a shriveling of his own talents, his own life, his own tastes, if that is the result of such association, though I surely doubt that it is. The teacher should be able to maintain a distance between his private tastes and his professional ones. Using the various popular culture media merely means that in a democracy, one teaches from democratic premises, with democratic assumptions, from and through democratic media, for democratic ends. That means that the instructor should never be embarrassed by or condescending to the degree of literacy or illiteracy one finds or to the means of eradicating that illiteracy. Everybody has to begin sometime at the beginning.

All people, no matter how humble, have the democratic right to access to the valuable and useful experiences of the past and present in order to improve or make more enjoyable their own lives. They cannot, in our democracy, properly be denied the tools of access to those experiences.

Which, of course, brings up an informative parallel. Asian-American children are doing so well in schools and colleges that questions are being raised as to whether they are smarter than other American kids. The statistics are impressive: Asian-American kids usually score some 30 points higher than other Americans on the Scholastic Aptitude Test, 520 out of a possible 800. Although Asian-Americans constitute only 2.1% of the American population, they make up 11% of the freshman class at Harvard; 18% at MIT; 25% at Berkeley. Does that mean that Asian-American kids are smarter than other American kids? Though the jury is still out on that verdict, there is every reason to believe that success depends more on motivation than native intelligence. Asian-American kids simply work harder.

University of Michigan psychologist Harold W. Stevenson feels that "they work harder largely because they share a greater belief in the efficacy of hard work." Stevenson added: "Japanese mothers gave the strongest rating to the idea that anyone can do well if he studies hard." Stevenson might have added that parents know very well that if students do not succeed early they will be condemned to a life in which they never can achieve the highest goals in their society. In Japanese society, success is built from one of the three elite universities and one's capabilities to matriculate in one of these schools are fiercely competitive and established early. Chinese mothers strongly agree in this particular work ethic. A typical Stanford Chinese student's comment was: "In the Chinese family, education is very important because parents see it as the way to achieve. With that environment it's natural to study. My friends are that way too. It's not a chore. They know the benefits."

Are we to conclude from these statistics that all other American students are stupider than the Asia-Americans? That their parents are stupider? Hardly. The evidence demonstrates that the Asian-Americans work harder. They are "merely entertained" less than the other American kids. So what should we do? Being realistic, we may as well confess that television and the other aspects of American entertainment and popular culture are not going away. One inalienable right that we are prepared to fight for is the "American Way" of life—and that way consists mainly of our popular culture. Since we are not going to put technology back into the undeveloped stage, why not use it to further our designs to create and promote conventional literacy? If Asian-American kids learn because their family tradition expects it of them, why don't we get the other American kids to learn because it is so easy and one uses the most enjoyable media to learn from, and because American society expects it of *them*? And rewards them for it. If the American way of life is so much fun, we should use it to learn to get even more fun out of it. The American way of life can become even more pleasurable and profitable for many more if educators use that means of pleasure and profit to promote literacy in the conventional forms.

Yet educators, people who presumably lead in the world of ideas, continue to face backwards, to remember the "good old days" when they were acquiring their wisdom and to teach wrong-headed ideas. Little wonder that American higher education is falling apart. For example, in 1987 Allan Bloom, professor in the Committee on Social Thought at the University of Chicago, published a book entitled *The Closing of the American Mind*. Picturing modernity as the enemy of the classics, and therefore of learning in particular, Bloom (*Chronicle of Higher Education*, May 6, 1987, p. 96) railed against television, "pop psychology," popular literature, and nearly everything else that was not written in the misty past. One of his guiding stars for "classics" was the works of Charles Dickens and the unforgettable characters that Dickens created. Apparently little did Bloom know that Dickens was the most "popular" writer of his day, turning out copy while the printer's devil leaned over his shoulder in order to make a living and avoid the debtors' prison. And Bloom, who curses stereotypical thinking, says that one of the great benefits of Dickens' writing is that his characters are "a complex set of experiences that enables one to say so simply, 'He is a Scrooge'," etc. In other words although he uses other words, Bloom desires the ease and convenience of the stereotype, the very rib-cage of popular literature of today.

Bloom stumbles over other dangerous misassumptions about education. One is that democracy helped kill off education: "The democratization of the university helped dismantle its structure and caused it to lose its focus." These are the words of the enemy of the people and of education in general, not of one who understands what education is for. Bloom also voices poisonous nonsense when he thinks of the purpose of education: "The old teachers who loved Shakespeare or Austen or Donne, and whose only reward for teaching was the perpetuation of their taste, have all but disappeared," he complains. Prof. Bloom apparently forgets that Shakespeare's plays were written for the very practical purpose of making the author a living on the stage, and Austen's and Donne's had their practical purposes. But mainly Bloom's words reflect the mentality of Matthew Arnold of the nineteenth century and merely demonstrate that many academics instead of wanting to generate free and innovative thinking for the twentieth century want to clone themselves and the past. An educational system that wants merely to clone itself and its history is going to be condemned to reliving the past. The frightening thing about Bloom's thinking is that apparently it is honey to many other academic bees who see in it salvation for their troubles. But it is more likely a Siren's song lulling unwary academics into a mess of troubles because it preaches against use of all modern thinking and theories, and surely against popular culture as one of the tools of instruction, with working with what one has.

In using popular culture to promote literacy, sometimes instructors have to be understanding and work from very little. For example, if a student in "composition" would rather perform on his guitar, if he would rather sing a song than write an essay, he should be encouraged, and the performance should be accepted as a "composition." If an "essay" consisted of a collage of pictures of rock 'n' roll stars, it should be accepted. From these parallel beginnings, actual literacy in conventional language can be encouraged. The person who sang a rock song or performed on his guitar could be induced to talk about what he had done, and then urged to write down his thoughts for those people not in class. The person who pasted up the collage could be asked to form some kind of connection, historical or cultural, between the pictures, and thus in effect do some "writing" that would promote his literacy. Acceptance of the different language is useful in bridging the gap between the two or three media, and through acceptance students are assured that the instructor lives in and appreciates the world that they are concerned with. The communication, the empathy, the understanding form a two-way street, and two-way communication.

With these purposes and techniques in mind no plan should be too low to begin on, and no idea should be assumed to be above the reach of the print illiterate until it has been proved to be so. Many Americans may have difficulty with even the simplest words and sentences. But these people are not necessarily stupid or unteachable: they simply have not yet learned the art of language use, and they have not learned because for one reason or another they have not been properly motivated. To teach such people, educators need liberated and active minds looking for ideas of today and tomorrow what will excite and motivate the minds before them. The field of these ideas remains constantly present.

There is no reason for the American educator to think that he will have to stop using the media when he has accomplished literacy in the print medium, that the potentials are short-lived and soon exhausted. Functional literacy through the media is only a beginning. This accomplishment can be like a person holding a piece of candy just out of the reach of a hungry child. As the child crawls toward the candy, it can be pulled back continuously—until, in theory at least, the child has become an adult. The bon-bon of media education can likewise be continually pulled back until the learner is accomplished in advanced degrees of literacy and knowledge, until he is, in fact, what we might call "educated." Properly presented the entertainment of life is an unending source of knowledge and training.

The point is to realize the possibilities and to get to implementing them. Illiteracy, drop-outs, fade-outs (arrested learners) are problems that should be attacked directly, not obliquely. Thus on the matter of effective education in the United States, William Bennett the Secretary of Education, should not be grandstanding by teaching history or philosophy to 8-year-olds in schoolrooms. He should be out on the streets of Detroit—and Washington and every community in the U.S.—asking drop-outs and fade-outs and illiterates why they are not in the classroom. He should be concerned with the very basics of long-range education—that is, keeping students in classrooms long enough for them to learn, then teaching them something while they are there. The task is to get them into situations conducive to our purposes and goals. As everybody knows, the people are learning, but they may not be learning what we think is of primary importance. But there is no doubt that the Prof. Blooms of academia can do a great amount of mischief if they continue to rely exclusively on the "classics" for wisdom and then do not understand them.

Academics are often uncomfortable in the presence of the multitude of ideas that the media and popular culture provide because they need the feeling of safety and assurance guaranteed by the old restrictions. Such people prefer the snugness found in the old forms of expression to the potentials latent in the new and unrestricted possibilities. Some see merit in the cliche being circulated by many of today's politicians of going "back to basics." Indeed there is much merit in the concept, other than the deceptive alliteration, provided we do not mis-remember what the basics are. The basics are age-old means of communication about the phenomena of life. The media of communication have been modernized and brought up to date every time the medium of communication has changed. When copying of texts by hand, one by one, gave way to rapid printing, the "basics" became tied to printing. When mechanical typewriters gave way to electric machines, nearly everybody happily changed machines and the "basics" underwent yet another technological advance.

Entertainment is also "basic" in nearly everybody's life, one of the primary drives which socialize society. Through the years the media entertainment have changed radically. Though many people like to cling to some aspects of the "old" entertainment, perhaps claiming that they are superior to the newfangled ones, most people have moved happily into the forms provided by the electronic media.

Society like technology in a literate world moves inexorably forward. But it moves along a trail which includes the past. In truth, popular culture *is* that past as well as its present. Popular culture has never left the basics— it *is* the basics, the fundamentals, the everyday, and indeed it should be so used. Only the technology of popular culture changes. Technological genies do not go back into bottles once they have been released. The practical and sensible thing, then, is for educators to realize the importance and opportunities of the technological society we live in and to utilize its equipment in the teaching of print literacy. The opportunities are great—and the penalties for failing are heavy and costly. Too costly, in fact, for us to afford. Either we go with the media or they go without us.

So popular culture which on the one hand seems to be destroying conventional literacy is actually providing people with the greatest and easiest access to practical functional literacy, to the basics, to getting people to remain in school, and to luring people into continued education long after their formal years are finished, if we will only realize the opportunity and take advantage of it.

Never before have so many people had such easy access to so many means of getting to the top and fulfilling the American Dream of success. That these media are not utilized to develop mediacy and love of learning constitutes one of the great and needless shames of our country and our time. Utilization of popular culture in this way would not, of course, cure the whole trouble. The literacy and education provided might not be of the casebook variety and might not be conventional literacy and education. But it would be communication, it would be functional literacy, and it would keep the human mind busy on "worthwhile" subjects. There would, of course, still be many people who would not or could not become literate in the conventional sense, who would, for one reason or another, not be interested in learning and using the mind. Perhaps the illiterate and the half-educated, like the poor, will always be with us in certain numbers. But literacy builds on its own accomplishments, just as education feeds on education. Literacy breeds love of learning; education breeds more love of education, and of literacy. Learning through popular culture is no panacea. But this approach would surely help alleviate the problem of illiteracy, of drop-outs and fade-outs and would provide bases for further development. Any assistance should be welcome and tried. After all, half of the American Dream is better than none—for individuals *and* for society.

Popular Books and Popular Culture

Ray B. Browne

Popular books—both fiction and non-fiction—with television and movies constitute the Big Three of communication in contemporary popular culture. Although the popular books—both the bestsellers and the not-so-wide-sellers— do not parallel television and movies in total number of people reached, they undoubtedly do rival the other two mass media in the influence they exercise. So popular books as one of the most influential media of popular culture must be understood for what they do to popular culture, for what popular culture does to them and how they should be read *vis-a-vis* popular culture.

Popular culture is the voice, the actions, the motivations, the results of all aspects of life engaged in by nearly all people. Popular culture is the traditions, the modes of life we inherit from our ancestors, use in turn and pass on—generally greatly modified—to our children and their children. Popular culture is entertainment and non-entertainment, the serious and the playful. It is the cultural atmosphere in which we live, the total blanket of our lives, the cultural "water" we swim in, the barometer of the weather of our lives.

Popular books are the voice and the ears of the people. Their purpose is to communicate to large numbers of people in a language they can understand and appreciate information about subjects which are or can become of interest to them. Thus, since life is so varied and people's interests so endless, popular books must be all-inclusive and all-comprehensive in the subjects they cover. They must try to present all of life. All one has to do to see how nearly popular books meet this criterion is to scan the shelves of any library or large book store. There one will find virtually every subject covered, to stimulate every taste and answer every question. The books constitute a mirror of society, comprehensive and revealing. As someone in *Blackwood's Edinburgh Magazine* recognized more than a hundred years ago, "Popular literature is a reflection of the period in which it flourishes—its active as well as its meditative life— its politics and its romance, and we rest assured that there is not a movement in it, not a force, not an atom of life which has not its counterpart in contemporary history....Literature, in fact, now implies far more than it did before. It is now a complete representation of society....It is to the historian what the dial-plate is to the time piece; it is a perfect index of the innumerable processes at work throughout the whole frame of society." What was true a hundred years ago is even truer today, as the number of phenomena of life has proliferated, with the attendant interests on the part of large or small numbers of people, at a time when every voice and every combination of voices demands to have a voice and a hearing in literature.

The value and power of popular literature as influences in popular culture have recently been attested to in the words of such eminent observers as Richard Hoggart, and T.S. Eliot.

British cultural historian Hoggart felt that "Literature at all levels has the unique capacity to increase our understanding of a culture" and therefore of ourselves. T.S. Eliot, cringing under the power of popular literature, observed: "I incline to come to the alarming conclusion," he said in *Essays Ancient and Modern*, "that it is just the literature that we read for 'amusement' or 'purely for pleasure' that may have the greatest...least suspected...earliest and most insidious influence upon us. Hence it is that the influence of popular novelists, and of popular plays of contemporary life, require to be scrutinized."

Popular literature achieves much of its power because it is conservative; by repeating it again and again, popular literature tends to maintain the status quo. The fact that one popular writer does what a predecessor has already done demonstrates the viability of the idea and the force it exercises in culture. For example, Peter Benchley in *Jaws* (1974) wanted to write a story about a sea adventure, one of the most popular possible, in which man fights sea monster, again a story popular since the classical times. In order to give his book a newness coupled with the power of the old, he chose a great white shark as man's adversary. Whales and blue marlins had already been used (the earlier in the Bible and in *Moby-Dick*, the latter in Hemingway's *The Old Man and the Sea*). The association of the new adversary does not vitiate or invalidate Benchley's story at all. On the contrary, the association of the four or more adventures enrich all four.

In another type, the fact that Jack Shaefer retold the classic Western story in *Shane*, in almost the exact prototypical setting as its ancestors enriches the classic story which has meant so much to the American myth of life in this country and in the Western states. Louis L'Amour's further development of the myth—this time in a reversal—only demonstrates, again, the power of the myth and the story.

The eminent critic Leslie Fiedler is undoubtedly right on the mark when he points out in addition to the conservation status also the subversive nature of popular books. They may confirm the status quo, to be sure, but at the same time simply because they are ubiquitous in subject matter and treatment they revolutionize their genres. Charles Dickens' novels, *Uncle Tom's Cabin, Gone With The Wind, The Circular Staircase*, Agatha Christie's various books, Graham Greene's *The Quiet American*, Ruth Rendell's various works, those of George Chesbro, Andrew Greeley, Rita Mae Brown, and countless others, are subversive in that they unconsciously change the content and the direction in which popular culture flows. These books are subversive, of course, because popular books just as much as so-called elite fiction are creative, and as conditions of life change the authors' approaches and development change also.

Some critics, unfortunately, cannot see the organic development and new thrust of popular books, the dynamics of creativity. Although an avowed fan of detective fiction, Jacques Barzun, felt that "anyone who attempts to improve on the mystery genre and make it a real novel suffers from bad judgement." John G. Cawelti, commenting on roughly the same restrictions of popular literature, said that the detective formula "operates to limit the expression of deeper and more complex cultural perspectives." Both comments illustrate how most such statements must be restricted to the time they are made and cannot be allowed to become guideposts of the future. One of the most powerful, and saddening, examples of this ephemeral quality of comments is seen in Alan M. Wald's book *The New York Intellectuals* (1987), where he has such eminent and persuasive critics of literature and society as Phillip Rahv, Lionel Trilling and Irving Howe demonstrate how much they were powers only of their own time, their own chemistry and their cultist following. Life soon passed them by, made them footnotes in history, made their comments insights to their times but otherwise merely reliques.

But other authors recognize the constantly changing nature of popular books and the society they operate in. The very successful American hard-boiled detective author John D. MacDonald, for example, recognized that popular fiction is a gloss on our daily lives. He correctly observed that "fiction at its most entertaining provides little hints, clues, nuances, which aid us in our endless deciphering of ourselves."

On a larger scale, others have felt that restricting an art form to itself is contrary to nature and inhibiting to its growth. Such thinkers have felt that all artifacts of society are the result of the society in which they are created and in which they work. Alan Gowans, for example, insists that art is not understandable, even definable, until one knows what the art does. "To know what art is," he insists, "you must define what it *does*. You can define art only in terms of function." The same must be said for all other expressions of human society. The popular authors, since they appeal to nearly all the literate audience in one of the oldest of the media of communication, are directly a part of society. They write of matters of concern to members of society, in a language which society can understand. Such writers look upon popular books as living and growing organisms, which expand and develop according to the demands of the readership, the creativity of the creators and the opportunities afforded by society.

Certain formulaic authors have approached their genres with different goals and have come away with different accomplishments. Graham Greene, for example, with a long line of spy novels to his credit, began by distinguishing between those works that were "entertainment" and others he wanted to write as "art." Finally, however, he realized that there is no real distinction, that the formulaic form can carry his message as well as any other, and he dropped his effort to keep the two separate. Other authors have felt even more strongly than Greene about the presumed limitations of formulaic stories, at least to begin with. Some have intended to use them as stepping stones to something more esthetically satisfying and respectable.

For example, the English author of crime fiction P.D. James, whose favorite author is Jane Austen, and who, like Henry James, learned art by writing popular literature, began by looking upon her works as serious endeavors, but as a step to something else: "...I saw the writing of detective fiction with its challenging disciplines, its inner tensions between plot, character, and atmosphere, and its necessary reliance on structure and form, as the best possible apprenticeship for a serious novelist." Through the years she has maintained her respect for the form itself. Each of her books has been, in her words, "a landmark in [her] gradual realization that, despite the constraints of this fascinating genre, a mystery writer can hope to call herself a serious novelist." Through the years she has developed this "serious" aspect of her works so much that she has expanded the restrictions of the genre and turned the form into psychology-crime stories.

Ruth Rendell, another of Britain's leading authors of today, has expanded her studies in detective fiction to include the psychology of crime victims and criminals and motivations for human behavior. In one study, *A Judgement in Stone*, (1977), for example, she demonstrated how illiteracy causes such frustration, alienation and paranoia that murder can result.

The American author Ross Macdonald also found the formula too confining and constricting. Though most of his books center on the hardnosed, softhearted detective Lew Archer, Macdonald never was content merely to be a writer of detective stories. He set his tales in southern California because, as he said, that part of America represents most vividly the raw edge of American society, where civilization has pushed itself nearly into the sea, and in so doing has created problems that it may never be able to solve. It is the attempt—and the necessity—to solve these problems that Macdonald concerned himself with. His books probe reality at large, not just the question of who committed a crime. This aspect of Macdonald's late work was recognized by born critics. Macdonald was severely criticized for presuming to write something other than detective fiction, as he did in *Sleeping Beauty*. But he continued to adhere to his definition of the crime story because it was the best medium, expanded as he enlarged it, for his probing into the working of the human condition.

Stephen King, the most popular author of horror stories ever to write, sees the genre as much more revealing of culture and America than that analyzed by any of his predecessors or fellow authors of horror stories. He expands the genre to make it almost a universal comment on human nature and the American scene.

Increasingly, modern writers of all genres, like George C. Chesbro, Joan Hess, Teri White of crime fiction, and dozens of others, are searching for the larger purposes in life and society, and are insisting that the humanities and humanitarian qualities of life be written into and read out of their books.

One of the more remarkably revolutionary authors of popular fiction today is Fr. Andrew Greeley. Greeley writes popular novels of many kinds, science fiction, crime fiction and novels of divine love. In all, he writes with a philosophy not found so much in the pens of other authors as in sermons from pulpits. Whatever genre Greeley is writing in, he usually is suggesting a sermon, trying to show that God loves everybody and that all worshipers should come back to God. In all his books Greeley is explicit in illustrating the need for both physical and spiritual love and the inseparability of the two in the eyes and plans of God. Greeley brings new meanings to the words erotic love. There is a straight-forward, clean, one almost says "pure" sex, beautiful and uplifting that inspires and enriches. It is something like the purity of the love Sir Galahad had in his Quest. In Greeley sex grows in a love of self, of companion, of community and a proper role in God's plan. Sex is a sacrament, a way of achieving grace and Godliness when used in its proper, fullest human sense. There is also throughout Greeley's works a Christian humanism which reaches out and has all people love all people and through that love to reach up to God. The books are William Blake's *Songs of Innocence* written about adults, still with innocence but also with innocent erotic love. William Blake's *Songs of Innocence* written about adults, still with innocence but also with innocent erotic love.

Rita Mae Brown, a leading feminist author, brings to her many areas of concern a fierce assertion of female liberty found in few other writers working today. She expands the horizons of humanism and makes them more encompassing and sensitive.

Thus in all the standardized formulaic bestsellers of the past, strange forces are demanding new definitions, new approaches, new appreciations of the various kinds of popular writing. The result is a merging of the genres. Romances are one extreme of romances of past, historical novels are more cultural than they have been, spy thrillers, historical romances, history, science fiction and crime fiction are becoming more general novels. Increasingly it is difficult to tell what kind of popular book you happen to be reading because all are becoming infused with "general" characteristics and ingredients.

Some of these general characteristics of popular books we have already touched on. Some should be more explicitly defined and described.

1. Popular books, far more than other "art" and morally neutral elite books, possess uplift and social purpose. Although many books are written merely so that the author can make money, if there is one ingredient that a majority of popular books contain it is response to and a catering to America's continued fascination with the puritanical insistence on improvement. In America, bestsellers are supposed to provide moral uplift and social purpose, with demonstration of the American ethic of freedom, liberty, Godliness, sex and timeliness, and now the liberation of women. There are numerous examples of all types.

An excellent example of the liberation of women in contemporary fiction is Irving Wallace's *Fan Club* (1974)—twenty-four weeks a bestseller in cloth. The book was apparently misunderstood because of its surface sex and violence which covered a much profounder message. Although the average reader might have got more of the surface message than the underlying one, there is no doubt that the underlying message got through.

The novel developed an idea Wallace had had in mind for years. Once on a train ride from Boston to New York, he overheard some trainmen in the sleeper talking about how they would give anything in the world to spend a night with Elizabeth Taylor. Wallace developed this idea in a novel in which he asked what if four men, acting out their fantasy, kidnapped a Hollywood sex goddess and raped her, assuming that she would eventually repay their violence with love. It is, of course, a ridiculous idea, but not outside the realm of violent men in violent America. The book was criticized for being both prurient and sexist. The charges against the book were peculiar, for in fact it was neither prurient nor sexist when compared with, say, Erica Jong's *Fear of Flying* which was popular at the same time. *The Fan Club* actually demonstrates how a woman—though a sex goddess and therefore in the minds of men presumably merely a "dumb blonde"—could outsmart four men, one of them a writer, and triumph, with three of the four condemned to death and self-destruction, and the writer too obtuse to learn anything anytime.

Perhaps more obvious, and more graceful and stronger, and more timely, was Leon Uris' book *Trinity* (1976). In eight hundred pages Uris embroiled readers so much in the reality and anguish of contemporary Ireland that their only regret when the book ended was that it finished too quickly. Perhaps even more universally compelling was a book about the world half a glove away—Colleen McCullough's bestselling *The Thorn Birds*, which gripped the imagination of all readers with its study of war and of fighting the elements to prevail in Australia. Not content with that historical development, McCullough next turned to a study of politics and society in the future, in *A Creed for the Third Millennium*, (1986) in which she set about investigating America after the turn of the century, when events force one person to become a dictator to save the world, but the women he loves determines to destroy him. In 1986 Lee Iacocca's autobiography, caught America in the midst of a felt hero-vacuum and demonstrated how even in America of the mid-twentieth century, a "ethnic" child can make it big. And Garrison Keillor's *Lake Wobegon Days* jerked the heartstrings of all readers—elite and popular—with its appeal to the nostalgia of growing up which has always been important in the American psyche.

2. Popular literature is generally long, and perhaps at times loosely written. Popular books need to be timely and therefore must be written and published rapidly. Generally, therefore, the author cannot devote as much time to style and brevity as the author of more deliberate books. Ross Macdonald used to exercise much care with his composition, deliberating with as much care in style as in plotting. He could afford to, since he wrote only one book a year, and was not propelled by the desire to make money, or even the compulsion to write. Others, however, are driven by the sheer desire to write, the need to make money, Michael Avallone, for example, who has written nearly 200 novels of various kinds, insists that a professional author should be prepared to write any time and "should be able to write *anything*: garden seed catalogues, the Bible, or minutes of the Last Meeting." Harold Robbins supposedly locks himself in a library and turns out a book in six weeks. Louis L'Amour, author

of the most effective series of western books of the last half of the twentieth century (with sales running over 150 million) runs his manuscripts through the typewriter once, has his wife check them for consistency, and then mails them to the publisher. Irving Wallace's latest book, *The Celestial Bed* (1987), with his usual ability to be right on the spot when cultural developments come to the forefront and erupt, treats the televangelists and their potential for trouble. Such timeliness, perhaps unparalleled in any other popular writer of our time, and the degree to which Wallace is read, demonstrates how bestselling authors need to respond to the cultural events and phenomena of their time.

Most writers try to check up and feel the pulse of their readers. Wallace's publishers include survey cards which are mailed back to the publishers and thence to him. Andrew Greeley receives hundreds of letters from the publication of each book. Other writers get responses in other ways. But they are generally read and responded to. John Jakes, the author of, among many books, the Kent Family Chronicles, recounted in an interview with Michael Barson, the reception of Volume VIII, *The Americans*, and the announcement that the series would not be continued beyond that volume:

I've really been astonished at the volume and the emotional intensity of the mail that has come in following the conclusion of the series.... I have letters from people who have stayed up all night, who have stayed up eighteen hours reading continuously. And I even have, I'm amazed to say, tearstained letters from ladies who cried as they finished the book, and immediately sat down to write a letter. A writer can ask for no more, no greater reward, than that kind of response.

Popular books tend to be wordy, though writers like L'Armour are not. Popular books are concerned with facts, with stories, rather than with character development, and are therefore sometimes wordy. But *life* is wordy, not artful. Therefore bestselling books promote the practice of reading. They should be praised for promoting reading, in our society where we condemn the lack of reading, and media that tend to foster "functional illiteracy."

Before the electronic media, we praised the long, sometimes dull, book. Dickens' books were long, marvelous for their stories, but virtually unreadable today. James Fenimore Cooper is long and unreadable today. Herman Melville and Henry James certainly took too long, in the eyes of some people, to tell their stories. But wordiness and brevity, like beauty, lies in the eyes of the reader. If Uris and Wallace are too long for the critics, they obviously are about right for the average reader.

3. Bestselling novels are sometimes accused of presenting life falsely and therefore mislead, even dangerously "seduce", the reader. To a certain extent this observation is accurate but in another it is incorrect and irrelevant. All art is by definition a falsification of reality, even the works of the realists, the naturalists, and surrealists. Irving Wallace's heroine of *The Fan Club* was more his creation than a duplication of Elizabeth Taylor, though Taylor is herself a falsification of life. The life presented in *The Thorn Birds* is more lovely and painful than reality would have us know. Sex is more steamy in

the so-called romances than it could ever be in life. But the London life in Dickens' novels is much more endurable than it was in real life.

4. Popular fiction is sheer fantasy. To a certain extent it is, thank goodness. *Watership Down* (1972) and *Shardick* (1974), both very popular novels by Richard Adams, were sheer animal fantasy. But Tolkien's works and *Alice in Wonderland* as well as *The Wizard of Oz* are fantasy. And the world has been brightened by these works. Fantasies should be encouraged; they are directly in line with children's books *of* all ages *for* all ages.

5. Contrary to what many critics say about bestselling literature, these books are always exploring new areas and new approaches. True, bestselling books, like popular culture in general, tend to be repetitious. Since they must be self-supporting and since one of the purposes is to make money, bestselling books like to trust in the success of success. Therefore when one book or one type of book has been successful, the success breeds many copies and duplicates. Thus the success of *Jaws* caused the publication of scores of other similar books. The so-called Romance, especially the Harlequin Romance, was so successful that authors began writing books like the originals, and numerous publishers began publishing the type because they realized that the books were covered with gold. But the wide sales of these types of books constitute no reason for condemning them. The condemnation was undoubtedly by those who would not or could not write similar stories and the condemnation was motivated by envy largely. Unfortunately, elite writers cannot forgive the popular writer his success. One is reminded of Nathaniel Hawthorne's condemnation of the widely-selling books being published in his time by women; he could not write them, they sold better than his books; therefore they were inferior.

Yet obviously not all popular fiction is copy-cat. Through the years the Harlequin Romance has changed. Beginning with a kind of chaste sex and a man-woman relationship that was suitable for the most conservative minded readers, where the woman maintained a pre-woman's Lib psychology, the formulas for the stories developed into a much steamier sex relationship in which the woman tended to have her own profession and personal and gender development until at the end of each book she met the man of her choice and generally decided that woman's happiest place was in the home. These stories developed from largely stay-at-homes in locales to all kinds of international travel, from the rain forests of the tropics to the sub-freezing zones of northern latitudes.

Furthermore, there have been many trail-blazers and pioneers in subject matter and style. Crime fiction, as we have seen, has come a long way from the conventional British so-called locked-room puzzle to the very broad-subject approaches currently being developed. Fr. Andrew Greeley has perhaps gone as far as any other popular writer in forcing novels to be expanded versions of what he thinks are God's teachings and plans for the human race. Popular Fiction has developed so far, in fact, that there is hardly any subject and hardly any approach and development that a reader might want that he won't find on the bestselling shelves.

The sheer breadth of subjects, approaches and development, in popular fiction, and the sheer weight of numbers in popular fiction have caused some drastic changes and developments in the type. Because of the economics of book-publishing demand that books sell in large numbers to be published and marketed, there has been a democratizing of books. Elite authors of the past who would not lowered themselves to write popular books, now, for one reason or another, are glad to try to cater to a more "popular" market and to write books that hopefully will sell in large numbers. They are seeing that the gap between the elite and the popular is not now as large as it used to be felt to be.

Thus economics have done what other political forces failed to do. Yet as a result of economic pressure authors in general have developed a respect for the general reading public which has not been there in the past. Yet with this new respect there has come a new and tighter tension, a feeling on the part of many that they will never let go. This diminishing minority are represented today by the current and writings of such people as Dwight MacDonald, Edmund Wilson, Stanley Kauffmann and William Gass. They base their thoughts on the philosophy of Plato, the political attitudes of Edmund Burke, Ortega y Gasset, to name just a few, and Matthew Arnold, who taught that there is an unbridgeable gap between the tastes and accomplishments of the elite and the unwashed millions. But luckily just as human nature has done much in the past to perpetuate the nonsense about "tastes" and "standards" in the arts, human nature, greed and desire for privilege has finally swung past the elite to the democratizing influence of the masses. To paraphrase Housman's famous line, greed does more than reason can to explicate man's ways to man.

In the vast and complicated world of popular fiction, then, what is the reader going to do to try to make sense out of it? If virtually every subject known to man is written on, in varying degrees of complexity and simplicity, how is a cultural critic, someone who is trying to see what all this adds up to in the real world, going to approach and make heads or tails of the vast flow of the material?

It should be kept in mind what bestsellers are and whom they serve. The strongest books are those which tend to give the fullest picture of the subject they strive to cover. Thus a book on race relations is strongest if it covers most or all of the aspects of the subject. Haley's *Roots* was successful because it gave an indepth and rich coverage of the subject. McCullough's novel *The Thorn Birds* was especially effective because it was the saga of a family's, and two individual's (Meggy and Ralph) growth and development. Benchley's *Jaws* was especially moving because it developed not only the strength of a great white shark but did it against and intertwined with man and man's nature. In other words, those books are strongest which are most inclusive. It follows then that the reader and the critic must get just as much out of the book— or even more—than the author put into it. Robert Frost, it should be remembered, said that whatever a reader found in his works was his whether he intended it or not. Most authors of bestselling books are not professional philosophers, psychologists, or persons pursuing a single line of thought. In the middle of the 1980s there are few novelists with only a single purpose—Betty Friedan, some other feminists, cultists, exorcists and others to the contrary notwithstanding. And even the authors with single purposes have to be much more inclusive than their single-mindedness might allow if they want to sell their books widely. Thus just as there are few novels written by narrow Marxists, or feminists, or Jungists, or environmentalists or sexists, or Republicans or Democrats, the books should not be read as single developments of single-strand points of view. They are more, and they must be read as reflections of life, not of those of propagandists or theorists.

The history of academic disciplines are those of continued and growing specialization. Thus political science and economics develop into different political and economic points of view, from Marxists to Keynesians and post-Keynesians, from supply-side to post-supply-side. Histories have to be rewritten according to the dictates of whatever political point of view is prevalent at a given time. Unfortunately literature also is subject to the whims of the latest discoveries in literary theories and methodologies. Thus in the thirties and forties, literature had to be subjected to Freudian and Jungain schools of thought. After that came the Structuralists, post-Structuralists, Constructionists, deconstructionists, myth-symbol, post-myth-symbol, etc. All such theories are merely tools of the trade, carpenters'—or engineers'—tools used by specialists to investigate one aspect of the subject. Granted these particular ideologies supply the tools for an individual to cut deep into the motivations and accomplishments of a piece of literature. But such approaches undoubtedly tend to serve only one master, and generally the conclusions are skewed, and simplistic.

For example, the British scholar Cora Kaplan (in *Formations of Fantasy*, 1987) tries to revitalize the tired old Marxian approach to Colleen McCullough's *The Thorn Birds* by calling it "a powerful and ultimately reactionary read." Concerning popular fiction in general, Kaplan urges that "Our priority ought be an analysis of the progressive or reactionary politics of the narratives to which they can become bound in popular expression." Her purpose is, of course, to "change" them.

Though much truth and revelation can become manifest under such scrutiny, without doubt the detritus thrown away as useless by the critic is in fact worth far more than the material utilized. The process is something like throwing away unrecognized gold mineral in order to get at the recognized silver in a lode of rocks.

Thus if one is going to get the full richness of the popular literature vis-a-vis popular culture, he or she must be the generalist. He must read the work for the cultural ingredients and overtones, for what the book contains about and says about society, not for some particular aspect.

Of all the single but inclusive themes that should be read out of popular books perhaps the humanism—the humanities—is the most important. Humanism can reflect all other points of view. The political, social, cultural, artistic, esthetic, the iconic, ritualistic, fetishistic, heroic—and all others contained in a work of art—all resonate down the large pipe of the humanities and humanism. The humanities contain the flow of all the other streams. The humanities are the individual strands in the cable that support the bridge over the chasm in the study of popular literature. These individual strands all work together as the total communication cable that allows all readers to exercise their individual and collective conclusions and add together the total impact and message of a popular culture bestseller.

The Suspense Process

George N. Dove

There has never been a shortage of critical approaches to popular formula fiction: Freudian, Marxist, structuralist, and formulaic, as well as the familiar humanistic interpretations. All of these schools have been represented in studies of the mystery, the spy story, the tale of the supernatural and the thriller, with varying degrees of success, but many critics must have wished, at some time, for an approach specifically intended for *popular* fiction.

There are two fundamental problems in the application of the traditional critical methods to the study of the popular formula story. One is the familiar danger of imposition of external dogma, whereby the critic loses sight of the original purposes of the writer and seeks to re-cast the story in terms of his own doctrinaire predilections. The other is the peril involved in going direct to the text of the fiction, with maybe a side-glance at the author but without consideration of one of the basic elements, the reader. Both of these dangers can be avoided in a critical approach that takes as its point of departure the relationship between author and reader.

Such an approach would seek to identify the disposition or "readiness" of the reader-consumer with the processes employed by the artist-producer. It would recognize such structures as formula and would take into account that convention and various cultural pressures are involved in the literary process. Most especially, it would be uniquely suited to popular productions, because it would require that the critic look through the eyes of the author, who is viewing his text through the eyes of his reader. The purpose of this criticism is to seek answers to such questions as *Why* did this writer handle this situation in this way? or *What* is he trying to do in this passage? Such an approach does not require that the critic project a typical or ideal reader; he looks for the reader only in the method of his author. The idea of *process* is that we take a functional approach, seeking to identify those processes or operations a writer employs to achieve a purpose. If that purpose is to sell well (which can be almost automatically assumed for the popular writer), by keeping his reader turning the pages so he will want to finish this book and buy the next one, he will try to use those proven suspense processes that have brought success to earlier writers.

"Suspense" is a term easier to use than to define. Most reviewers, people in the book trade, and even novelists either use the word to signify a sub-genre and consider it interchangeable with "mystery," or reserve "suspense" for that type of narrative characterized by menace, danger, and violence.[1] A more useful definition is the one advanced by Marie Rodell, "the art of making the reader care what happens next."[2] This conception has two advantages: it identifies suspense as process rather than as literary type, and it defines in terms of the response of the reader, without whose participation the idea of suspense is inherently meaningless.

What I am proposing here is that it is possible to identify a Suspense Process that is discernible, with formulaic modifications, in the mystery, the spy story, the tale of the supernatural, and the thriller.

When really effective suspense is developed, there is a special kind of relationship between author and reader, which permits the writer to generate a whole set of messages and signals to get the reader involved in the story and to keep him that way. When these transmissions are working properly, the story becomes a "book you just can't put down" and a treasure to author and publisher. The Suspense Process may be thought of as the product of a private lecture delivered by the narrator, who stands beside the screen on which the story is unfolding and nudges his listener along with "Watch this now" or "Just between the two of us...." In the standard detective story, the author may play the role of magician, the talented fraud who artfully misleads with false messages and signals; we love him for it and expect him to do it well.

Reader-involvement, then, is by definition the essential ingredient in successful suspense, and any skillful writer knows that violence, action, and menace alone are not enough; much more important is that bag of tricks, sometimes frankly (and accurately) called "hooks," that transform reader-observer into reader-participant. Alfred Hitchcock makes an important distinction between *shock* and *suspense* with this illustration: if a bomb explodes under the table around which the Board is meeting, killing everybody in the room, that is shock. But when the bomb is ticking along during the meeting and the camera keeps cutting away from the discussion and showing the timing device as it moves from 8:08 to 8:12 to 8:14, that, says Hitchcock, is suspense.[3] This is a good illustration of the principle, because it reminds us that there are three elements involved, not just one. First, there is the bomb, the impending menace, which is the reason for telling the story in the first place. Note, too, that the thriller formula implies a kind of tacit agreement that the writer will *do* something with that bomb: the menace will be ultimately disposed of, one way or another. Second, there is the ticking clock, the time element that triggers the sense of impending crisis. Finally, and most important, there is the moving camera, which is basic to the suspense process because its motion tells the viewer that something is going to happen, supplies him with an insight not shared by any of the people around the table, and thus makes him a participant in the narrative. Not only that: the very act of repeatedly going back to the bomb prompts the viewer to ask, "Why is he doing that?" and if he has had previous experience with the formula, he knows that the narrator is tacitly keeping his options open. Something may yet happen to prevent that explosion.[4]

Notice that a definition of suspense that goes no further than the bomb may neglect a lot of good suspenseful story-telling, because it limits the process to dependence on simple menace.[5] To stop with the clock is almost as unsatisfactory, because it limits the viewer's interest to that of onlooker; that ticking clock adds piquancy to the situation, but it is still not basic. The moving camera is the signal that not only asks the viewer, "How do you think I can work this out?" but puts him into such a position that when the Chairman announces that the meeting is almost over, the viewer can't resist commenting, "Hoo, boy, is it ever!"

There are several ways of setting the "hooks" and getting the reader involved in the story. One is to make him a party to privileged information, with the result that he is no longer just a puzzled onlooker. The technique is handled with special skill by Michael Crichton in *The Andromeda Strain*, a work that bristles with esoteric scientific jargon of such awesome nature that the lay reader may feel intimidated. Crichton, though, carefully lets his reader in on a few elements unknown to the scientists, and the resulting state of superiority is an invitation to participate.

Now of course these things are done in almost all fiction, "serious" as well as popular, mimetic as well as formulaic. There are, however, in the popular formula story two principles operating that are practically axiomatic. The first is that there are, in the formula story, almost no "free" motifs, that is, those elements that can be omitted from a story without disturbing the causal connections between events.[6] Every person, incident, or other element is likely to be important. A standard situation in spy fiction is the one in which the secret agent takes his seat on a plane or bus and is immediately engaged in conversation by a garrulous fellow-passenger. Now the reader, after just a little experience with the formula, knows the talker is not there merely for atmosphere or to provide information: the author-beside-the-screen is signalling us, "Watch this fellow. He may be danger!" The second axiom of the popular formula story is that complete and satisfying resolution is assured; conflicts always result in victory or defeat, and mysteries are always solved. The reader can safely assume that there is, in the popular mystery, no such thing as paradox without resolution, and the question that impels him to finish the story is not *Can* this be solved? but *How* is the writer going to handle this one? More than any other type of fiction, the popular formula story assumes an understanding between writer and reader that convention will be honored. The detective may not know the solution, and the guilty party may go unpunished, but the reader knows the answer.

The operation of the Suspense Process, then, is largely conditioned by a sort of private contract, which provides assurance that the game will be played within certain agreed-upon bounds. The reader can thus proceed with confidence that all paradoxes will be resolved and all conflicts brought to unambiguous conclusions; thus assured, he soon becomes accustomed to watching for his writer's signals and listening for his private messages, in the same way that a sports fan heightens his enjoyment by recognizing the importance of formations, sequences of plays, and subtleties of timing.[7] Controlled as it is by convention, the total effect of the Suspense Process is much more functional than substantive, deriving its dynamic not so much from the fact that our author is doing something as the reason he is doing it. Thus popular fiction need not be obvious in technique; quite frequently, what a writer says is less exciting than what he does not say.[8]

We must distinguish between "messages" and "signals": although they produce the same ultimate effect, they differ somewhat in operation. Messages have content which is in itself germane to the narrative, like the knowledge of that bomb under the table in Hitchcock's definition. The fact that the reader knows it is there, reinforced by the fact that the Board members do not, makes him more than just an onlooker. Signals, on the other hand, may or may not be elements in the story, their real function being that they serve as triggers of the reader's interest. Have you ever noticed, for example, how the mere statement of exact time in a story catches your attention? We are probably not spellbound by the statement that Lady Chattsmere was serving tea to the Vicar in her drawing room one day, but if our author goes on to add, "It was exactly 3:16 P.M.," we are immediately curious, regardless of whether the time was important to the episode. There are two things to remember about the place of signals in the Suspense Process: since they are by nature repeatable, they usually become conventions, and they themselves need not influence the outcome of the story. Their importance lies not so much in what they say as in the fact that they are there.

This is not the place to undertake a discussion of the psychology of suspense, but there are several apparent operational principles by which messages and signals accomplish the involvement of the reader. One is the principle of focus or specification, as in the example. "It was exactly 3:16." Now, if the author adds next, "At that moment a tall man dressed all in white turned into the lane above Lady Chattsmere's house," adding a Solitary Figure to the Exact Time, it would be an insensitive reader who could put the story down without finding out what is so important about the figure and the moment on which his attention has been focused. Another is the act of interruption, departure, or contrast, which has the effect of breaking into a pattern with some element that is noticeably at variance with the earlier tone or direction, like a sudden change in mode, point of view, or tempo. Yet another is the principle of intimation or indirection, usually expressed as hints or suggestions, and usually most effective in the mystery or the ghostly tale. Finally, there is the principle of confidentiality, which has the effect of heightening tension by letting the reader in on a secret, like the crucial mistake made by one of the scientists in *The Andromeda Strain.* Any of these principles may produce occasions, singly or in combination, for the strategies employed by skillful writers to get us hooked.

We will first examine the messages a writer works into a story to give the reader certain privileged information and to get him involved by means of information not shared by the characters. It is this kind of reader-knowledge that makes the difference; in the Hitchcock definition, the basic element is what the reader is told by that shifting camera. This kind of knowledge can even affect our sympathies and the commitment of our loyalties. In Forsyth's *The Day of the Jackal* we find ourselves pulling for the would-be assassin, contrary to normal standards of decency and justice, because we know him, have watched him prepare, step by painstaking step, for the murder of Charles de Gaulle. Not so in Knebel and Bailey's *Seven Days in May*, where General Scott is seeking to oust the President; we know the President, but Scott is the outsider.

"To appreciate a mystery," says E.M. Forster, "part of the mind must be left behind, brooding while the other part goes marching on."[9] The principle operates especially well when the writer feeds the reader some information early and lets it lie there for a while, leaving him to wonder whatever became of it. Mystery writers will sometimes begin with what looks like a major element—an episode, a character, even a partially developed plot—and then make a change to an entirely different matter, without reference to the original element for fifty or a hundred pages. The suspense is heightened for the reader, who races along to find out what it was that happened back there in Chapter I. Another way of capitalizing on the "brooding" effect is the device Du Maurier uses in *Rebecca*: by the time we finish the first chapter we have all the basic information regarding the narrator, her husband, the other chief characters, and the fate of Manderly. As a result of these confidences, we become participants and find ourselves "marching on" and looking back, mindful that, in keeping with those two axioms of the popular formula story, everything will be cleared up before the novel ends.

The device works well in the thriller. There is a scene in Benchley's *Jaws* where some especially vulgar city visitors arrive at the beach, followed shortly by a brassy TV news team drawn by the sensation of the shark attacks. The pleasurable irony of the scene is considerably heightened because the reader knows the real extent of the danger and watches all the posturing and staging in expectation that the real menace may show himself. It is especially effective in the tale of the supernatural. Straub furnishes the reader of *Ghost Story* considerably more information than any character in the story has. Thus, when a very pretty young woman remarks, "I know some people who are interested in the occult," the reader will surely murmur, "I'll just bet you do!" At this point the reader is the only one who knows that she is a ghost. Sometimes a writer can set his reader charging ahead to the extent that he can use something like the football draw play on him, tricking him into making false assumptions and then springing the trap. This is a favorite device of detective story writers, and in the hands of someone like Agatha Christie it becomes a fine art.

There is one special kind of message that might be called the Promissory Plant: it is a small piece of information tucked into a story almost unobtrusively but also with an assurance that it will become important later. Thus Blatty concludes Chapter I of *The Exorcist*: "By midnight, all in the house were asleep. There were no disturbances. That night." The "hook" is those last two words, with which the author assures us that there *will* be disturbances in subsequent nights. In the detective story these "plants" may be clues, and in the thriller they serve as promises that the biggest action is yet to come.

Some of these are plants for the reader to remember, and some, just as obviously, are for him to forget. The old man who seems to be the only survivor of the catastrophe in *The Andromeda Strain*, and the pointed reference to "extraterrestrial life" early in the story, are open promises of things to come. On the other hand, the reader of Tey's *Miss Pym Disposes* will probably forget the allusion to "our only crime" by one of the students in the women's school, a remark that seems only conversational in context, but proves finally to be a critical admission. It should not take long to sensitize most readers to the importance of these messages, with the result that a skillful writer knows exactly what buttons to press in order to make his readers care very much what happens next.

In the Encounter-type story these promissory plants frequently have a cumulative effect even to the extent that they determine the structure of the narrative right up to the point at which the reader has a full understanding of all the factors converging on the denouement. It would take an almost superhuman resolve for the reader of Hailey's *Airport* to put the book down at that point at which the wounded plane is finally approaching touchdown, knowing as he does that there is a stuck plane still blocking the runway, a demonstration of angry residents inside the terminal, a love quadrangle to be resolved, and an impending suicide. Almost any hack can develop sensational cliff-hangers through the use of menace, but the tension Hailey develops is the result of those messages planted from the beginning of the narrative, that add up to a powerful drive.

To this point we have been discussing the *messages* an author sends his reader, most of them significant story elements in themselves and most of them supplying knowledge not generally shared with the characters in the narrative. We are ready now to consider that set of *signals* used to build a reader's feeling of suspense, conveying a type of information that is not substantive in the development of the plot: often, as we shall see, these signals have no bearing on the outcome of the story. Most of them have become conventions of the Suspense Process and consequently also serve as automatic triggers of reader-interest.

A familiar illustration of the use of the signal is the social-event-as-harbinger-of-crisis. Just let the mother in a menaced household announce, "I'm having a few friends in to dinner tomorrow evening," and the reader can brace himself for all hell to break loose. It happens in *Jaws*; after a weekend free of shark-attacks, Ellen Brody makes such an announcement, and before her dinner party is over another shark, this one human, has entered the picture. The same thing happens in *The Exorcist* and in *Ghost Story*. The classic example is the fancy dress ball in *Rebecca*, where the impact is heightened by the narrator's innocent foot-in-the-mouth questions, like "What will Mr. de Winter say?" In this signal, as in the others, it is not the event itself but the suggestion of what is coming that stimulates suspense.

We have already cited the two most commonly used conventional signals, the Solitary Figure and the Exact Time. Other familiar examples are the change in mode, as in an unexpected shift from realism to fantasy, the Fool-to-Worry (as when the protagonist decides that he has been disturbed over nothing) and the Expendable S.O.B., somebody on the "sympathetic" side who makes a nuisance of himself and becomes the predictable first victim of the menace, prompting the reader to remark, "Just as I expected!"

At several points in this discussion we have taken note of a habit of writers of popular formula fiction of calling attention to the author's own participation by making the reader ask, "Why is he doing this?" Whenever a writer repeatedly returns to some apparently minor character, or abruptly drops a subject and does not return to it for fifty pages, the question of Who? or What? becomes less important than Why? or How? When an author can draw us into the raising of such questions, he has made us participants and has accomplished the real goal of suspense.

Notes

[1]During the 1970s *The Writer* featured a number of articles on suspense by such successful authors as Joan Aiken, Brian Garfield, and Babs Deal. Almost habitually, they refer to "the suspense genre" and to "this type of fiction." Most of them seem to assume that menace constitutes the only motivation for suspense; Bill Pronzini goes so far as to say, "Without *menace*, of course, there is no suspense." (89, No. 2 [Feb. 1976] 16).

[2]*Mystery Fiction: Theory and Practice* (New York: Hermitage House, 1952), p. 71.

[3]Cited by Ed McBain in *Eight Black Horses* (New York: Arbor House, 1985), p. 245.

[4]For a good discussion of the ways a writer or director can achieve an extra dimension of suspense by keeping his options open, see John G. Cawelti, *Adventure, Mystery, and Romance* (Chicago: The University of Chicago Press, 1976), pp. 17-18.

[5]As Dennis Porter puts it in "Backward Construction and the Art of Suspense" (*The Poetics of Murder*, ed. Glenn W. Most and William W. Stowe [New York: Harcourt, 1983] p. 330), "...With mere progression there is simply a rush to the pleasure of a denouement that turns out to offer no pleasure at all."

[6]Those that can not be omitted are "bound" motifs. David N. Feldman, "Formalism and Popular Culture," *Journal of Popular Culture*, IX (Fall 1975), 394.

[7]Stuart Hall and Paddy Whannel point out that the art of the English music hall was stylized and conventional, and they argue that "the quality of the performance seems to have increased directly with the degree of familiarity with, or recognition of, the conventions which could be expected." *The Popular Arts* (New York: Pantheon, 1965), p. 57.

[8]Thus Carolyn Wells on *The Woman in White*: "The secret of Collins' power lies not in mere description but in suggestion. He excites us not by what he tells us but by what he does not tell us." *The Technique of the Mystery Story* (Springfield, Mass.: The Home Correspondence School, 1913), p. 40.

[9]*Aspects of the Novel* (New York: Harcourt, Brace, 1927), p. 87.

Popular Culture and Film Studies

Gary Edgerton

Metatheoretical Concerns in Popular Film Theory

The America ideology is not to have any ideology.
(Edmund Wilson, letter to William Faulkner, 1956)

Typically perceptive and provocative, the social and literary critic, Edmund Wilson, acutely understood America's reflex aversion to those who frame their topics in overtly doctrinaire ways. From his formidable, modernist sensibility, the strikingly atheoretical and pragmatic impulse of the majority of his fellow citizens obviously was a quirk to be lampooned and a source of pique and frustration. From our protracted vantage point, however, America's congenital distrust of the dogmatist and his or her orthodoxy can also be viewed as an ideological posture in and of itself.

Pluralism in the United States is a discourse that is rooted in a broader, liberal tradition that dates back to Hobbes and Locke. America's innate suspicion of each new "ism" is much more than the culture's propensity to be anti-intellectual, although Wilson's quote underscores this apparent tendency. The nation's seeming lack of commitment to any one single ideology is more a democratic expression that acknowledges alternatives, and at least in theory, allows for opposing viewpoints and explanations.

The ideology of pluralism also serves as the foundation and organizing principle for all of the film scholarship that has emerged from the movement in popular culture studies during the past quarter-century. The subsequent discourse in popular film is far from homogenous in orientation; it is marked by a wide variety of useful and valid theories and methods. At the same time, there are five similar and connective attitudes that do indeed set this area of film studies apart from other camps of research and writing about the cinema. Reviewing these five basic assumptions is a constructive place to start, since they underlie the most current and prevailing methodologies employed in the study and analysis of popular film.

Although various kinds of popular film theory and criticism appear in nearly every existing motion picture journal from time to time, the most committed and seminal forums in this area of inquiry are *The Journal of Popular Film and Television* and the *Journal of Popular Culture*. A summary perusal of these two periodicals reveals a wide range of research postures and

41

approaches. This eclecticism is a notable strength by which a free selection of ideas from as many different sources as possible is consciously promoted. What results is an intricate web of often interconnected, but sometimes diverse critical voices.

The lack of overall closure understandably unsettles scholars from some quarters. This adherence to pluralism is a view that is far from unstructured and unsystematic however; it is a frame of reference itself that is central to understanding how film is studied from a popular culture perspective. *This tradition holds that motion pictures (and all the other media arts for that matter) are phenomena that are far too complex to be adequately explained by any one all-encompassing theory. Moreover, no theory or critical methodology is sacrosanct, no matter how popular it may be at a given moment.*

Theories are perceived as fluid, framing devices that are always subject to change and further refinement. Methods are likewise seen as tools to be used, adapted, modified, or combined with each other whenever a research problem warrants such coaction. That is not to say that some theories and methodologies have not been preferred over others in the history and development of popular film scholarship; for example, variants of genre, socio-cultural, institutional, political, and feminist criticism are prominent and commonly-used methods. The point here is that the particular agenda of research should determine the approach, not the other way around; and it is generally accepted that no one theory or method, however fashionable, should become orthodoxy and thus stifle free expression in the field.

The second assumption involving film and popular culture is probably the most self-evident: *This line of inquiry has always placed motion pictures in their cultural context. The first allegiance of this genre of film criticism has steadfastly remained the surrounding milieu, not the medium.* Movies and the other media arts are always important to the cultural critic; each communication technology allows for a new orientation by which to structure and analyze human perceptions, thoughts, and sensibilities. Still, the apparatus, in and of itself, is only meaningful in its relationship to the broader conditions, institutions, and discourses that engulf the coordinating process of filmmaking/ film-watching.

From the beginning, popular film scholarship has made a concerted effort to stress the role of the mass audience, and how this grouping affects and is reflected in the resulting movie content; how massive and complex technical, economic, aesthetic, industrial, and ideological forces mobilize to mass produce and distribute motion pictures worldwide; and finally, how the stories, myths, and symbols of the cinema are a composite of many perspectives which, in turn, are subject to the interpretations of numerous mass publics who are separated from each other by time, place, and outlook. The key is that popular film criticism has always spotlighted the *processes of culture,* rather than just conceiving of the film artifact as a hallowed and immutable art object. This predisposition has freed the subsequent discourse to consider pre-filmic, filmic, and post-filmic considerations in such a way that all are seen as affecting and impinging on one another. The motion picture is, therefore, placed within a larger system of cultural significance, as are its stages of conception, production, and reception.

This focusing of attention on the dynamics that undergird the entire film culture and its processes leads inextricably to a third assumption: *The emphasis in popular film theory and criticism veers beyond the supposed meaning that is found within any particular motion picture to how that meaning is produced and received. Furthermore, cross-disciplinary approaches are usually necessary when analyzing the intricate workings by which meaning is socially constructed and later apprehended.* Popular film scholarship is never text-oriented alone. Close readings of individual motion pictures has always been more the domain of other schools of cinema studies. Scholarship in popular culture and film, in contrast, has customarily placed its research subjects within a broader framework of forces as a means of uncovering the socio-historical, cultural, and to a lesser degree, psychological mechanisms that largely determine shades of meaning.

Meaning in this way is not understood to exist in any static, one-dimensional form which is seemingly bound within the confines of the film artifact just waiting to be unlocked and released by some all-purpose methodology. The significance of any film topic is instead perceived to be flexible and many-sided, and the researcher needs to cultivate theories and knowledge from numerous fields and related disciplines to be able to more fully comprehend its subtleties and implications. Most of popular film scholarship is accordingly interdisciplinary or multidisciplinary in nature, and this tendency ultimately reflects its rootedness in the traditions of the field of popular culture and American studies.

Popular film theory and criticism has also accentuated the viewpoint and orientation of the mass consumer, rather than the professional movie critic or scholar. This discourse generally relies on critical approaches that reveal public voices and their versions of reality, not theoretical postures that are designed to teach the so-called naive and uninitiated viewer how to appreciate film art as an object which is lofty and sublime. A fourth assumption, therefore, is that *motion pictures are studied because of their immense popularity and vast influences on the culture, not despite these characteristics.*

As one of several forerunners to the postmodernist film criticism of the 1980s, the popular culturalists began the process of reformulating the usual structures and categories that were traditionally reserved for art, media, and perspective in the 1960s. The customary boundaries between fine, folk, and popular art were questioned and rethought. The film culture was no longer conceived of referring merely to an art form or even Hollywood, but to a broader state-of-mind that envisioned the popular arts in general as intrinsic and intimate parts of our world and environment; in the words of Gene Youngblood, movies became "expanded cinema," and the term evolved in such a way as to include all the electronic media, especially television and video.

The border between what were once considered private and public perspectives also grew increasingly indistinct as the media environment became ever more recognizable and pervasive. Movie content was no longer thought of as a one-of-a-kind, personalized statement by an auteur, but the articulation of broader points-of-view which are the products of the culture at large and represent various segments of its mass audience.

As a result, popular film studies followed an alternative, conjectural route by so thoroughly focusing its attention and interest on those factors that are most public and masscult about motion pictures. This unhesitating concern for the "popular," in turn, liberated popular film scholarship to resee and transcend the usual aesthetic boundaries that were being applied to motion pictures; recognize the many relationships that exist between all the media arts; entertain heterogeneous viewpoints, and challenge the customary suppositions and demarcations that had previously been established about film art and culture in the field.

The final assumption that propels and actuates the study of film from a popular culture perspective is the belief that *popular film theory and criticism should be as democratized as the media art that it strives to define, interpret, and analyze.* No motion pictures are off-limits for the pen (or word processor) of the popular culturalist; from the viewer-friendly, high-tech extravaganzas of a Steven Spielberg or a George Lucas, to regionalist renderings by a Horton Foote or a John Sayles, to pornography, documentaries, or experimental films and videos, there are no tacit barriers on what can or cannot be researched, studied, and reviewed. The resulting critical reaction is similarly devised by scholars who see themselves not as detached and distinguished experts, but as full-fledged members of the respective audiences that attend to these various kinds of films; and their subsequent writings are intended and designed to be read, discussed, debated, and hopefully appreciated by fellow viewers.

Popular film analysts are schooled in a vast number of theories and methodologies. Some are more easily understood in lay terms than others. The newer British and European-based cultural theories particularly demand a specialized knowledge of how perceptions, signs, story and language structures, and discourses work that are for the moment at least beyond the purview of the average filmgoer.

Popular motion picture theorists and critics accordingly feel a corresponding obligation to decipher and demystify any conceptual models and wordings that are markedly arcane. Popular film scholars are generally committed to informing themselves of all the various theoretical postures that are being debated in the discipline, while at the same time making an extra and concerted effort to imperceptibly assimilate any of the more difficult, though useful critical formulas into their books and essays, so that these publications can ultimately make sense to the proverbial film lover on the street. The basic rule-of-thumb is to avoid particularized jargon, as much as possible, if in fact the same speculative frameworks and methodologies can be presented in simpler and less alienating language. The discourse in popular culture and motion pictures is not aimed at only a few specialists in film studies, but ideally it will have meaning for the audiences that are reflected in and affected by movie content and culture as well.

Popular Film Theory and Method

Reality is socially constructed and...the sociology of knowledge must analyze the processes in which this occurs. (Peter L. Berger and Thomas Luckmann, *The Social Construction of Reality*. 1966)

There has surely been a turbulence in film studies for more than 15 years now, where the influx of a variety of new theories, such as semiotics, structuralism, phenomenology, different types of psychoanalysis, and poststructuralism have successfully challenged and supplanted the more traditional or classical ways of thinking about motion pictures. Much of this upheaval has certainly been for the good, as the more static and supposedly immutable models of aesthetics and culture have been replaced by methods that reveal how our perceptions and values are actually the result of our social enmeshment, not some other more absolute barometer. Needless to say, this theoretical implication was initially disconcerting for the world of film, as it was for philosophy, anthropology, the sociology of knowledge, linguistics, psychology, and literary studies well before it impacted on the study of media.

The effect of what is generally referred to in the aggregate as contemporary critical theory has transcended many fields and disciplines, and has been as decisive for popular film theory and method as it has for other areas of cinema studies. Today the way popular film scholars approach the concepts of genre, culture, the institution of moviemaking, politics, and gender have all been greatly altered and enhanced by these revisional perspectives. To paraphrase the above quote by Berger and Luckmann, meaning in the film culture "is" understood to be "socially constructed," and the respective methods for examining the media "must analyze the processes in which this occurs."

Over the years, the discourse in popular film has shown a propensity towards a handful of dominant critical views. The two most important are arguably the study of genres and socio-cultural criticism. Like all the principal theories of popular film, the general explanations about "what a motion picture genre is" and "how it works" have progressively matured through a traditional to a modernist to a postmodernist phase, much as many of the movie genres themselves have evolved. Genre theory actually dates back to Aristotle, and was first applied to the popular arts in the 1920s. *The genre perspective generally examines how story formulas are composed of a system of conventional areas which incorporate cultural meanings, mythic archetypes, and social preoccupations into a broadly recurring style and format. This critical view focuses attention on the processes by which the genre is constructed, how its supertext is structured and develops, and how the genre is received and understood by various mass publics over time.*

The first stage of movie genre criticism was essentially static and reductionistic in scope. Prior to the mid-1960s, analysis was primarily centered on the motion picture category itself; in this way, a classical or ideal representation of the film genre was envisioned, and subsequent motion pictures were compared and contrasted with what was considered the essence of the genre. Several crucial shortcomings in both theory and method arose from this initial speculation about the nature of genreness.

The theoretical projection of a perfect type lifted much of the critical dialogue about film genres from the more secular spheres of society, culture, industry, and economics. The intention was to raise the discussion of motion picture art and genre studies to a new level of respectability that approximates what were then the more standard goals of the fine arts, such as truth, beauty, universal quality, and timelessness. The result was evidently a conceptual shortsightedness that wrenched the genre idea from those very factors of context and environment that ultimately determine its meanings.

The traditional approach, moreover, reduced the method of genre criticism to a taxonomical exercise of creating conventional categories, such as plot structure, setting, characterization, icons, themes, and techniques; counting the frequency of examples in each area of classification; and then making inferences about the inherent meaning invested in each of these assorted items. Much of the resulting criticism is only valuable in hindsight in that it focused attention for the first time on the notion of popular movie genres and thus provided a base on which more modernist readings would eventually follow. Occasionally, though, film critics, such as André Bazin in his essays on the American western and Robert Warshow in his writings on the gangster and the westerner in *The Immediate Experience*, would instinctively transcend their limitations in theory and method with striking examples of socio-cultural insight, overall brilliance, and a lively appreciation for the importance of popular cinema.[1]

A new kind of self-reflexive and experimental sensibility entered the domain of film studies in general, and genre theory in particular, during the 1960s. A modernist perspective began to gradually replace the more traditional aesthetic and cultural models by reperceiving the relationship between motion picture art and reality as being much more ambiguous in its parameters, values, and meanings. Many camps of American film criticism adapted versions of the auteur perspective that had been germinating in French theory during the preceding decade. The popular culturalists, somewhat in reaction to this development, fashioned an alternative brand of modernist movie criticism that was more oriented to the public outlook of the mass audience than to the personal directives of an auteur.

The key is that both the genre critics and the auteurists were slowly widening their scope of analysis to include the process of filmmaking/film-watching, although neither camp had yet consciously realized the full impact of this overriding dynamic. The popular film theorists, moreover, acknowledged the role that the mass audience played in motion picture production by influencing the industry to either repeat or ignore generic formulas, depending on the previous response of the marketplace. During the late 1960s and into the 1970s, the influx of what was called new theory soon reasserted the idea that the film process was subject to more encompassing human structures or socio-historical contexts. The various applications of cinesemotics, cinestructuralism, and psychoanalytic film criticism coalesced into a research attitude that affirmed how meaning in the cinema is manufactured by the processes of film, history, and culture, and is subject to the complex interplay between movies, ideology, and society.

The modernist attitude of popular genre criticism, much of auteurism, and especially new theory, provided the whole of film studies with a clearer recognition and understanding of the overall filmic process, as well as how the ongoing movement of this process and its interaction of parts shape and frame the styles, symbols, genres, and myths of the cinema. Popular film scholarship, as evident in the culture journals, John Cawelti's *The Six-Gun Mystique*, and Jack Nachbar's anthology *Focus on the Western* for example, were busy examining the role that mass culture was having in the formation of movie genres and their respective meanings.[2] New theory also impacted directly on genre studies with the appearances of such works as Jim Kitses's *Horizons West*, Colin McArthur's *Underworld USA*, Will Wright's *Sixguns and Society*, and Ann Kaplan's *Women and Film Noir*.[3]

John Cawelti's provocative and pivotal 1978 essay, *"Chinatown* and Generic Transformation in Recent American Films,"* is a useful place to consider how the methodology of genre criticism evolved from its traditional beginnings to its full-fledged, modernist expression during the late 1970s. In this piece, the author's basic premise that "traditional genres" transform along with "the cultural myths they once embodied" undermines the notion of the ideal and unchanging supertext, which was a romantic projection that had been obsolete for some time. From the modernist perspective, generic parameters are forever realizing themselves afresh with each new invention in form and cultural meaning in the relevant film category. Cawelti also links these "generic transformations" to the growing sophistication of the mass audience, to the "imaginative needs of our time," and to creative contributions by specific auteurs.[4]

Popular genre criticism was now operating on a much more sophisticated level of theorization than it was in its traditional phase. The modernists were conceptualizing an interlocking cultural process that assumed systemic input from the realms of authorship, the film medium and institution, the mass consumer, and the force of social ideologies in the creation of meaning in individual generic texts or supertexts. In method, popular film scholars were in turn inacting a two-fold technique: they were firstly identifying conventional mutations in the genre's classical form, and then attempting to trace these changes back to their source. For example, Cawelti cites how a movie like *Blazing Saddles* lampoons the traditional western by "inver[ting the] expected implications" (i.e., employing a black sheriff) and "breaking...convention by the intrusion of reality."[5] These instances are next related to the altered sensibilities of both the mass audience and the filmmaker, Mel Brooks, who together no longer ascribe to the cultural myth of the old west as it once was.

Secondly, the genre critics were performing more macro-analyses of how the generic supertext itself was splintering into a number of different and comparative versions. In the case of Cawelti, the author intriguingly separated "generic transformation" into four separate manifestations or categories, which directly corresponded to varying attitudes within the mass culture towards these once inviolable generic myths.[6] The important point is that the broader generic parameters were now conceived of as being able to accommodate more than one, and sometimes contradictory generic models (i.e. the western and the anti-western). Cawelti also perceptively noted that "the present period of American filmmaking will seem in retrospect an important time of artistic and cultural transition."[7] As was previously happening in a number of other arts, such as architecture, painting, literature, and experimental film and video, commercial movies were presently entering a period of postmodernist expression and criticism.

Postmodernism is an eclectic approach which combines disparate elements of past artistic styles into a new and viable formal arrangement. Genre films specifically, such as *Silverado* (western), *Gremlins* (horror), or *Mad Max* (the road movie) for instance, combine conventions from the past and present and ironically disconnect both versions from their accepted traditional and modernist meanings. As in the example of *Silverado*, what is to be made of a genre picture that splits the cowboy hero into four, dissimilar and offbeat parts where each character evokes a different phase of the genre's development: the juvenile western; the adult western; the social western; and the anti-western? How has popular motion picture theory and criticism adapted to an era where genres, myths, symbols, and styles of previous decades are increasingly recycled and oftentimes blended with whatever happens to be new?

In the 1970s and early 1980s, the poststructuralists provided film studies in general with a view of language, narratives, and signs which insists that no values are fixed, and no meanings are certain. Generic significance is therefore perceived to be contingent on the encompassing capacities of cultural discourses and socio-political ideologies, as well as generated through the interaction between media consumers and the movies they attend. In 1985 and 1986, three special issues of *The Journal of Popular Film and Television* devoted to genre studies offer several interesting applications of contemporary genre theory from a distinctly postmodernist vantage point.

John Cawelti's lead article, "The Question of Popular Genres," provides an overview perspective on this critical approach, and then calls for more attention to the promise and potential of reader/viewer response theory.[8] Robert Eberwein next applies the assumptions of this theoretical perspective when he argues in "Genre and the Writerly Text" that the generically fragmented films of today demand viewer participation to complete the construction of meaning that is taking place between moviemakers, these genre films, and the mass consumer.[9] In his recent publications, Gregory Waller has continued to build on previous popular culture scholarship when calling for an increased regard for the role that other genres, arts, and media play in the formation of the multigeneric films of the 1980s.[10]

The key development in all of these recent examples of generic research and method is the mutual recognition that individual differences in perception and perspective comingle on the personal, public, and cultural levels throughout the filmic process to socially construct the meanings we create. Relative meaning in the postmodern sense is, furthermore, not to be construed as being non-ideological, valueless, and non-committal, but instead extremely subtle, many-sided, and probably more complex and challenging than ever anticipated.

Along with genre studies, the second principal and complementary outlook that has compelled the discourse in popular culture and motion pictures is socio-cultural criticism. The preceding discussion on genre theory and method, in fact, is grounded in the basic premises of this critical view. *The socio-cultural perspective presumes that movie content and culture simultaneously influence and reflect the society and era from which they originate and belong.* On the one hand, the vast effect of the film world on human behavior is profound, and in general, not easily discernable by any exact measure. Literally hundreds of increasingly reliable and telling studies are nevertheless appearing. This research seeks to chart how different segments of the mass audience are moved, altered, and modified in action and outlook by their participation in and exposure to the milieu of motion pictures.[11]

The aspect of the socio-cultural perspective that is most fully developed and apparent in the dialogue concerning popular culture and motion pictures is irrefutably the examination of how mass society and its many publics are portrayed, however indirectly, in the structure, products, and material conditions of the movie industry and culture. Popular film scholars assume a role that ideally combines the skills of a cultural critic, historian, and anthropologist in their search to uncover the population's conscious and unconscious transmissions within the filmic and extra-filmic realms of the cinema.

The central assumption of popular culturalists in this line of film research is that movies and their surrounding institutional and industrial contexts are products of a given time and civilization; moreover, motion picture content and culture mirror the concerns, beliefs, myths, fantasies, desires, fears, and aspirations of various social pluralities in both hidden and overt ways. It is, therefore, the goal of popular film critics to detect and reveal these literal and latent thought processes, ideologies, feelings, moods, and discourses with their respective theoretical views and methodologies.

This impulse to consider film artifacts and their diverse groupings as barometers of cultural sentiment thoroughly permeates the previous discussion about genre studies. Generic transformations, in particular, are perceived as being inextricably intertwined with movements and shifts within the society at large. The socio-cultural perspective, nevertheless, holds wide-reaching implications that transcend beyond genre to non-genre, or "art" films, and post-genre offerings, such as movies that contain a myriad of conventions from many generic categories but ultimately fulfill the formal and audience requirements of none.[12]

Movies as a mirror can be discerned in settings, storylines, individual signs and symbols, stars and characterizations, and the use of filmic styles and techniques. Social predispositions and predilections are also evident in the manner by which Hollywood and all the other venues of the motion picture industry have evolved and continue to develop; in the patterns of speech, body language, construction, transportation, and lifestyle that the movie institution exhibits; and in its inclination to symbiotically share with some reciprocating arts, media, and portions of culture, and subsume or discard others. In all these multifarious relationships and formal characteristics, certain practices, belief structures, and myths are evidently highlighted, while others are suppressed. The essence of socio-cultural methodology is to identify these societal preferences; and, in turn, distinguish and infer whatever evidence and insights are available about the more encompassing processes of culture, history, and the continuing human condition.[13]

A final note is to again emphasize that there is no all-purpose method or research agenda; these selections depend entirely on what is most appropriate for the questions asked, and what the scholar can reasonably hope to discover. There are scores of critical models available in journals, texts, and anthologies which analyze certain elements and features of popular film and culture as they relate to discrete topic areas and institutions, including race, age, gender, regionalism, politics, art, business and the economy, religion, education, mass communication, and the family.[14] There is also a strong and vital tradition that already prevails which investigates motion pictures as historical documents, and the film establishment as an "unconscious historian."[15] The point is that there now exists two generations of popular film scholarship that has embraced the notion that movie entertainment and culture represent more than just escapism; they offer an abundant and lush invitation into the imagination and dreams of a society and its history. We as viewers and researchers need only to continue to revise the theories and to refine the methods that are necessary to recover the shades of meaning that lie waiting for us to share.

Notes

[1]André Bazin, "The Western, or the American Film Par Excellence," and "The Evolution of the Western," in *What is Cinema?* Volume II, trans. Hugh Gray (Berkeley, California: University of California Press, 1971); and Robert Warshow, *The Immediate Experience* (New York: Doubleday Anchor, 1964).

[2]John G. Cawelti, *The Six-Gun Mystique*, 2nd Edition (Bowling Green, Ohio: Bowling Green State University Popular Press, 1984); and Jack Nachbar, ed., *Focus on the Western* (Englewood Cliffs, New Jersey: Prentice-Hall, 1974).

[3]Jim Kitses, *Horizons West* (Bloomington, Indiana: Indiana University Press, 1969); Colin McArthur, *Underworld USA* (London: Secker & Warburg/British Film Institute, 1972); Will Wright, *Sixguns and Society* (Berkeley, California: University of California Press, 1975); and E. Ann Kaplan, ed., *Women and Film Noir* (London: British Film Institute, 1978).

[4]The term supertext refers to the ever-fluid and dynamic generic parameters that are determined by the cultural interchange between filmmakers, individual genre films, and the movie audience. John G. Cawelti, *"Chinatown* and Generic Transformation in Recent American Films," in *Film Theory and Criticism*, Third Edition, ed. by Gerald Mast and Marshall Cohen (New York: Oxford University Press, 1985).

[5]*Ibid.*, p. 513.

[6]Cawelti's four-part model of generic transformation includes (1) humorous burlesque, or a lampooning of the genre; (2) the cultivation of nostalgia, or a romanticizing of the generic myth; (3) demythologization, or a demonstration that the

generic myth is unreal or obsolete; and (4) the affirmation of the myth for its own sake, or the presentation of the generic myth as unreal, but then a confirmation of the myth as "a reflection of authentic human aspirations and needs."·

⁷*Ibid.*, p. 520.

⁸John G. Cawelti, "The Question of Popular Genres," *The Journal of Popular Film and Television*, 13 (Summer 1985), pp. 55-61.

⁹Robert T. Eberwein, "Genre and the Writerly Text," *The Journal of Popular Film and Television*, 13 (Summer 1985), pp. 63-68.

¹⁰Gregory A. Waller, *The Living and the Undead: From Stoker's 'Dracula' to Romero's 'Dawn of the Dead'* (Urbana, Illinois: University of Illinois Press, 1985); Waller, "Mike Hammer and Detective Films of the 1980s," *The Journal of Popular Film and Television*, 13 (Fall 1985), pp. 108-125; and Waller, "Re-placing *The Day After*," *Cinema Journal*, 26 (Spring 1987), pp. 3-20.

¹¹For extensive bibliographies on film audience and effects research see: Bruce A. Austin, *The Film Audience: An International Bibliography of Research with Annotations and an Essay* (Metuchen, New Jersey: Scarecrow, 1983); and Austin, "Research on the Film Audience: An Annotated Bibliography, 1982-1985," *The Journal of Popular Film and Television*, 14 (Spring 1986), pp. 33-39.

¹²For two interesting discussions on post-genre offerings see: Eberwein; and Christopher Sharrett, "The Hero as Pastiche: Myth, Male Fantasy, and Simulacra in *Mad Max* and *The Road Warrior*," *The Journal of Popular Film and Television*, 13 (Summer 1985), pp. 80-91.

¹³For some overview literature on the socio-cultural perspective see: Michael T. Marsden, John C. Nachbar, and Sam L. Grogg, Jr., eds., *Movies as Artifacts: Cultural Criticism of Popular Film* (Chicago: Nelson-Hall, 1982).

¹⁴Two useful bibliographies on popular movie content and culture are: Larry N. Landrum, "Sources for the Study of Popular Film," in *Movies as Artifacts: Cultural Criticism of Popular Film*, pp. 239-264; and Landrum, "Recent Work in Genre," *The Journal of Popular Film and Television*, 13 (Fall 1985), pp. 151-158.

¹⁵See: *Film and History*, a quarterly created by the Historians Film Committee of the American Historical Association; John E. O'Connor and Martin A. Jackson, eds., *American History/American Film: Interpreting the Hollywood Image* (New York: Frederick Ungar, 1979); and Peter C. Rollins, *Hollywood as Historian: American Film in a Cultural Context* (Lexington, Kentucky: University of Kentucky Press, 1983).

Taking Inventory:
Stock Elements of American Feature Films

Paul Loukides

In "An Apology for Poetry," written in the 1580's, Sir Philip Sidney comments that of the various kinds of poets—and poetry—"some [are] termed according to the matter they deal with, some by the sorts of verses they like best to write in."

Were Sidney a popular culturist writing today, he might comfortably reflect that film genres—like literary genres—are either termed according to the matter they deal with—as the Western, gangster film, war film or disaster movie, or the manner in which they are presented—as with the film noir, the musical or the animated film, and that others are termed by their theme as with the buddy film, the anti-war film, or the celebration of family film.

For the popular culturist interested in cataloging, describing and analyzing the patterns of American popular film, is it perhaps time to suggest that our traditional focus on film genres is outmoded?

Can it be that our genre classifications confound more often than they illuminate because of our inability to decide on even the fundamental premise of genre? If we idiosyncratically classify films in terms of themes, or subjects, or treatments, or plots, or locales, and call the resulting group a genre, then we have created a meaningless taxonomy of film.

If we cannot settle the question of premise, then *Bonnie and Clyde* is a gangster film, an outlaw film, a tragic love story and a celebration of violence. *Butch Cassidy* is a Western, a buddy film, an adventure romance and a death of the West film. If *Jaws* is a disaster movie, then so are *Halloween* and *Friday the 13th*. Given an open premise, *All the President's Men, Ghandhi, Patton, Sgt. York, Lawrence of Arabia, Midnight Express, Moulin Rouge* and the *Lou Gehrig Story* belong in the same genre because of their biographical/historical dimension.

Genre studies have not, of course, been fruitless; they have simply not fulfilled their early promise. It is by looking at the best of genre studies that we begin to see the direction post-generic studies might take. The most illuminating genre studies—like those of the classic Western, the classic gangster film, the film noir, and the atomic monster—draw their strength from their identification and analysis of sub-generic elements rather than from the creation or codification of genre patterns.

Without exception, the conventions that underpin any concept of film genre are most clearly and precisely described not in terms of genre-structures, but as conventions which exist across generic lines. These conventions—stock characters, stock actions, stock plot devices and stock themes—are the foundation of the popular arts and of all generic forms, and offer fruitful ground for study.

What this paper proposes then is the redirection of critical attention away from the study of film genres toward a more detailed study of the distinct lesser conventions of popular film. Rather than focusing our attention on the "buddy film" or the "Sci Fi" film or the "Western," would we not learn more about American popular film by careful classification and analysis of the stock characters, stock actions, stock plot devices and stock thematic motifs which are the primary components of popular film?

Like traditional folk songs, or folk tales, popular films endlessly play variants on a standard—and limited—number of narrative devices. If we are to become more exact in our attempts to find both the changing and enduring patterns of popular culture, we would do well to catalogue the components out of which popular films are constructed. If a major goal of the study of the popular arts is an understanding of the cultural mores of those who produce and consume those arts, then the study of the component conventions of popular film will, perhaps, lead to different kinds of understanding than those afforded by the study of individual films or film genres.

The study of stereotypes and stock characters in popular film offers one point of focus for sub-generic studies. For the most part, analyses of stereotypes and stock characters seem to be initiated largely out of offense taken with Hollywood's negative stereotyping of women, blacks, Indians, Italians or other large coherent social groups. While much of the scholarship on these groups has been excellent and illuminating, not nearly enough attention has been focused on the diverse collection of stereotypes and stock figures that people American film.

One advantage to focusing on stock characters as they appear in a wide range of films is that such attention can help reveal the interpenetration of popular arts and culture. Because stereotypes and stock characters are relatively easy to identify with some precision, it is possible to date their appearance and/or disappearance from popular film and thus begin to chart their evolution within a changing social context.

To take one example, it seems likely that we will not again see any number of "immigrant grandmothers" of the kind brought to flower in *A Tree Grows in Brooklyn*. In the 1930's and 1940's, a large portion of the American film going audience still lived with the immigrant experience; two generations later, the last great wave of immigration is far removed from the psychic and emotional lives of the audience. Nana, from the old country, is no longer a stock figure of either American life or American movies. Like the Stepin Fetchit character and the loving Mammie, Nana has lost her symbolic value in movies because of historically documentable changes in American society.

The stereotype and the stock character—whether they be buck-toothed Japanese, tragic mulattoes, supercilious English butlers, thieving young hoods, or ignorant hillbillies, are filmic evidence of the matrix of cultural assumptions held by the audience. Would we not do well to systematically document their use?

Equally illuminating—but even less often studied—are the conventions of incidental action and dialogue that form the visual and verbal texture of conventional film. Such conventions are part of our informal folklore, yet where would we look to get a well documented or comprehensive view of the fashions that these conventions enjoy?

Is it only imagination, or did more heroes chain smoke in the 30's and 40's than in the 70's and 80's? Were the apartment bar and the bottle in the desk drawer more common in the 30's and 40's? When did modern heroes stop putting on their hats? When did going to a restaurant replace going to a nightclub as the thing to do with urban leisure? When did the gestures of adjusting french cuffs or smoothing a girdle stop being signals for readiness? How many heroes feed pets? How many villains keep aquariums? When was it first "too quiet?" Does anyone still say "No, we mustn't" or "We can't go on like this?" When did sticking a gun in someone's mouth first appear in film? When did kicking in doors replace the heavy shoulder? Have mothers entirely stopped explaining to adolescents that father loves them in his own inarticulate way? Do bartenders still say "What'll it be?" Do lovers say "Darling!" or "You shouldn't have." And who first said on film, "Have a nice day"?

The conventions of incidental action and dialogue are clearly not without significance; they afford the popular culturist evidence of the very thread of the cultural cloth. That there are just some things a man has got to do is not just a credo for the gunfighter. Until we have documented this dimension of film, how can we begin to understand the interpenetration of popular film, and the American experience?

A third area on which we might focus is clearly an important component of all narrative genres. The stock plot device—the formula complication of plot and the formula resolutions of complex situations—are as familiar as the movies and literature. Aristotle's scene of recognition, or the classic Western's gunfight, or the movie chase, or the death of the villain, are the fundamental components not only of well-defined genres, but of all popular narrative arts.

The function, history and the evolution of these conventions needs to be documented. While the Motion Picture Code may give us the direct motive for the ritualistic death of the villain, the just punishment of the adulteress, the salvation of the good/bad hero, and the last minute rescue of the innocent, the Code will not explain why the hero is so often captured by the villain (re: James Bond), why the woman never stays in the car as instructed (or at home, or other safe place). In how many films do soldiers going to war play out a scene of conflict between love and duty? Given the new dimensions of violence, do the dying get less chance to speak now as their lives ebb away? When did it become fashionable for policemen to have scenes of conflict with their superiors? Are there periods of greater or lesser popularity for the stock devices of instant antipathy which leads to romance, Cinderella transformation of spectacled women, love at first sight?

The stock plot device—whether a jealous misunderstanding, or a seemingly poor rich man, or a shoot-out on main street, takes its form from the cultural assumptions of the historical moment. Without the stock plot device, the rituals of popular film could not be enacted, and yet we have barely begun to catalogue or analyze these fundamental units of the popular film.

Intimately tied to the use of the stock plot device, but a convention in its own right, is the stock thematic motif. Again, the strictures of Motion Picture Production Codes are helpful in defining these motifs. The inevitable punishment of the criminal, the obligatory unhappiness of the adulterer, the sure piety of the minister were the stock thematic premises of the Code. These, and other thematic motifs, are at least as familiar to a modern audience as the great chain of being and the divine right of kings were to Elizabethan audiences.

Often these thematic motifs are articulated as stock motives; at other times they are so clearly understood in their implicit form that they need never be mentioned. The gunfighter may remind us of his code; the bride-to-be will not. How many films include the stock theme that men should be strong and women should be loving? How many films assume women are fulfilled by men, marriage and children, while men are fulfilled by achievement outside the home? We hardly need parents' groups to tell us that films casually suggest that violence is an acceptable—even praiseworthy—solution to problems. In how many films is running away (or retreat) anything but the coward's way? Has there really been a shift in the dominant attitude toward war? Are the filmic assumptions about war, patriotism and individual responsibility the same in 1983 as they were in 1953? When did we stop assuming that virginity or innocence or marital fidelity were worth preserving? Can film makers assume that audiences know that parents naturally love their children, that every man dreams of success, or that big business is corrupt, or that it's not winning that counts, but sportsmanship? At what point in history did the assumption of white supremacy or the validity of imperialism begin to fade?

Endlessly repeated, rarely challenged, stock thematic motifs seem to encapsulate bits of American folk wisdom. Yet as frequently as these thematic motifs occur, they have been neither well catalogued nor broadly studied. To begin to understand the cultural assumptions of those who produce and consume popular film, we must delineate the entire spectrum of stock thematic motifs within the popular film.

Cataloging, describing, dating and analyzing the uses of stock characters, stock actions, stock plot devices and stock themes offers a means for furthering our understanding of popular culture and the complex matrix which creates and supports it. What is clear is that we have only begun to deal with the most complex questions of the dynamics of change in the popular arts. To further our studies we will need analytical tools which can be used to systematically describe and document the components of hundreds of films. A concentrated focus on the stock elements of film—across genres and across decades—can provide new and useful insights into the patterns of American film and American culture.

History and Popular Culture

Carlton Jackson

There are at least two major categories of historian, each of whom tends to despise the other. One type is the "Sociological-Philosophical," (SP), while the other is "Popular-Journalistic" (PJ).

On any subject, the first thing a SP historian looks for is focus. What is the context of the subject in the larger world? What are you trying to prove with your pursual of it? How do the pieces fit and what do they mean once they are put together? Without rationale, there is nothing.

The PJ historian attempts to find a slant, an angle, a particular way of treating a subject. He will want his writing to "say something" to the generation in which he lives, while the SP historian's focus is very often an end in itself; going no farther than the time of the subject under discussion.

The PJ historian is apt to believe that the discipline of history belongs to literature rather than to any of the "social sciences." In fact, the PJ historian turns up his nose at the very phrase "social science." If it is social it can't be a science, he will probably argue, and if it is a science it can't be social, because science is predictable, and social mores are not. Of course, the SP historian thoroughly disagrees with this point of view, arguing that history *is* a science, with clearly forecastable roles, holding Von Ranke's oft quoted phrase, "Geschicte wie es eigentlich gewesen war," as the highest possible creed.

Whenever a SP historian goes into a new city, the first thing he is likely to do is visit a museum, or two or three. On the other hand, the PJ historian will probably take a walk (and, more than likely, he's familiar with that phrase in other connotations), turning down every street he comes to out of curiosity about what's around the corner. He will also visit a few bars, and find out what the "commoners" are thinking. An SP historian had rather find out about the "commoners" from books on the subject.

The SP historian believes that history is made up of thesis, antithesis, synthesis, rationality, and elitism. The PJ historian will emphasize slices of life, and try to put them together into a whole, without forever making the point that everything has got to *mean* something. He certainly will not agree with the elitist "great man" thesis, or to any particular rationality in the universe.

The SP historian will probably maintain that the more education a person acquires, the more rational that person will become. The PJ historian might well tell you that an education is supposed to open a mind and make it amenable to things, both physical and spiritual, that it does not comprehend, more *liberal*

57

in things it confronts. Perhaps it was this kind of process that caused such a great intellect as Horace Greely's to believe that one can actually communicate with those who have departed this earth. In fact, Gilbert Seldes, in his book, *The Stammering Century*, pointed out that the educated person was much more apt to embrace doctrines of spiritualism than the uneducated, conservative masses.

To summarize the differences, the SP historian lives for focus, rationale, theory, scientific predictability, and methodological elitism. The PJ historian will stress angle (subtly different from "focus," in that once it is established, it becomes as "modernistic" as it can be), prefer the phrase "social studies" over "social sciences," readily mix with the populace to see what's on their mind, and have a beer or two with them, while his counterpart, the SP historian is sipping wine and nibbling cheese at a local reception.

These differences have gone a long way in producing one of the great academic quarrels of our time. They are at the heart of the legitimacy or non-legitimacy of "Popular Culture." Of course, the SP historian does not believe in "Popular Culture." Of course, the PJ historian does. The SP historian would never be caught dead at a Popular Culture Association meeting; the PJ historian can hardly wait for the next one. Of the two types history-at least immediate history-the PJ historian is probably the more useful to society.

The Uses of Popular Culture
for
Political Science

James Combs

Academic disciplines are always in danger of acquiring a bad reputation. Like the proverbial widow across the tracks, they can come to be seen as too fast; or like the equally proverbial old maid librarian, to be seen as too slow. In the former instance are those disciplines, and interdisciplinary agglomerations, that acquire a reputation for being trendy, hopping aboard the bandwagon and beating the drum for whatever new intellectual fashion is parading through town at the moment. But even though funning in the sporting houses of academia is dangerous enough for one's health and reputation, equally damaging is acquiring the reputation for intellectual chastity, never daring to passionately embrace anyone or anything, dooming oneself to a life of sterility and unadventuresome caution. I fear that for the uninitiated, and the snobbish, popular culture has acquired the reputation, undeservedly so, of being loose and trendy; but it is also the case, I suspect, that political science has acquired the reputation, more deservedly so, of being intellectually chaste, the old maid of the social sciences committed to the sterile rites of the familiar and safe.

Political scientists thus tend to think of people who study popular culture as a bit debauched, and certainly too gaudy for their tastes. Conversely, popular culturists will express the opinion that political scientists have all the flair of undertakers. Certainly their national conventions confirm for many observers this impression: popular culture conventions are lively, diverse affairs, where as far as paper and panel topic anything goes, and the hotel bar is always full; political science conventions, by contrast, are quiet to the point of somberness, where paper and panel topics are indistinguishable from years past and confined to safe and dreary subjects, and where evenings in Chicago or New Orleans are enlivened by collections of middle-aged men in brown suits trekking a block down the street from the hotel to get the dinner for ten at a recommended Chinese restaurant.

Such a contrast may be unfair, but it points up the difficulty of bridging the gap between two academic disciplines with such diverse backgrounds and reputations. Political scientists will often opine that the study of popular culture (and, now, "popular communication") is so much silliness, and can be safely

59

ignored as another form of naughty fluff relegated across the academic tracks to the illegitimate status it deserves. But like so many other people or things of dubious reputation, they do it an injustice, and could learn much from it. They probably do not regard what popular culture scholars find as valid evidence, and do not see the political relevance. This position is taken, recall, in the wake of the communications revolution and the popular culture explosion of the past several decades. As an experiment, glance through the political science journals from 1981 to 1989, and you will find scant attention to the fact that a former movie actor has been President during then. Political scientists ignore popular culture at the peril of missing a major source of knowledge about the conduct of politics in a world with a vast and important popular culture. To understand Ronald Reagan, I contend, one has to know about more than demographic shifts, neoconservative ideology, and party unities and disunities. The student of politics interpreting Reagan would be well advised to understand the persistence of the nostalgic myth in American culture; to ponder the history of Hollywood and the heroic expectations it gave iconic shape to; to read of the rise of celebrity culture, and the merger of show business and politics; to grasp the rhetorical importance of political folklore derived from the common culture; in a word, to not dismiss Ronald Reagan as a fool or an aberration but to see his rise to power in the context of the development of popular trends culminating in the merger of Hollywood and Washington, and to call for the use of the popular culture literature to enrich our understanding of politics.

Here I would like to point to some ideas, and illustrative examples, that I hope might stimulate some adventurous political scientists, and popular culture scholars, to pursue the relationship between politics and popular culture. Political scientists (such as students of "public opinion") will, I think, find that their understanding of politics is enhanced by understanding "the culture of the populace." And popular culturists will, I have a hunch, come to see that "politics," correctly conceived, is a process that includes a good bit more of popular culture than one might think. In any case, I hope what follows has some constructive impact on relating the two distinct areas of inquiry.

Political scientists have developed the concept of *political culture*, a flexible and widely used notion that connotes the extent to which culture, both subjective and objective, gives politics its distinctiveness and variety. But little effort has been made to incorporate the "participation" of popular culture in the politics of different countries. Popular culture is an increasingly important part of the general cultures of modern mass societies, and should be seen as more important for the specific political culture. The growth of popular culture as a legitimate activity and force is part of what I call *the logic of a popular society*, the principle, first observed in detail by Tocqueville, that the democratic ideal is not limited to politics but extends also to culture, made most manifest in the legitimacy of mass choice and the supremacy of mass taste. A popular society combines politics and culture in ways hitherto unforeseen, since it celebrates both popular culture and popular politics.[1] To understand the "logic" of such a society, one must grasp not only the cultural determinants of politics, but also the political determinants of culture. For popular politics is always "populist" in the sense of its obeisance to popular will and appeal to norms of popularity. Popular political folkways are at least as important as elite political mores. The logic of such a society suggests that political and cultural process are indistinguishable, since their conduct occurs in a politico-cultural mosaic that blends together in the minds of both populace and political strata. "Presidential popularity," for instance, is both a political and a cultural phenomenon, gathering political power from public opinion and popular support. But popularity is not just the result of political acts; it is also the result of cultural representation. Presidents and Presidential candidates are very much aware that they are public cultural beings whose popularity depends in no small measure of their representation of, and obeisance toward, popular norms of cultural conduct. This may range from marital fidelity to celebrity associations to displays of a "common touch" in campaigning, but they are not in a strict sense political acts in the usual definitions of power and politics. But they are very much politico-cultural acts, part of the political logic of a popular society. A political figure in such a society is not only a political representative, he or she is also a cultural representation, a metaphor of popular power exercised in a popular political culture.

There is, then, an interplay of influence between political and cultural processes, often in diffuse, covert, and unconscious ways that are agonizingly difficult to understand. The facile language of "cause-and-effect" and "shape-and-reflect" cannot fully capture relationships that are kaleidoscopic and mercurial, an ongoing process of popular communication and political comprehension that may be ultimately unmeasureable, although certainly not unfathomable. The student of the relationship of politics and popular culture need not despair because what she or he studies is like nailing jelly to the wall. Similar problems have long bedeviled art and cultural historians: what is the relationship between culture and the artifacts of culture, and what else is being thought and done at a particular time and place? In large measure, we are dealing here with the *aesthetic dimension of politics*, the extent to which cultural imagination intersects political process. We are used to thinking of politics as a pragmatic and realistic enterprise characterized by the struggle for power to realize practical results. But power is rarely exercised in raw and naked terms: rather, it is couched in symbolic terms and values, conducted with regard for dramatic force, interpreted as either beautiful or ugly, and evaluated in cultural context. The practical and dominative dimensions of politics are complemented by the aesthetic, transforming political process and event into story and symbol. In that regard, Machiavelli himself has been underinterpreted: his Prince is a political figure of violence (*forza*) and cunning (*froda*) but also a manipulator of appearances and mobilizer of opinion (*fantazia*).[2] Political aesthetics involves the mobilization of popular imagination for political purposes, accompanied at the cultural level, at least in countries with freedom of speech, by independent and often critical aesthetic treatments of political processes. In both cases, political understanding is enhanced by translating abstract processes into concrete narratives. In order to influence the public domain of opinion and support, the politician must master political discourse, including the symbolic convergence of the popular aesthetic imagination on political stories. Thus politics in a popular society tends public discourse towards the analogical, and makes much public action metaphorical. A President may not be able to do much about altering the history and labyrinthe politics of the Middle East, but he can identify heroism and villainy in political rhetoric, and reassure us that our "presence" in the region, punctuated by low-risk and well-timed "military theatrics," insures that the story will turn out the way we would wish it to.

Not only does popular culture have political uses for politicians, politics has popular uses for those who consume popular culture. For popular culture always occurs in a political culture and at a political time, so even the most avowedly apolitical creation can offer clues as to political habits and temporal "climates of opinion." But here let us avoid a pantheistic theory of politics that sees political significances everywhere, and be parsimonious: the careful observer can select for analysis ostensibly "non-political" artifacts of popular culture that represent important politico-cultural mythemes and folklore which, if correctly and deeply interpreted, will enhance our understanding of political reality. Such analysis, however, requires awareness that political reality is created out of communication, is dynamic and temporal, pluralistic and changing, continuous and emergent, asserted, negotiated, and undermined. Political reality is a struggle for power over the definitions of situations, and if people define political things as real, they are real in their consequences. Here the aesthetic dimension of politics blends again with the pragmatic and dominative: those who have the power to define conventions and situations as real are calling appearances reality, giving a political aesthetic the ontological status of truth. But "official" reality is not the only reality we encounter. We also find popular uses and gratification in the aesthetic realities of popular culture. We are interested in popular fare for a variety of reasons, including our desire to know what's happening. We find definitions of reality, mythemes and conventions applied to a present, in the artifacts of popular culture. Our experience with popular culture is a source of *political learning*, whereby we encounter aesthetic definitions of reality that help us to learn what's happening. Since political reality is one of the processes out there that is happening, then in often covert and unintentional ways popular culture is a political teacher from which we learn concrete stories and symbols that aid us in coping with the unfolding processes of politics. Popular culture is a source of political attitude and opinion by dramatizing what has happened, what is happening, what might happen, and the kind of thing that always happens. Popular culture helps us develop a *political vision*, an aesthetic imagination of politics. For that reason alone, popular culture is amenable to political interpretation, since it is an increasingly important source of political knowledge, what we "see" in and what we expect of political reality. We live in a world of "mediated political realities," in which politics is part of a cultural mosaic of popular activity and learning.[3]

Let us specify three related concepts that identify the process by which a political vision might derive from our experience with popular culture. When people undertake a popular activity—reading a book, watching TV, attending a movie, playing golf, and so on—they are engaged in *play*. Play is an activity of choice, occurring in the interludes of social rhythms, sought for pleasure and distinguished from work. Play-activity, either active or passive, involves us in an imaginary social world that usually has certain conventions and rules of conduct. But play is not meaningless nor inconsequential: mankind at play, *homo ludens*, is engaged in active learning that may not be confined in applicability to simply that sphere of action. Popular play stimulates aesthetic imagination that may serve as metaphors for other areas of cultural life. A child, after all, is expected to learn from children's books the relevance of "the moral of the story" to cultural life beyond the confines of the story; we should expect no less from, say, middle-aged women reading romance novels or teenagers listening to their favorite musical groups. Their orientation in such activities are playful, pleasurable, and usually without conscious regard for the "lessons" learned or larger applications of what story or song augurs: but this does not mean that learning does not take place, nor that analogical connections to the larger world cannot be made. The second component of this process, then, is the subjective vision enriched by popular play, what we here term *fantasy*. Fantasy is the subjective component of play, the ludenic imagination playing at relating self and world. The fantasist is at play building and using a vision that provides metaphorical punctuation of the relationship between self and world in which we are interested in knowing. The fantasizing process helps us piece together a mosaic of concrete images that form a political vision. But such a vision is not simply a static picture of politics. Rather it, and all other social fantasies, are given narrative form in "dramatizing communication," both through subjective fantasy and shared fantasy. Our visions of the world (and self) are given the dynamic structure of *story*, that "the play" of our lives and our social visions acquire the logic of dramatic representation. In informal ways, our political vision takes on narrative and dramaturgical expectations that do not necessarily correspond to political processes nor the realities of elite political conduct. If our political visions are formed by the dramatic logic of popular plays, then our fantasies about political events may include expectations acquired from popular culture that do not inhere in the actual course of political events. But if it is the case that in a popular society such shared visions on the part of mass publics are something that politicians find it prudent to heed, then the actual conduct of politics may be affected by mass political visions which are derived from traditions of popular culture and not from direct or rational political experience.[4]

Let us here offer an example. Students of American popular storytelling have long noted the recurrent appeal of a type of cultural story called "the captivity narrative." The story takes many specific forms, but always involves Americans who are held against their true will by aliens who mean them harm. This story began with the popular narratives of colonials taken by the Indians, and clearly involved deep-seated fears of alien absorption, satanic possession, and sexual ecstasy. But in always new form it has persisted down to the present, and its political relevance persists because of the power of the story. If a free people should not be held hostage by aliens, and if we have narrative traditions of rescue (such as with the U.S. Cavalry rescuing settlers held by the Indians), then popular expectations may affect the importance accorded hostage situations. In other words, popular expectations have become an integral mytheme in the political culture, a consideration of the exercise of power. And indeed, it can be argued that our popular desire for dramatic resolution of captivity narratives has adversely affected the Presidencies of Carter and Reagan, in the former case with the failure to resolve the Iranian embassy captivity (including the failure of the U.S. Cavalry ride in and rescue them), and in the latter by embroiling the President in a politically embarrassing and debilitating scandal in order to ransom a few Americans held in Lebanon. Similarly, in the 1980s, the captivity narrative persisted in popular culture in the foreign fantasy of hordes of MIA's held in Indochina, and resulted in much symbolic political effort to assure MIA families and the public that no effort was being spared to bring these (likely non-existent) hostages home from their captivity. Too, a great deal of domestic effort was devoted to the fantasy of the great hordes of missing children kidnapped by heinous aliens (even though statistics showed that most missing children were not taken by strangers), with faces of the missing everywhere. Whatever the psychic roots of this recurrent story might be, the popular roots and consequences of it are clear enough for politicians to recognize its importance and even to take grave political risks to affect a happy resolution. The captivity narrative is a clear example of how recurrent habits of popular thought, emergent in a political present through play, can create a popularly shared fantasy that makes dramatic expectations a political consideration.[5]

Too, we must examine the other side of the relationship between populace and popular culture, so to speak, and understand the political context and significance of the creators and creations of popular culture. We have said that populations use popular culture as a source of political learning, and that politicians use popular culture for political purposes. But it is also the case that popular culture may be usefully studied without trying to specify the mercurial process by which populaces learn or politicians use. The most solid evidence we have from popular culture are the creations themselves, because like any art form, they provide *aesthetic recognition and articulation of politics*, and perhaps more importantly, of the "non-political" cultural and temporal context of the conduct of politics. Such popular artifacts as movies, radio shows, novels, and comics are the surest evidence of political realities unfolding in place and time, and can be interpreted for their immediate and larger significance in understanding culturally-enfolded politics. There is a sense in which popular art is a process of learning too, wherein creating a popular artifact is an aesthetic way of dealing with political reality. This can range from a purely propagandistic intent to the murkiest awareness of politics, but even the most "non-political" of popular creations may reveal something of politics if carefully interpreted.

Let us illustrate by reference to the movies, perhaps the most complex and subtle of all forms of popular communication, and by the popular traditions and responses they have represented over time. Like all other popular art forms, the movies' relationship to reality is metaphorical, a symbolic engagement of human relations that recognizes and articulates an aesthetic conception of socially significant transactions. Movie making is characterized by both commercial and aesthetic considerations, utilizing conventions of popular aesthetics to strike responsive chords in popular audiences. Since both commercial and aesthetic responsiveness is crucial, the movies—either specific important movies, movie genres that change over time, and "clusters" of movies with similar themes—represent both enduring and particular mythemes in play-form. If it is the case that movies tell stories about human relations important to a culture-in-time, then this includes power relations: who has power? how is it exercised? for and to whom? Is it malevolent or benevolent? what does it tell us about the nature of politics? what does it tell us about political reality? what is the relationship between metaphors of power and the actual exercise of power?

Movies, then, can be analyzed as symbolic realities, metaphors of power relations in aesthetic form with attention to conventions of popular storytelling and audience expectations. If they depict power relations, it is within the confines of the ritual play of dramatic structure. Movies that offer important representations of politically relevant relations are *rituals of power*. In a ritual universe, generic dramas of suspended and analogical reference are enacted, giving ceremonial form to some basic action pattern or historical truth. A ritual of power gives concrete demonstrative enactment of power relations, either by the creation of a normative universe which shows how power should be exercised in a justly ordered world, or by the creation of a "fallen" universe which shows how power is "in fact" exercised in an unjust and disordered world. The popular heritage of myths about the exercise, proper and improper, of power is combined with the immediate fantasy about political reality to create popular film dramas that recognize and articulate universes of power. Ritual dramas may reaffirm fundamental normative relations of power, or confirm fantasies of corrupted arrays of power, but in either case they provide metaphorical understanding of the political moment in relation to the larger politico-cultural world.[6]

This approach gives the inquirer sensitivity to the history and structure of a major popular art form, allows for the role of the dynamics of creativity and immediacy, and permits us to make valid, although never directly demonstrable, inferences about the relationship of movies and politics. There is a danger, of course, in defining "politics" out of existence, seeing in every movie political significance in the conflict and resolution of the story. But when we see alterations and trends in movie genres over political time, recurrent political archetypes that reappear concomitant with renewed political tensions, and "clusters" of films that are synchronic with an unfolding political era, we are observing popular evidence of political change from which we may draw valid inferences. The Western as genre, for instance, has had many uses over time, and one can look at a specific political time such as the late 1960's and see Westerns (*Little Big Man, The Wild Bunch*) which use the genre to show power as capricious whim and savage force, improperly inverted in an immoral universe, and a political world committed to indiscriminate and self-destructive violence. Too, the political archetype of the Russian as villain was revived in the 1980's with renewed tensions, and the attribution of political culpability, with "the evil empire." Like their Cold War predecessors, the Russians (*Firefox, Rocky IV, Rambo*) became paradigms of evil, combining both subhuman and superhuman qualities as icons of menace. However, the unbearability of such menace in the earlier Cold War led us to "displace" such menace in the "cluster" of early 1950's science-fiction films which placed the political fantasy of feared invasion, annihilation, or dehumanization from extrahuman and demonic beings from "outer space." We could, however, defeat them, as we did in the 1980's with "Rambolina" in *Aliens*, justifying self-defensive genocide. In all cases, these movies communicated something about power relations in the world of politics, and can be said to be indicative of movements of power conceptions in historical practice.

It remains to be seen how far the idea of movies as rituals of power can be extended, but it can be argued that other genres—the swashbuckler, the survival film, the gangster film, and others—can be interpreted politically. The gangster film, for instance, is always about illegitimate power exercised in extralegal ways. But different eras, and audiences, may call for different political interpretations. In the early 1930's, the gangster may represent the menace of the business ethic, the tragedy of possessive individualism, and the collapse of the moral order; for the early 1970's, by contrast, the gangster may represent the last bastion of rational self-interest, wherein one has to put oneself under the authority of an illegitimate power who can protect your interests, and provide justice, in a world where the "proper authorities" are corrupt or incompetent, and bring familial warmth and individual prosperity in an atmosphere where one surrenders freedom of choice for the protection of a political "godfather" and his "family." Both eras had different political "climates of opinion." To understand them, comparing the ritual uses of the gangster film may give us aesthetic insight into how popular artists, and perhaps we who attended the movies, conceived these times.

The concept of rituals of power might well be applied to other forms of popular creation, by asking the kind of political questions we have suggested. Popular books, for instance, reveal much of changing attitudes about roles—role relations, role conceptions of heroism, villainy, and foolery, fantasies of power in alternative universes—all of which may be sensitive indicators of politically relevant moods and trends. When fantasies of superheroism emerge (such as in the 1930's and 1970's), it may be the case that popular participation in such a ritual of power indicates a yearning for the emergence of a political superhero who is seen to possess extraordinary powers and able to perform superhuman acts. To understand Ronald Reagan, we would have to understand the popular context of frustration and delimitation of the 1970's, with the concomitant emergence of movie rituals of uncomplicated power in the form of Luke Skywalker, Clark Kent, and Indiana Jones. To take another example from popular books: when students of role relations study the antifeminist backlash of the 1970's and 1980's, they can find much material to contemplate in popular fantasy novels of restored male domination and female submission (as in the *Gor* series and romance novels). If there is a congruence between popular and political role expectations, then it may be the case that it will appear in the various forms of popular creation.

In the larger view, students of popular culture should investigate the hypothesis that as the sophistication and ubiquity of popular culture expands, so does its influence. If that is the case, then it may follow that the political influence of popular culture expands accordingly. The logic of popular politics would overwhelm more traditional constraints and expectations. For example, the categories of political hero and popular celebrity would merge entirely. Prior celebrity status might become a virtual requirement of significant political success, and we would increasingly evaluate political actors by the extent to which they conform with the folkways of celebrity. Thusly, the blending of show business and politics introduces popular standards of political theatricality that makes political campaigning, for instance, into dramatic performances. In a broad historical sense, it may be the case that the expectations of role performance that popular culture has taught us is creating a new American self, a "theatrical self" that takes David Riesman's famous formulation one better: rather than tradition-directed, or inner-directed, or other-directed, we are now *performance-directed*, oriented toward the theatrical presentation of self in everyday life. If that is so, then it may be that we are now oriented toward politics as performance, and evaluate political actors on the basis of performative principles, political events by their theatrical satisfactions, and political observers by their critical faculties. Politics in such a world *is* theater, what has been called the politics of simulation.[7]

These notions are based on a kind of "maximum consequences" theory, whereby I argue that popular culture has had far greater impact on politics and other areas of social life than many social scientists and historians will admit. Indeed, observers of the present in the twenty-seventh century might well speak of the "popular culture revolution" of the twentieth and twenty-first centuries. We can here hypothesize that popular culture has contributed to an alteration in consciousness, what I call the *supercession of fantasy over reality*. It may be the case that our experience with popular culture has altered our cognitive assumptions and foci to the point that fantasy supersedes reality because we *prefer* fantasy. We spend more time in "artificial social relations" with fantasy figures than with palpable ones; on balance, the amount of time, effort, and wealth spent on play outstrips work; and our psychic ability to absorb multivarious forms of entertainment increases. We expect to be entertained, and dwell in the imaginary social world of our entertainment. Entertainment has become the "ritual center" of our lives, serving the sacred function of aesthetic enlightenment, diversion, and satisfaction once reserved for religion. Indeed, religion itself has become entertainment, as part of the process by which the profane and sacred are merged. Not only do we "project" ourselves into fantasy worlds, we "introject" fantasy into our lives. Ourselves become simulated amalgams of popular experience, "as if" beings who do indeed live out our fantasies.[8]

This idea remains to be proven, but if in any sense such a process is under way, then it will give credence to the corollary notion that increasingly politics *is* fantasy. In a world of political theater, political skill and success come not so much from the adroit use of force and fraud as much as appearances. Political fantasy superseders reality as well, requiring that political communication be play, that political imagination be fantasy, and that political action be dramatic. It may be the case that successful states of the future will be *popular theatocracies*, made so by their ability to utilize the histrionic resources of theater in order to stimulate and direct the play of popular fantasy. Such new orders have the clear potential to acquire dystopian traits of the Orwellian and Huxleyian varieties, wherein popular aesthetics becomes a major and subtle resource of domination and manipulation. In such a world, command of the popular imagination through the control of political reality is the defining feature of power. In the wake of scarcities, environmental depletion, and permanent warfare, the chief function of the state will be to provide political entertainment.[9]

If such brave new political orders are in fact coming into existence in the "mass-mediated" and "post-modern" world, then we will witness a fundamental transformation of politics. In a popular theatocracy, politics *is* play. Our experience with politics would be limited to the structured play-forms of mass communication controlled by the state. We would "know" a world of political romance full of progress, justice, and victory, and devoid of failure, conflict, and defeat. We would play with recurrent and satisfying stories that serve the functions of romance, fulfilling us with political fables of adventures consummated, mysteries unraveled, villainies foiled, and heroes triumphant. The politics of play would return us to a kind of political childhood, with future states in a new Grand Inquisitorial role: take our freedom, but entertain us.

These cosmic musings do demonstrate, I think, that the intermingling of politics and popular culture is not necessarily a benevolent process. Too, my thoughts here should remind us of the research task before us. Not only must we delineate the political uses, and abuses, of popular culture, we must also analyze historical and popular trends that let us forecast what the popular politics of the future might be like. The political future may be benevolent, or sinister, or merely preposterous, but in any case popular culture will play an important role in defining what it will be. The student of politics and popular culture, then, has a diagnostic function, attempting to analyze popular symptoms in order to infer the political health of future bodies politics. It is not an easy task, but it is one from which we should not shrink. We will have to be bold in asserting the validity of political interpretations of popular culture, and build a body of literature that supports our ideas. Finally, we will have to retain the wonder that motivates our study. We must wonder, with the poet William Blake, whether we become what we behold, and conversely, whether we behold what we become.

Notes

[1]Not all societies, of course, are "popular societies" in the sense we mean it. The United States is, I suspect, the model for what other societies are becoming, or fear they are becoming. There are more constraints on populism in Western Europe, but they are succumbing more and more to the logic of a popular society. Other systems have powerful institutional or ideological constraints. The Communist countries have an "official" popular culture, but unofficial popular culture (rock, for instance) is potentially a more vibrant force. Countries with strong traditional or elitist forces (Iran, China, Chile) fear and ban popular culture as a subversive force, but it remains to be seen as to whether they can escape the historical logic of the expansion of popular society as a principle.

[2]K.R. Minogue, "Theatricality and Politics: Machiavelli's Concept of *Fantasia*," in B. Parekh and R.N. Berki (eds.), *The Morality of Politics* (London: Allen & Unwin, 1972), pp. 36-47.

[3]cf. Dan Nimmo and James Combs, *Mediated Political Realities* (New York: Longman, 1984).

[4]The classic study of play is Johan Huizinga, *Homo Ludens* (Boston: Beacon Press, 1956); see the discussion and bibliography in James Combs, *Polpop* (Bowling Green, Ohio: Popular Press, 1984); see also M.A. Salter (ed.), *Play: Anthropological Perspectives* (West Point, NY: Leisure Press, 1978); Elizabeth Atwood Lawrence, *Rodeo* (Knoxville: University of Tennessee Press, 1982); Clifford Geertz's influential "Deep Play: Notes on the Balinese Cockfight," *Daedalus*, Vol. 101 (1972), pp. 1-37; James S. Hans, *The Play of the World* (University of Massachusetts Press, 1981).

[5]The definitive work on the captivity narrative has yet to be published, but for openers see Richard Slotkin *Regeneration through Violence: The Mythology of the American Frontier, 1600-1860* (Middletown; Wesleyan University Press, 1973).

[6]The literature on ritual is vast, but the political implications of popular ritual remain virtually unexplored. For a suggestive discussion of movies, see Vivian Sobchack, "Genre Film: Myth, Ritual, and Sociodrama," in Sari Thomas (ed.), *Film/Culture* (Scarecrow Press, 1982), pp. 147-165; see too Dudley Andrew, "Film and Society: Public Rituals and Private Space," *East-West Film Journal*, Vol. 1 (Winter 1986), pp. 7-21; for television, see Daniel Dayan And Elihu Katz, "Television Ceremonial Events," *Society*, Vol. 22, no. 4 (May/June 1985), pp. 60-66.

[7]I discuss this in my yet unpublished *Dreaming Heroic Dreams: Ronald Reagan and American Political Culture*; the intriguing if elusive concept of "simulation" has been given much impetus by Jean Baudrillard, most graspable in his *Simulations* (New York: Semiotext, 1983).

[8]The evidence for this is not conclusive, but see the work of John Caughey, *Imaginary Social Worlds* (Lincoln: University of Nebraska Press, 1984).

[9]See some of the articles in Robert Savage (ed.), *The Orwellian Moment: Hindsight and Foresight in the Post-1984 World* (Fayetteville: University of Arkansas Press, forthcoming 1989).

Dramatic Conversations:
The Relationship Between Sociology and Popular Culture

George H. Lewis

In its most vital and vibrant forms, the culture of a people—especially that portion of their culture that is acknowledged to be *popular*, is, at its core, an argument about the meanings of destiny those people share. Popular culture, then, is a voice, or many voices, engaging in what sociologist Robert Bellah, in his 1985 landmark study of American culture, *Habits of the Heart*,[1] calls "dramatic conversations" concerning the things that centrally matter to a people. As such, these dramatic conversations of popular culture are, or should be, of central concern to sociologists, engaged as they are in the task of seeking to understand and explain the complex webs of social relationships and meaning we all weave.

And yet, there has been a curious relationship between sociology and popular culture—at times almost a relationship of strangers, where one would expect openness and the intimacy of sharing. Sociology seems most at fault here, zealously guarding its disciplinary boundaries and, although utilizing the stuff of popular culture in many of its best studies, almost never openly admitting this use by name. Popular culture, on the other hand, has benefited a great deal from the attention paid it by those sociologists who have not been afraid to strike up a relationship and engage in dramatic conversations outside the traditionally forged boundaries of their discipline. What has emerged over the years, is a case of strange relations between two disciplines who may at times and in darkest night share the same bed, but who most certainly will never admit to this sharing in the bright light of day.

Obvious Things Unobserved: Popular Culture in American Sociology

In "A Scandal In Bohemia," Sherlock Holmes remarks that "the world is full of obvious things which nobody by any chance observes."[2] With some few rare and fine exceptions, this has been true historically with respect to the serious study of popular culture by sociologists—most especially American sociologists.

Until the great intellectual shake-up of the discipline which coincided with the social and cultural turmoil of the late 1960's in America, American sociology was primarily focused in the direction of developing as an experimental science, in search of general and quantifiable laws of social behavior. Axiomatic theory and mathematical sociology were all the rage. If it couldn't be quantified, it seemed, it was not worth serious study. And, of course, culture was not a concept easily quantified.

The academic baby boomers, raised in the cultural and social storms of the 1960's, challenged this sociology with the social, moral and intellectual concerns of their generation. Sociology, they felt, should more closely and responsibly address this world of human beings, the warp and woof of everyday life. Moreover, there should be *understanding* involved, not just a sterile, manipulative count of numbers. Verstehen, resurrected from the writings of Max Weber, was born again as a method of sociological inquiry, usually accompanied by equal parts of empathy and activism. Whatever their political bent, most of these new sociologists would have easily agreed at the time that those of their academic establishment fit Bob Dylan's portrait of a thin man very well. "There's something happening, and you don't know what it is, do you, Mr. Jones."

With the waves of social protest washing higher outside the academy—over the airwaves and in the streets—increasing numbers of these newer academics began to look to culture, especially popular culture, as both instigator and indicator of this protest and change. The search for meaning became a central concern for many of these new members of the discipline, who had turned their faces in the direction of culture. It was no accident, then, that areas of study such as ethnomethodology, symbolic interactionism, and a study of contemporary cultural variables and their relationships to social structures arose nearly simultaneously in the American sociology of the late 1960's, along with a rebirth of interest in critical theory and the Frankfurt School. More than just fringe elements, these concerns took a tenacious hold and refused to be shrugged off, no matter how viciously they were slapped at by disciplinary mainliners.

The blinders of empirical preoccupation worn by many of the American sociological establishment cannot be blamed completely for why the study of culture—and culture as meaning—had been so often overlooked. One must lay some of the blame at the door of the concept itself. Culture, as abstract as the concept is, has always been difficult to operationalize for research purposes. This problem is only exacerbated in the arena of popular culture, where one finds a wide variety of categories that have been proposed to differentiate elements, but no uniform set enjoying general acceptance. Terms such as "mass culture," "popular culture," "folk culture," "elite culture," "taste culture," and "kitsch" abound in the literature, both sociological and otherwise. Unfortunately, the analytic utility of the distinctions offered among these concepts may well be more limited than their champions will concede. And, too, many of the distinctions and definitions bruited about, originating as they did in philosophical-ideological debates about the "worth" of mass culture in the 1940's and 1950's, are less than the evaluatively neutral categories they should be in order to be useful in the social sciences.[4] In sum, as Gregory Stone once remarked about the concept of "play," the concepts of culture found in the literature by sociologists have been wrapped in so much ideological toilet paper they look round; whatever cutting edges they may have once enjoyed have been dulled and blunted.

Historically there has been a problem with aesthetics as well. Excluding for the moment whatever "elite" culture may be, as Edward Shils has pointed out, "the real fact is that from an aesthetic and moral standpoint, the objects of mass culture are repulsive to us."[5] This aesthetic bias of the academy has convincingly been traced to literary criticism of the eighteenth century[6] and has, it seems, become a kind of paranoia of many social scientists who work and live in this "elite" cultural academy. As a marginal person, the sociologist dwells between the hard scientists who scoff at his or her claim to scientific status and the humanists, who feel the scientific method is an inappropriate means to understand humanity. The commitment of science to rationality clearly puts it on one side here, while the commitment of humanism to people over science puts most of art and literature on the other. But sociology simply cannot move to one side or the other. In such an atmosphere, the study of aesthetically sanctioned art and literature has generally been seen as acceptable, but the taking of *popular* culture seriously has, only too often, invited scorn and thinly veiled ridicule from both ends of the academic spectrum.

Those few American sociologists who have chosen to take this academic flak from both colleagues and bystanders have profited greatly from their studies in the area of popular culture. Belatedly, others in the discipline have seen the worth of such studies and have given grudging approval to serious research that leans in this direction—though usually, in order to receive the attention it needs for publication, such studies have clothed themselves in the more traditional concepts and concerns of the discipline, sneaking in the term "popular culture" deep in the text and seldom, if ever, using it in the title of the study. Indeed, *even in the 1980's* it is a rare issue of any mainstream American sociological journal that carries an article that deals directly with the stuff of popular culture,[7] though a solid minority of research papers on this topic now are regularly delivered at national and regional conventions— something that was not true until at least the mid-seventies. In addition, there has now been established a grass roots section of the American Sociological Association on the Sociology of Culture. Only two years old and one of the fastest growing sections of the ASA, it finally offers an ongoing and sociologically "legitimate" arena in which some serious study of popular culture (along with elite culture, literature, art and so on) can be undertaken.

Beyond Our Borders: Conversations Overseas

In turning to sociology as practiced beyond American borders, one finds some striking differences in the acceptance and analysis of popular culture, although in nearly all cases, serious concern by sociologists hardly can be said to have begun until the 1950's.

The Western Europeans, reacting against the empirical juggernaut of American sociology, have, since at least the early 1960's, pushed their research emphasis in the direction of culture and cultural studies. In England, this research has revolved around leisure and the popular culture of the working classes. Much of the work in this area has been done in research centers, such as the Centre for Contemporary Cultural Studies at the University of Birmingham and the Centre for Work and Leisure Studies at the University of Salford. Qualitative in nature, these British studies seek to uncover the *meaning* in popular culture for those who consume it, with a special interest in how the communication involved in this popular culture varies by social class level.[8]

In France, Pierre Bourdieu at the Center for European Sociology in Paris has, through the 1970's and 1980's, developed his important theory of culture codes.[9] Bourdieu argues that cultural artifacts have symbolic codes embedded in them that make sense only to those socialized in these codes. For those from different social strata, cultural objects are viewed through non-applicable or misleading codes which cause a confusion of interpretation, while those from the same social stratum, who know the codes because they were socialized in them, will interpret, understand and appreciate the cultural object in question. Much of Bourdieu's empirical work, in support of his theory, has been drawn from the popular culture of France.

Studies in Eastern Europe and the USSR center more around leisure research—how many radios are owned, who attends cultural events, how popular are urban parks and other attractions. As such, many of these studies are empirical nose (or radio) counts, and explanation or interpretation—when offered—is likely to be buried in ideologic, party line cliche and excess.

In Sweden, research centers around thoroughly empirical studies of mass communication and its effects. Swedish researchers, heavily data oriented, have moved to the vanguard in developing and refining the concept of cultural indicators,[10] having drawn much of their inspiration in this area from George Gerbner's important American work on violence and television.

In turning to the Far East, it is vital to understand that there has never been the sort of distinction made culturally between "popular" culture and any other form. Although it is clear, for example, in Japan that certain cultural forms have been produced, consumed, and enjoyed within a very rigid system of social stratification, the culture "of the people" has never been denigrated as being aesthetically inferior to any sort of "elite" culture, nor have efforts to study it been seen as any less valid than other types of cultural or social studies.[11] Therefore, a goodly number of the problems Western sociologists have had in studying popular culture are not in evidence in Eastern sociology.

Finally, it is imperative to mention the work of Third World sociologists, most of whom spend their research time documenting the impact and effects (seen to be largely negative) of Western popular culture on the developing nations. This is an important, white-hot issue, and is at the center of many "dramatic conversations" initiated and sustained by these sociologists. Thus, the stuff of popular culture is extremely visible in Third World sociology, from the analysis of work songs and social protest in South Africa to the ideological impact of Donald Duck comics in Chile and other Latin countries of the Americas.[12]

Obvious Things Observed:
Sociological Contributions to Popular Culture

Even though popular culture has historically been much less than a central concept of intellectual focus for much of sociology (and especially American sociology), those sociologists who have examined it have made some tremendously important contributions to its study. In a chapter as limited in length as this must be, it is impossible to present these accomplishments in any great detail; however, I have identified four major areas in which I feel sociological contributions have been especially impressive.[13] Interestingly, even though popular culture research *per se* gives one little prestige within the academic borders of mainstream American sociology, many of the major contributions to a sociological understanding of popular culture have come from American sociologists.

Figure One
Major Sociological Contributions
To the Study of Popular Culture

I.   The Creation and Content of Culture, and the Transmission of Meaning
    A.   Studies of symbolic interaction
    B.   Sociological contributions to the study of semiotics
    C.   Popular culture in the developing field of cultural indicators
    D.   Content and document analysis, especially comparative and over time
II.   The Organizational Approach to Popular Culture Industries
    A.   Occupational roles, careers and constraints on artists
    B.   Description and working of popular culture industries
    C.   Relationship between culture industries and the larger societal environment
III. Analysis of Audience Composition
    A.   Development of concepts of taste culture and culture class
    B.   Studies of audience stratification by social class and the implications of this
    C.   Studies of subcultures and their definition within the mass audience
IV.   The Impact of Popular Culture on Its Audience
    A.   Studies of cultural hegemony, power and control
    B.   Development of the theory of culture codes and their implications
    C.   Studies of the impact of Western popular culture on the developing nations
    D.   Studies of the effects of portrayals of sex, violence and pornography on attitudes and behavior

The Creation and Content of Culture, and the Transmission of Meaning

Twin tasks that sociologists (and, to a much greater extent, anthropologists) have set themselves is the study of how culture is created and shared, and the symbolic content of culture thus produced. From anthropology, sociologists have learned and borrowed a good deal from the works of persons such as Clifford Geertz, Mary Douglas, and Claude Levi-Strauss—influential figures in the field of the interpretation of culture.[14] From their own discipline, sociologists have tapped the intellectual roots of symbolic interactionism, as established in the early works of thinkers such as George Simmel, W.I. Thomas and George Herbert Mead.[15] These intellectual tools have been brought to bear on the subject matter of popular culture—how is the created meaning of this symbolic material developed, shared and transmitted?

The cornerstone of symbolic interactionism—the focus of concern—is that of a common set of symbols and understanding that are possessed by people in a group.[16] Studies in sociology that adopt this perspective in examining popular culture perhaps begin with Howard Becker's classics of the 1950's, "Becoming a Marihuana User," and "The Culture of a Deviant Group: The Dance Musician"[17]—studies in which Becker traces the creation of meaning involved in marijuana use and the developing "world views" of jazz musicians concerning both their music and their audiences. Becker has more recently moved into the areas of photography and the arts, examining the creation and meaning involved in what he terms "art worlds."[18] Another recent and excellent example of work in this tradition is H. Stith Bennett's study of learning how to be a rock musician,[19] while the portrayal of male and female role models, and their transmission in the popular culture of American advertising has been effectively examined by Erving Goffman.[20]

Many who work in the area of symbolic interaction look a good deal to children in their research, assuming the key elements in kids' worlds are the symbols and understandings that make their social environment symbolic. Colin Lacey has looked hard at the cultural symbols (such as caps and blazers) that become imbued with meaning in the world of the English grammar school,[21] while in America, Gary Alan Fine has produced numerous studies of popular culture of children from this perspective, including studies of little league baseball, children's gossip and humor, and the creation of shared fantasies and social worlds in "Dungeons and Dragons" and other such role playing games.[22]

In turning more directly to the study of cultural symbols from the structuralist, interpretative perspective, one must mention the semiotics of Roland Barthes' French studies of popular culture, which have ranged from examinations of artifacts such as soap operas and wrestling to ornamental cookery,[23] Mary Douglas' British studies of popular food in cultures,[24] Michael Foucault and Jeffrey Weeks' studies of sexuality,[24]a and M. Gottdiener's recent analysis of mass culture from the semiotic perspective.[25] Although this interpretive, semiotic approach is stronger in anthropology than it is in sociology (and stronger in European social science than it is in American), it has shown power and promise in applications by sociologists.

Another developing tradition in the sociological study of popular culture is that of the cultural indicators approach, an empirical charting and analysis of imagery in popular culture and what it reveals about important issues such as violence, ethnic stereotyping, or sexism. Charting trends in popular culture content via this approach and that of content and document analysis, is a research activity that seeks answers to questions such as what kinds of values appear continuously in a culture and what kinds of values appear to have shifted over time? Studies in this tradition range from George Gerbner's influential and on-going work on violence in American television to Karl Erik Rosengren's studies of changes in the Swedish value system to Herman Lantz's studies of American family values in the 1600's, as reflected in the colonial magazines of that period.[26]

More traditional content analysis studies of popular culture—an approach that does have a longer history in sociology than perhaps any other—include Patricke Johns-Heine and Hans Gerth's influential study of American values in mass periodical fiction from 1921-1940; Elizabeth Long's examination of the American Dream and the post-WWII novel; James Carey's study of courtship patterns as they were reflected in popular songs from 1955 to 1966; Gaye Tuchman, Arlene Kaplan Daniels and James Benet's 1978 edited collection of studies of the images of women in the mass media, and Gunner Andren's Swedish study of ideology in American advertising.[27] Interestingly, although there have been—for sociology—a relatively good number of studies of popular culture done in this content analysis tradition, many of them have only found publication in journals outside the field—in areas such as public opinion, journalism and studies of communication.

The Organizational Approach to Popular Culture Industries

One of the most promising developments in the study of popular culture, especially in its creation and distribution, has been the attempts by sociologists to draw from the theoretical frameworks of industrial and organizational sociology and from the sociology of occupations and professions and apply these frameworks to the stuff of popular culture. Sociological research in this tradition has sought to answer questions such as the following. How do systems of production affect the content and impact of popular culture? What are the interrelationships between culture industries and the larger institutions of society? Do these systems place constraints on one another and if so, of what nature?

A pioneer study of the American broadcasting industry was done in the late 1940's by Paul Lazarsfelt, working with Frank Stanton.[28] This work, known as the "Columbia School" research, was the touchstone upon which most subsequent sociological studies of cultural industries have relied. These studies, which reached a critical mass only in the 1970's when increased attention began being paid to popular culture-even in American sociology, seem to naturally break down into three major organizational approaches.

The first approach focuses on occupational roles, careers, and the interaction of popular culture organizations with the individuals filling them. Studies in this area examine the ways in which people participate in the production of popular culture. Because of assumptions held by many in American sociology concerning the lack of quality of popular culture and the lack of creativity involved in producing it, there has been relatively little emphasis placed on the creator as artist, and a good deal of emphasis placed on the production and distribution of popular culture items. This emphasis is nearly the exact opposite of that found in the sociological study of art and literature, where the creator as artist receives focal attention.

When the artist has been looked at, it usually has been in terms of various strategies he or she uses to insulate him-or-her-self from the tensions between self-concept as independent creator and a dependence on external sources of financial support. Howard Becker has examined this with respect to the jazz musician, Ken Mullen has looked at public house performers in Britain, R. Serge Denisoff has focused on Waylon Jennings' career in country music and George H. Lewis has researched popular artists in Hawaii.[29]

The second general approach concentrates on the organizational arrangements by which the activities of persons in the popular culture industries are integrated into a production system. Most of the theoretical framework utilized in this area has been taken directly from industrial sociology and the sociology of organizations, and includes work such as Paul Hirsch's organizational set analysis of the film, recording and book industries, in which he found a great deal of similarity in the ways of dealing with a high risk product, especially in terms of systems of production and distribution.[30] Richard Peterson and David Berger have examined the relationship between economic factors such as market concentration and structure and innovation in popular culture in the music industry,[31] R. Serge Denisoff has traced the creation of popular culture through the constraints of the music business,[32] and George. H. Lewis has focused on the promotion of popular culture in the culture industries.[33] Most recently, Douglas Kellner has offered a critique of this approach from the perspective of critical theory, which makes a number of important points concerning this way of analyzing popular culture.[34]

Finally, studies in this area have focused on the relationship between the culture industries and the larger societal environments in which they operate. In moving to the international level, Francesco Alberoni has developed a fruitful framework of analysis, in which he views the cultural industries located in the United States as an "epicenter."[35] The effects of this epicenter vary. There are regions of high acculturation, such as West Germany; areas of partial acculturation, such as Spain; areas of disintegration in which this form of popular culture is disruptive, such as in Latin America; and areas of new antithetical cultural syntheses, such as Mainland China.

Other studies of the interrelationships between the popular culture industries and their social environments include Benetta Jules-Rosette's work on the production of tourist art in Africa, Cornelia Butler Flora's study of the effects of various state systems in Latin America on the production and content of the fotonovela, and Jeremy Tunstall's analysis of Anglo-American media systems throughout the world.[36]

Although studies using the organizational approach are sometimes difficult to locate, as they are published in many different places, geographically and discipline-wise, taken together they offer one of sociology's most important contributions to the study of popular culture.

Analysis of Audience Composition

The empirical sociological contribution to the great popular culture debate about whether there really is such a thing as a huge "mass" public who consumes culture or, rather, a series of smaller "taste publics" of differing demographic, social and cultural composition, has been a large one. In 1967, Herbert Gans first used the term "taste culture" to refer to the set of cultural strata in a society that roughly parallels the strata of social class of that society.[37]

What Gans had in mind was the fact that members of a society—all members, from upper to lower class—have definite ideas as to the worth of popular cultural material. These ideas have a strong influence on what they choose to consume and enjoy, therefore, there exists a sort of cultural stratification of taste in society which roughly (but not exactly) parallels its social stratification.

There are other important demographic variables that help define taste as well, factors such as age, education, religion, race and geographic area lived in. These variables have been examined in various sociological studies, such as Michael Brake's study of youth cultures in America, Great Britain and Canada, George Comstock's analysis of the American television audience, and Richard Peterson and Paul DiMaggio's investigation of the listeners of country and western music.[38] Many of the findings uncovered by researchers such as these suggest that social class based lines of distinction are not necessarily those along which popular cultural tastes break down most definitively, especially in advanced industrial societies with their conditions of relatively high social mobility, greater discretionary income, easy credit, efficient distribution of cultural goods, high diffusion rate of products, conspicuous consumption and relatively great amounts of leisure/consumption time. All these factors seem to contribute to a blurring of the social class-cultural consumption correlation and a strengthening of the effects of other demographic variables on the popular culture audience. In sociology, the term "culture class" has been coined to refer to that aggregate of individuals who seek out similar popular culture forms, even as this aggregate is non-definable in the traditional, social class sense of taste culture.

Studies of audience composition in sociology have also focused on subcultures within the larger public, both in the sense of defining these subcultures and in analyzing what cultural artifacts are created and consumed by the members of them. Studies of this sort range from Edward Sadalla and Jeffrey Burroughs' analysis of the characteristics of consumers of vegetarian, gourmet, health, synthetic and fast foods to Richard Hebdige's study of punks and other youth subcultures in Great Britain.[39] In the cumulative sense these sociological studies, done over several years now, reveal that it is quite apparent

that the linkages between what people consume in the arena of popular culture
and who these people are is a very complex one.

The Impact of Popular Culture on Its Audience

The effects of popular culture on those who are exposed to it has received
a good deal of attention in the sociological and social psychological literature.
Of concern here are issues such as to what extent are people manipulated and
controlled by popular culture that is created and controlled by the State or
other powerful institutions; to what extent does familiarity and understanding
of cultural artifacts solidify one's position in a class structure; what effects
does popular culture, created in America and other industrial nations, have
on a Third World audience; and what effects does popular culture portrayals
of sex, violence and pornography have upon its audience?

Students of cultural hegemony trace their intellectual roots to the work
of Antonio Gramsci, who accounted for the fact of the non-revolutionary nature
of the working classes in Europe to the bourgeois domination of the thought,
the common sense, the life-ways and everyday assumptions of the total society.[40]
This domination was made possible by their control of culture and their shaping
of its content. In Germany—and later, in America—the Critical Theory of
Frankfort School scholars such as Theodor Adorno and Max Horkheimer
presented the dominant forms of commercial, popular culture as crystalizations
of authoritarian ideology.[41]

Most recently, this position has been taken in the work of Raymond
Williams and Todd Gitlin in their work on the television industry, and the
work of Dick Hebdige and Simon Frith in the area of popular music.[42] In
their eyes, the content of popular culture, as created and distributed by the
culture industries, serves to reinforce the dominant ideology of the power
structure and to define and justify in the eyes of its audience, the structure
of power in society.

This argument is a common theme in the work of Third World sociologists,
who argue that the dominant ideologies of the (mainly) capitalist nations are
being spread via their popular culture and are effecting the life-ways and everyday
assumptions of the members of the Third World. Ariel Dorfman and Armand
Mattelart have analyzed what they term "imperialist ideology" as it exists in
the Disney comics distributed in Chile, Hidetoshi Kato has shown that, in
Thailand, the popular heroes with children are Japanese television stars, rather
than local persons, real or fictional, and Jeremy Tunstal has documented how
the Indian film industry has grown up economically and thematically linked
with Hollywood in both the form and symbolic content of its productions.[43]

In turning to the social psychological studies of the effects of popular
culture on its audiences, it is important to note the studies of Elihu Katz,
who has traced the effects of opinion leaders within the audience on the
interpretation of popular culture materials.[44] These opinion leaders can act
as a buffer between the individual and the persuasive structure of the popular
culture industry, and can also translate cultural materials into terms
understandable to local world views and frames of reference.

Pierre Bourdieu, in France, has developed a different view of the effects of popular culture on its audience.[45] Bourdieu argues that cultural artifacts have symbolic "culture codes" embedded in them that make sense only to those socialized in these codes. For those from foreign cultures (or even from different social strata in the same culture), cultural objects are viewed through non-applicable or misleading codes. Such exposure will cause a confusion of interpretation until (if ever) the relevant code is mastered.

An important implication of Bourdieu's position is that, if the dominant culture is a code into which some people are inducted from birth and which others must master, then debates over the "value" of popular culture artifacts are highly political in nature, since they involve the argument that the "worth" of a cultural object is equated with the social worth of the consumer, with respect to his or her position in the class structure.

Other political questions about the effects of popular culture spring up, like mushrooms after a spring rain, around the topics of sex and violence. What Paul Lazarsfeld said some years ago about such questions, and the studies they have generated, still holds true—"the effects of television on children is controversial not because some people are against crime and others for it; it is controversial because so little is known that anyone can inject his prejudices or views into the debate without being proven wrong."[46]

The basic point of debate here is whether popular culture reflects and reinforces people's values and attitudes, thus possibly contributing to causing behavior congruent with these values and attitudes or whether popular culture can actually change values, attitudes and behaviors. Although a great deal of empirical evidence concerning this question has been amassed in social psychology over the last thirty or so years, it is in the main contradictory, with studies ranging from strong reinforcement of values, to behavior change, to no effects at all.[47] What the data have done, in general, is to underscore the fact that the relationship between popular culture and its audience is an extremely complex one—one that could use a good deal more thorough and unbiased attention paid it by social scientists.

Finale: Academic Boundaries and the Conversations of Culture
Having taken a brief look at the relative lack of impact that popular culture has had in the field of sociology, and the larger influence sociological theories and methods have had in explaining and giving meaning to the stuff of popular culture, one is struck by the stiffness and artificiality of academic disciplines—especially those in the social sciences. As Alasdair MacIntyre has pointed out, it seems the very nature of a narrowly professional social science—something many in sociology have been pushing the field toward—that it is specialized and that this specialization leads to a disavowal of knowledge of the whole or any part of the whole that lies beyond its strictly defined domain.[48]

That this is true with respect to sociology can be seen, sadly, in the fact that much of the best sociological study of popular culture is *not* published in the journals of the field—and when it is, it is "disguised" and cloaked in the conventional terminology of the tried, true and "acceptable" variables of sociological study. One is struck by the richness of the work that sociologists have done in popular culture, yet at the same time saddened that a great deal of this good work is not known, read, nor taken seriously by those who consider themselves as professional, mainstream types in the field.

And, although this is far more true with respect to American sociology than it is across the rest of the world, the fact is that most sociological study of popular culture has been done by a minority of persons who—for various reasons—have not been afraid to step across academic boundaries and engage in the conversations of culture. In so doing, they have amassed an impressive body of empirical and, to a slightly lesser extent, theoretical work—work that one hopes will only grow in depth and importance over the coming years. As Robert Bellah and his colleagues suggest in *Habits of the Heart*, one of the very few well respected and widely read recent works that is unashamed of its use and interpretation of popular culture, an invigorated sociology must break through the "iron curtain" between the social sciences and the humanities if it is to move forward, bringing the traditions, ideals, and aspirations of society into juxtaposition with its present reality—a reality all too often polished and reflected in the mirrors of popular culture. As they conclude; "by probing the past as well as the present, by looking at 'values' as much as 'facts,' such a social science (would be) able to make connections that are not obvious and to ask the difficult questions.[49] Would that more of these questions get asked, and answered, in dramatic, boundary-busting conversations with popular culture."

Notes

[1]Robert Bellah, et al, *Habits of the Heart* (Berkeley: Univ of California Press, 1985).

[2]Arthur Conon Doyle, "A Scandal In Bohemia," in *The Adventures of Sherlock Holmes*, (New York: Berkley, 1963), p. 10.

[3]These solid exceptions include Herbert Blumer's work in the 1930's on film audiences, Paul Lazarsfeld's work in the area of mass communications in the 1930's and 1940's, David Riesman's lifelong involvement with popular culture, Leo Lowenthal's important work in the 1950's and early 1960's on the emergence of the popular culture critique from the intellectual configuration of the eighteenth century, Herbert Gans' work on taste cultures in the 1960's and 1970's, and Robert Bellah's extraordinary look at American culture in 1985. See Herbert Blumer, "Molding of Mass Behavior Through the Motion Picture," in James F. Short (ed), *The Social Fabric of the Metropolis*, (Chicago: Univ of Chicago Press, 1971), pp. 117-137; Robert Merton and Paul Lazarsfeld, "Mass Communication, Popular taste and Organized Social Action," in Lyman Bryson (ed), *The Communication of Ideas*, (New York: Harper Bros., 1948), pp. 95-118; David Riesman, et al, *The Lonely Crowd*, (New Haven: Yale Univ Press, 1950); Leo Lowenthal, "Historical Perspectives of Popular Culture," *American Journal of Sociology*, 55 (1950), pp. 323-332; Herbert Gans, *Popular Culture and High Culture*, (New York: Basic Books, 1974); Robert Bellah, et. al., *op cit.*

[4]Zev Barbu, "Popular Culture: A Sociological Approach," in CWE Bigsby (ed), *Approaches To Popular Culture*, (Bowling Green, Ohio: Popular Press, 1976), pp. 39-68.

82   Symbiosis

[5]Edward Shils, "The Mass Society and Its Culture," in *Culture For the Millions?* Norman Jacobs (ed), (Princeton, NJ: Van Nostrand, 1961), p. 13.

[6]Leo Lowenthal, *op cit.*

[7]In the course of research for this paper, the author checked the seven major American journals of sociology that could conceivably carry articles and research reports on popular culture (*American Sociological Review, American Journal of Sociology, Social Forces, Social Problems, Social Science Quarterly, Journal of Social Psychology,* and *Sociological Perspectives*). In these seven journals, since 1980, there had been only two articles published that related relatively directly to popular culture, and neither of these had the term "popular culture" in their titles. M. Gottdiener, "Hegemony and Mass Culture: A Semiotic Approach," *American Journal of Sociology,* 90, 5 (1985), pp. 979-1001; and Ann Swidler, "Culture In Action," *American Sociological Review,* 51, 2 (1986), pp. 273-286.

[8]See, for example, Richard Hoggart, *The Uses of Literacy,* (London, 1957) and Michael Smith, "Work, Alcohol and the Public House," (Salford: Centre for Work and Leisure Publication, 1982) for good examples of this work.

[9]The most complete statement of this important school of thought to date is Pierre Bourdieu, *Distinction: a Social Critique of the Judgement of Taste,* (Cambridge, 1984).

[10]For a good overview of the Swedish effort, see Karl Eric Rosengren, "Cultural Indicators for the Comparative Study of Culture," in G. Melischek, KE Rosengren and J. Stappers (eds), *Cultural Indicators,* (Vienna: Akademie der Wissenschaften, 1984).

[11]See Hidetoshi Kato, *Japanese Popular Culture,* (Tokyo: Charles Tuttle, 1959).

[12]Ariel Dorfman and Armand Mattelart, *Para Leer al Pato Donald: Communicacion de Masa y Colonialisma,* (Bueno Aries: Siglo Veintuno Argentian Editores, 1972).

[13]The European-based International Sociological Association, in 1978, published a trend report on popular culture which documents many of these contributions in greater detail. See George H. Lewis, "The Sociology of Popular Culture," *Current Sociology,* 26, 3 (1978), pp. 1-162.

[14]See Clifford Geertz, *The Interpretation of Cultures,* (New York: Basic Books, 1973); Clifford Geertz (ed), *Myth, Symbol and Culture,* (New York: Norton, 1974); Mary Douglas, *Culture,* (New York: Russell Sage Foundation, 1977); Claude Levi-Strauss, *The Raw and The Cooked,* (London: Jonathan Cape, 1970).

[15]The term "symbolic interactionism" was coined by Herbert Blumer in the 1960's. For his intellectual roots, see Kurt H. Wolff (ed), *The Sociology of George Simmel* (New York: Free Press, 1950); Paul J. Baker, "The Life Histories of W.I. Thomas and Robert E. Park," *American Journal of Sociology,* 79 (1973); and George Herbert Mead, *Mind, Self and Society,* (Chicago: Univ of Chicago Press, 1934).

[16]Herbert Blumer, *Symbolic Interactionsim,* (Englewood Cliffs, NJ: Prentice Hall, 1969), pp 15-16.

[17]Howard Becker, "Becoming A Marijuana User," *American Journal of Sociology,* 59 (1953), pp. 41-58; "The Culture of a Deviant Group: The Dance Musician," in *Outsiders,* (Glencoe: Free Press, 1963), pp 79-100.

[18]Howard Becker, *Art Worlds,* (Berkeley: Univ of California Press, 1982).

[19]H. Stith Bennett, *On Becoming A Rock Musician,* (Boston: Univ of Mass Press, 1980).

[20]Erving Goffman, *Gender Advertisements,* (New York: Basic, 1981).

[21]Colin Lacey, *Hightown Grammar: The School As A Social System,* (Manchester: Manchester Univ Press, 1970).

[22]Gary Alan Fine, "Little League Baseball and the Creation of Collective Meaning," *Sociology of Sport Journal,* 2 (1985), pp 299-313; "Social Components of Children's Gossip," *Journal of Communication,* 27 (1977), pp. 181-185; *Shared Fantasy: Role Playing Games As Social Worlds,* (Chicago: Univ of Chicago Press, 1983).

[23]Roland Barths, *Mythologies,* (New York: Hill and Wang, 1975).

[24]Mary Douglas, "Deciphering A Meal," *Daedalus*, 101 (1972), pp 61-81; *Food as an Art Form*, (London: Studio International, 1974).

[24a]Michael Foucault, *History of Sexuality*, (London: Constable, 1979) and Jeffrey Weeks, *Sexuality and Its Discontents*. (New York: Routledge and Kegan Paul, 1985).

[25]M. Gottdiener, "Hegemony and Mass Culture: A Semiotic Approach," *American Journal of Sociology*, 90, 5 (1985), pp 979-1001.

[26]See George Gerbner, *et al*, various 1970's-1980's editions of the *Violence Profile*, (Penn: Univ of Penn Press); Karl Erik Rosengren, "Cultural Indicators: Sweden, 1945-1975," in *Mass Communication Review Yearbook*, (London: Sage, 1981), pp 61-87; Herman Lantz, *et al*, "Pre-Industrial Patterns in the Colonial Family in America," *American Sociological Review*, 33, 3 (1968), pp 413-426.

[27]Patricke Johns-Heine and Hans Gerth, "Values In Mass Periodical Fiction, 1921-1940," *Public Opinion Quarterly*, 13, (1949), pp 105-113; James Carey, "Changing Courtship Patterns in the Popular Song," *American Journal of Sociology*, 74 (1969), pp 720-731; Gaye Tuchman, *et al* (eds), *Hearth and Home: Images of Women In the Mass Media,*, (New York: Oxford, 1978); Gunnar Andren, *et al, Rhetoric and Ideology In American Advertising*, (Stockholm: Liber Forlag, 1978); Elizabeth Long, *The American Dream and The Popular Novel*, (NY: Routledge & Regen Paul, 1985).

[28]Paul F. Lazarsfelf and Frank Stanton, *Radio Research*, (New York: Duell, Sloan and Pearce, 1944).

[29]Howard Becker, "The Professional Dance Musician and His Audience," *American Journal of Sociology*, 56 (1951), pp. 136-144; Ken Mullen, "Control or Compromise? Occupational Autonomy and the Public House Performer," (unpublished, 1985); R. Serge Denisoff, *Waylon*, (Knoxville: Univ of Tennessee Press, 1983); George H. Lewis, "Beyond the Reef: Role Conflict and the Professional Musician in Hawaii," in Richard Middleton (ed), *Popular Music: Continuity and Change*, (Cambridge: Cambridge Univ Press, 1985), pp 189-198.

[30]Paul Hirsch, "Processing Fads and Fashinon: An Organizational Set Analysis of Cultural Industry Systems," *American Journal of Sociology*, 77, (1972), pp 639-659.

[31]Richard A. Peterson and David G. Berger, "Cycles In Symbol Production," *American Sociological Review*, 40, 2 (1975), pp 158-173.

[32]R. Serge Denisoff, *Tarnished Gold*, (NJ: Transaction, 1986).

[33]George H. Lewis, "Uncertain Truths: The Promotion of Popular Culture," *Journal of Popular Culture*, 1977 (in press).

[34]Douglas Kellenr, "Critical Theory and the Culture Industries," *Telos*, 62 (1985), pp 196-206.

[35]Francesco Alberoni, "Society, Culture and Mass Communication Media, *Ikon*, 19 (1966), pp 29-62.

[36]Bennetta Jules-Rosette, "Alternative Urban Adaptations: Zambian Cottage Industries as a Source of Social and Economic Innovation, *Human Organization*, 8, 3 (1979), pp 225-238; Cornelia Butler Flora, "From Escape From Reality to Reality Therapy: The Fotonovela and the State in Latin America," in George H. Lewis (ed), *Symbols of Significance*, (Paris: International Sociological Association, 1984), pp 27-49; Jeremy Tunstall, *The Media Are American*, (New York: Columbia Univ Press, 1977).

[37]Herbert J. Gans, "Popular Culture In America," in Howard Becker (ed), *Social Problems: A Modern Approach*, (New York: Wiley, 1967). Also see Gans, *Popular Culture and High Culture*, (New York: Basic Books, 1974).

[38]Michael Brake, *Comparative Youth Culture*, (London: Routledge and Kegan Paul, 1985); George Comstock, *et al, Television and Human Behavior*, (New York: Columbia Univ Press, 1978); Richard Peterson and Paul DiMaggio, "From Region to Class: The Changing Locus of Country Music," *Social Forces*, 53 (1975), pp 497-506.

[39]Edward Sadalla and Jeffery Burroughs, "Profiles In Eating," *Psychology Today*, 1980, pp 12-17; Dick Hebdige, *Subculture: The Meaning of Style*, (London: Methuen, 1979).

[40]Antonio Gramsci, *Selections From the Prison Notebooks*, (New York: International Publishers, 1971).

[41]Theodor Adorno and Max Horheimer, *Dialectic of Enlightenment*, (New York: Seaburg, 1944).

[42]Raymond Williams, *Television: Technology and Cultural Form*, (New York: Schocken, 1975); Todd Gitlin, "Prime Time Ideology: The Hegemonic Process in Television Entertainment," *Social Problems*, 26, 3 (1979), pp 251-266; Richard Hebdige, *op. cit.*; Simon Frith, *The Sociology of Rock*, (London; Constable, 1978).

[43]Ariel Dorfman and Armand Mattelart, *How To Read Donald Duck: Imperialist Ideology in the Disney Comic*, (New York: International General, 1975); Hidetoshi Kato, *Essays in Comparative Popular Culture*, (Honolulu: East-West Center, 1975); Jeremy Tunstall, *op. cit.*, pp 119-122.

[44]See, for example, Elihu Katz, "The Two Step Flow of Communication," *Public Opinion Quarterly*, 21, 1 (1957), pp 61-78.

[45]Pierre Bourdieu, *op cit.*

[46]Paul Lazarsfeld, *op cit.*, p 101.

[47]See George Comstock, *et al.*, *Television and Human Behavior*, Vols 1 and 2, *op. cit.*; F. Scott Anderson, "TV Violence and Viewer Aggression: A Cumulation of Study Results, 1956-1976;" and the President's Commission of *The Effects of Pornography In Society*, (Washington, DC: Gov't Printing Office, 1986) for various and conflicting conclusions concerning the effects of popular culture on its audience.

[48]Alasdair MacIntyre, *After Virtue*, (South Bend: Univ of Notre Dame Press, 1981).

[49]Robert Bellah, *et. al.*, *op cit.*, p 301.

Demography and Popular Culture

Arthur G. Neal
and
H. Theodore Groat

The word "demography" is from the Greek words *demos*, meaning people, and *graphy*, a combining form used to denote the act of writing about or describing. In the broadest sense, then, demography may be defined as the science dealing with the description of human populations. Initially, these descriptions address the topics of population size, composition (e.g., age, sex, race), and distribution (e.g., region, state, rural, urban). However, the interests of demographers go far beyond the mere description of these major demographic variables. For example, demographers also are interested in determining whether or not these variables are changing, and if so, the nature and extent of the changes taking place.

There are only three ways, demographically speaking, that any given population can change: (1) people are born into it (fertility); (2) people die out of it (mortality); and (3) people move into or out of it (migration). These three basic demographic processes, in turn, determine changes in population size, composition, and distribution. In its narrowest sense, demography is concerned largely with the statistical and mathematical measurement of population phenomena. More broadly, however, it also involves the explanation and analysis of a wide variety of population facts. For convenience, demographers typically distinguish between the largely statistical realm of formal or *mathematical demography*, on the one hand, and the broader area of population studies or *social demography*, on the other. Social demographers strive to analyze, explain, and understand the underlying sociocultural forces that influence, or are influenced by, a wide variety of population phenomena. Sometimes the phenomena studied are large scale, macro level trends such as Nineteenth Century fertility decline in Europe or the historical westward migration of the American population. Other times demographic studies are directed more at the micro level of analysis, such as attempts to understand contraceptive decision-making among teenagers or the consequences in later life of having grown up in a small versus a large family.

Social demography, then, uses a great variety of nondemographic factors as either predictor or outcome variables. As a predictor, for example, religion is used to explain differences in birth rates; income is used to explain differences in infant mortality; and job opportunities are used to explain the volume and direction of migration streams. Similarly, such outcome (or dependent) variables as voting behavior, crime rates, or mental illness, may be attributed to differences in age composition.

The incredible impact of the postwar "baby boom" on virtually all facets of American social and cultural life is a classic example of how change in a basic demographic variable—fertility—may be felt for decades throughout the entire society.[1] To illustrate, the baby boom resulted in a "youth culture" in the 1960s which led ultimately to a greater tolerance for deviant behavior of many kinds, new attitudes towards sex and drugs, and vast markets for new products. Changes in age composition due to the baby boom, in fact, undoubtedly affected all aspects of the business world. Currently, the U.S. divorce rate is likely to remain high as the baby boom generation passes through their 30s and early 40s, the ages when divorce is most frequent. Of course, when this large cohort reaches the oldest ages, when medical needs are greatest, the nation's total medical bill likely will surge far beyond current levels. While the baby boom is a particularly graphic example, it seems safe to say that there are virtually no societal conditions—past, present or future—that do not have a demographic dimension.

From the above, it is apparent that sociocultural and demographic phenomena are not only interrelated, they are inseparable. Virtually all facets of social and cultural life are implicated, both as causes and as consequences, in demographic behavior. In the pages that follow, we draw upon four examples to elaborate some of these connections between popular culture and fertility-related behavior. These examples are drawn from our own research in the areas of adolescent sexuality, the value of children, stereotypes of the "only" child, and sterilization decision making.

Adolescent Sexuality, Pregnancy, and Childbearing

As has been widely publicized, approximately one million adolescents become pregnant each year in the United States. While about 400,000 of these pregnancies are intentionally aborted, about half end in live births. Moreover, the majority of these births are to unmarried mothers, nearly half of whom are under age 18. The United States leads all Western, developed nations in its rates of adolescent pregnancy, abortion, and childbearing, despite the fact that American adolescents initiate sex and engage in sex no earlier, and no more frequently, than their counterparts elsewhere.[2] This difference is especially striking among females under age 15, who are more than five times as likely to give birth as females anywhere else in the developed world. In the United States, more than 10,000 babies are borne each year by females in this age group.

Seldom does a week go by without the media—television or radio, newspapers or magazines—making reference to what is commonly referred to as an "epidemic" of teenage pregnancy. Almost any popular magazine or newspaper reminds us of the disturbing facts, although the birth rates among adolescents have actually declined somewhat since the 1970s. Yet parents and professionals, researchers and policymakers, continue to debate the meaning of these social and demographic trends, frequently calling for immediate responses to this "impending crisis." Indeed, the facts do seem to warrant a crisis label. Certainly the personal and public costs that result from unintended pregnancies and untimely births are much too high to warrant an indifferent response. Discontinued educations, reduced opportunities for employment, unstable marriages, low incomes, and increased health risks to the children of teenage mothers are a few of the most obvious and immediate personal costs. In addition, the combined public spending for welfare, medicaid, and food stamp programs in the mid-1980s for families begun by a birth to a teenager was nearly $17 billion.

Two questions concerning adolescent fertility dominate the attention of most demographers and other social scientists who research these issues: (1) why is there so much sexual activity among unmarried teenagers, especially at such early ages, and (2) why are sexually active teenagers, especially American teenagers, such poor contraceptors? There are several ways in which cultural variables are implicated in tentative answers to each of these questions.

Since the 1960s there have been several changes in both the structural and cultural features of American society that have helped to promote early entry into sexual activity while at the same time inhibiting the successful practice of contraceptive behavior. For example, the *opportunities* for young people to have sexual intercourse are greater perhaps than at any other time. The generally free and easy mobility of very young adolescents to come and go as they wish, free of close parental or any adult supervision, means that if youngsters want to have sex they will certainly have no difficulty finding a place to have it. In many families only one parent is present, and in the others both parents typically work outside the home. Concomitantly, there has been a substantial shift in the mechanisms of social control for adolescents from parents to peers. This peer control, in turn, has fostered an adolescent subculture in which liberal norms regarding sexuality have been continuously supported by the media.

Without research evidence to substantiate a causal relationship, we may nonetheless explore the role of the media in the transfer and/or reflection of adolescent values on sexuality. Only the most naive would fail to see the sexual symbolism and stimuli inherent in much advertising for such teen products as jeans, make up, and hair styling materials. The values of being sexually attractive as well as sexually experienced also are reinforced by a plethora of low-budget teen "exploitation" films, music videos, popular lyrics, and television.

Children, especially during early adolescence, watch a lot of television and see a lot of movies. Content analyses have shown increases in the frequency of sexual references on television during the 1960s and 1970s, during the same period that the country experienced a major increase in sexual activity among teenagers. Frequently in movies and television programs aimed at adolescents, for example, there is depicted some variant of lovers being "carried away" by their passion. We have all witnessed the "slump to the floor" act in a movie or television scene: the man and woman look deeply into each other's eyes, madly embrace, and slump passionately to the floor (or couch, bed, boat deck, lawn, etc). Fade out, and nobody doubts what is going on!

What almost invariably is *not* going on is concern for contraception. Unlike many other activities that require conscious effort, pregnancy is very likely (given sexual intercourse) unless something is done to prevent it. It has been suggested that if it were the other way around, civilization would have long since died out. The reason for this is that making the decision to use contraceptives takes a certain toll—i.e., it requires motivation, resources, time, and knowledge. Decisions to use contraception require changes in behavior, the overcoming of inertia. So we should not be very surprised that the risk of unintentional pregnancy is highest during the first months following an adolescent's sexual debut. This is because effective contraceptive use is inextricably associated with the process by which early adolescents come to define themselves as sexually active, to become aware of pregnancy risk and its consequences, and to develop the motivation to prevent pregnancy by taking appropriate contraceptive measures.

Approximately half of all teen women are unprotected against pregnancy at their first intercourse. Not surprisingly, then, half of all first premarital pregnancies also occur within the first six months of sexual activity—more than 20 percent within the first month. How are we to explain the ineffective and sporadic nature of adolescent contraceptive behavior?

Part of the explanation, of course, is that accurate sex and contraceptive information are not readily available to American youngsters. But most teenagers know about at least some kinds of contraception, such as the pill and "rubber," and are educated in the basic biological facts of human reproduction. Knowledge of sex and contraception clearly is a necessary but not sufficient condition for the effective practice of contraception. What else, then? There is reason to believe that broader societal attitudes and values regarding sex and contraception also may have an important effect on contraceptive use. Teenagers seem caught between a general permissiveness, on the one hand, and a kind of institutional conservatism, on the other.

The "sexual revolution" of the 1960s unquestionably helped to demystify sex; yet in many ways there currently are present in American culture a set of "schizoid" values straddling the transition between traditional and contemporary sexual values. Traditionally, based to a large extent on Christian/ Judaic interpretations of the Bible, sex was to be non-erotic and clearly procreative in its purposes. Later the double standard, by which sex was defined as woman's duty and man's pleasure, became an additional value. Each of these sexual values has its contemporary opposites: sex for pleasure rather than procreation, and a single standard whereby erotic sex is deemed as appropriate for females as for males.

Yet the change from traditional to contemporary values, especially in the United States, is inconsistent and incomplete. Everywhere the media glorify youth and sexuality while ignoring contraception. The message to teenagers is clear: have sex, and don't worry about pregnancy. Thus young people are not equipped emotionally or intellectually for effective contraception, especially in the early stages of their sexual relationships. Until recently, contraceptives have not been advertised in popular magazines and newspapers, nor on television. But more importantly, concerns with birth control have not been included in the scripts of media presentations to which young people are most exposed. Situation comedies, for example, and teen movies in general, seldom depict young lovers engaging in conversation about contraception or even expressing concerns about unintentional pregnancy. It is ironic that sex is so approved and condoned, at least covertly, while strong taboos continue to surround the topic of contraception. But for society fully to accept contraception would be tantamount to a full acceptance of sex as erotic and non-procreative in nature—sex for pleasure. From this perspective, teenagers will be brought fully into the sexual revolution only when the larger society presents them with a new message: both non-procreative sex and contraception are "good," "healthy," "responsible," "clean," and "normal." Another irony worth noting is that contraception (at least condoms) may at last be popularized by the media in their attempts to cover the real and imagined horrors of the AIDS epidemic.

The stereotypes of contemporary culture provide major reference points for decision making and action at the individual level. While the sexual themes of modern advertising and mass entertainment tend to promote and encourage sexual involvement on the part of teenagers, other themes in popular culture provide reference points for avoidance behavior. The negative images of the "only" child is one of the more interesting forms of public perception that is clearly in error. As young married couples decide on the number of children they would like for themselves, there tends to be an avoidance of the one-child family because of the perceived negative consequences for the only child who grows up without sibling socialization.

Stereotypes of the "Only" Child[3]

During the first half of this century, "expert" opinion provided ample evidence to support the fears of married couples about the negative consequences of having an only child. In an often quoted study by an early psychologist named Bohannon, published in 1898, only children were viewed as below average in health and vitality, less regular in school attendance, and less successful in their academic performance. Further, he regarded only children as having less command of themselves socially than other children and noted that many of them indulged in imaginary companionship in order to compensate for inadequate social contacts.

More recent studies have expressed corroborating views. G. Stanley Hall, a prominent psychologist, wrote that being an only child is "...a disease in itself." A Viennese psychiatrist, Wexberg, warned that only children have a boundless egotism, tyrannizing their friends and suffering no other gods beside themselves. Writing in the late 1960s, Messer, a professor of psychiatry, concluded that only children are at a decided disadvantage compared to sibling children. And in the late 1970s, George Crane, a psychologist, psychiatrist, and syndicated columnist, advised against marrying an only child because onlies are less capable than siblings of sharing with others.

Thus prominent views on only children, up to the present time, have supported Bohannon's conclusions. And these opinions have not been limited to the academic journals. Popular magazine and newspaper articles, for example have reported such judgements on the only child to the general public. Crane's comments are a recent example of this; and a historical example would be a 1927 article in *Liberty* magazine which strongly warned its readers about the dangers of "onliness." This latter piece incorporated an illustration showing a child, scepter in hand, seated on a throne. Below were two miniature parents looking on in a submissive way.

Collectively, the literature as well as folk attitudes toward only children seem most frequently to concentrate on two personality traits: selfishness and dependency. Only children are presumably self-centered, egotistical, selfish, and just plain "spoiled." Moreover, the only child is commonly thought to be a "shrinking violet," inclined toward an over-dependency on doting and over-protective parents.

Being without siblings, of course, the only child is viewed as never having to share with brothers or sisters, never having to compete for attention and affection, and never having to experience the crisis of "dethronement" from his central place within the family. Implied here is the clear notion that a realistic perception of one's self depends on the checks and balances provided by sibling relationships. Yet the research comparing onlies and siblings on sociability, sharing, and selfishness generally indicates that in most respects the only child comes out ahead in terms of popularity and the ability to get along with others.

Similarly, the shrinking violet stereotype does not stand the test of empirical research. Dependency is likely the most extensively studied personality attribute of only children, and the results are fairly unequivocal. In short, only children excel in being independent and self confident. If anything, the research strongly points toward overly dependent children as more characteristic of large families.

Only children have also been characterized as lonely, underachieving, maladjusted, and unhappy. None of these notions, however, is consistently supported by the research evidence. As Terhune[4] suggested in his conclusion to an extensive review of the literature, "The only child, it seems, it more maligned than maladjusted." Indeed, the only child is shown by the personality research to be in many respects just the opposite of what most people believe. Compared to sibling children, onlies are more independent than dependent. Said to lack sociability, onlies are shown to be more aptly characterized as out-going and popular. And there seems little question that only children excel in a characteristic which is usually considered healthy and desirable, *viz.*, self esteem.

In fairness, however, the most objective conclusion to be drawn from all this is simply that the burden of proof is on those who persist in taking the negative stereotype of the only child as scientific fact. There are, indeed, tenuous threads of evidence which lend limited credibility to some of these stereotypical attributes. After all, where does self esteem end and egotism begin? Considering the weight of the evidence, however, and taking into account the numerous methodological flaws, shortcomings, and contradictory findings of the research evidence, only children do not seem likely to suffer disproportionately from any significant disadvantages.

Most of the research on onlies has been conducted with samples of children or adolescents. To the extent that personality differences between onlies and siblings do exist, however, the important question for most people would be the degree to which these attributes really make an important difference in later adult life. To determine this, measures of behavior throughout the life cycle would seem to be more appropriate. In other words, if growing up as an only child does have negative consequences, this could better be determined through making a study of outcomes in adult life, rather than concentrating on the personality characteristics of children.

This was the logic that led us to analyze a large national data set which included information collected by the National Center for Health Statistics from a probability sample of nearly ten thousand adults between the ages of 15 and 44. This survey provided detailed information on family formation, fertility expectations, contraceptive use, employment histories, education and income, and many other social and economic characteristics of both husbands and wives. If growing up as an only child really does make an important difference, we reasoned, such a difference should show up in later life in differential rates of educational and income attainment, and occupational placement. Similarly, if sibling socialization is really important for learning to cooperate, share, or get along with others, this should be reflected in later life in such outcomes as age at marriage, marital stability, and marital adjustment and happiness.

The results of this study were conclusive and consistent. There are no measurable disadvantages in adult life of having been an only child. If anything, there may be some very slight advantages to having been an only child in terms of such crucial achievement areas as education, occupation and income.

The implications to be drawn from this research are quite clear. The decision to have more than one child in order to avoid having an only child are misplaced. No evidence was found of any negative consequences for onlies, compared to siblings, in patterns of behavior in adult life.

The Value of Children

At the turn of the century, several perceptions were held of the value of children to their parents that now have been superseded. These included the views that children are necessary for a couple to have someone to look after them in old age; that children are necessary to demonstrate one's masculinity or femininity; that children provide some degree of continuity from one generation to another; and that children help to perpetuate one's own immortality. These reasons for having children have receded into the background. The vast majority of recently married couples in the United States do not regard these values to be important ones as they decide for themselves to have a child or an additional child.

The value of children to their parents has taken on several new dimensions in recent years.[5] The major advantages of children to recently married couples relate to emotional need gratifications. The major reason that couples give for bearing and rearing children is "to have someone to love and to be loved by." Thus, the symbolic advantage of children resembles the symbolic advantage of pets. Each is seen as a love object, and each evokes emotional gratifications from meeting the survival needs of those in a dependency relationship. Through performing caretaker functions, parents receive love and affection from the children who are dependent upon them. The prolonged dependency of infants and children upon others for survival leads to the development of intense and reciprocal social attachments. Through a smile, a hug, a kiss, or some other form of affection, children confer the primary rewards that their parents had previously expected from them.

Within an advanced industrialized society, children have lost most of their utilitarian and instrumental functions, and these have been replaced by the value assigned to intimate and emotional involvements. In addition to the value of children as love objects, most couples also place emphasis on "the fun of watching them grow and develop." The pleasure of watching growth and development in the nurturing and training of children finds a counterpart in the pleasures of gardening. In each case, the value of growth and development derives from perceptions of orderly progression both in the physical world and in the human constructions of reality. The expected rewards from observing the growth and development of children is enhanced by perceptions of children as "necessary for having a complete family" and from perceptions of the qualities of children as an outgrowth of personal qualities and initiatives.

Beyond the satisfactions obtained from affiliation needs and from having a complete family, the perceived values of children among individual couples are many and varied. Some feel that the advantages of children include "adding something exciting to my life," "having someone carry on a part of me," and "a sense of personal accomplishment." Only a small proportion of the married couples today regard children as being very important for the fulfillment of sexual love, for establishing oneself as a mature person or for spiritual fulfillment.

The disadvantages of children to their parents have also taken on new dimensions in recent years. Children are seen as interfering with freedom of movement and with the leisure lifestyles that many young people have adopted. Further, the bearing and rearing of children poses many obstacles to the young married woman who wishes to pursue a career and to have continuous involvement in the labor force. Children have become very expensive, and the financial cost of children has increased dramatically in recent years. In part, the increasing cost of having a child or an additional child stems from the emphasis young couples place on producing "quality children." As the value of a large number of children has declined, an increase has occurred in the levels of aspiration that couples hold for the children they do have.

Many couples are caught up in positions of ambivalence toward children. These are the couples who see both many advantages and many disadvantages to having and rearing children. In the absence of a clear set of plans about what a couple wants for themselves, the pattern of family formation tends to become one of aimlessness and drift. Under these circumstances, the use of contraception is likely to be haphazard, and as a result, the first child is likely to be an unplanned child. Decision-making has, in effect, been taken out of the hands of the individuals involved and having a baby comes to be experienced as an occurrence, as "the will of God," or as something that just happened.

The attitudes of some couples are hostile toward children. These are couples who emphasize the few advantages and the many disadvantages of having children. The behavior of children is seen as destructive and unpredictable, and a major generation gap is perceived as inevitable between parents and their children. Images of "children as monsters" took on a special prominence in mass entertainment during the 1970s. A series of "devil baby movies" appeared and drew upon the theme of the hidden enemies within our midst. Rather than an image of "innocence," the destructive potential of children came to be emphasized.[6]

In the more extreme cases of commitment to career plans and to leisure lifestyles, couples are simply indifferent to children. In these cases, neither the wife nor the husband actually pay much attention to the topic of children. Indifference is expressed through working out an agenda in which children are seen as having both few advantages and few disadvantages. These couples are not really concerned with the place of children in their overall life plans. Yet, as "the biological time clock" begins to run down, some women recognize that the failure to make a conscious decision about having children becomes within itself a type of decision. Because of the irreversibility of the life course, an increasing number of women are deciding to have a baby before the opportunity escapes them. Through postponing their childbearing until they are in their thirties, many professional women are now having their first birth long after the age at which family size has been completed for most American women.

Sterilization Decision Making

In comparison to previous generations, couples now are postponing marriage to a later age, having fewer children, and completing their desired family sizes sooner. The average woman in the United States today will have had her last child by the age of twenty-eight to thirty. Because of the decrease in family size and the increase in life expectancy, childbearing and childrearing will occupy a less important place in the overall life activities of American men and women. The reduction in family size is due primarily to increased effectiveness in the use of contraceptives and to a psychological separation of sex from reproduction.

The commitments to smaller family sizes are reflected in the increased popularity of sterilizations. Currently, sterilization is the leading form of birth control in the United States. It is a relatively safe surgical procedure that virtually provides a life-time guarantee against unwanted pregnancy. However, given the generally irreversible nature of the surgical procedure, along with the stigma and misconceptions associated with its uses in the past, the rapidity with which sterilization has spread among American couples is truly remarkable.

In making a decision on sterilization, there are several major forms of uncertainty that individuals and couples must resolve for themselves.[7] These include the place of children in life plans, concern for the potential effects of an unwanted pregnancy, and notions about the physical and psychological effects of surgical tampering with one's sexual physiology. The considerations that enter into sterilization decisions are often based on faulty information, limited information, or no information at all. Popular misconceptions and personal values are blended as couples decide for themselves whether to have a sterilization and whether the specific procedure will be a vasectomy or a tubal ligation.

Intentionally seeking finality to childbearing is an idea that generates anxiety for many people. In part, the anxiety stems from the irreversibility of the surgical procedure and in part from the psychological stress of closing off a future option. While there is the possibility of later regrets about having had an operation, there is also the more immediate prospect of possibly having an unwanted pregnancy. Further, eliminating the fear of pregnancy has the prospect of enhancing the frequency and the pleasure of sexual intercourse.

Generalized fears of surgery and specific beliefs about human sexuality produce special forms of anxiety about sterilizations. For example, many men who hold "macho" images of themselves also hold intense levels of fear of any kind of surgical tampering with their sexuality. Vasectomies are confused with castration, and sterilization is viewed as reducing one's interest in having sex. Some also hold that one's capacity to biologically reproduce is necessary for being "a complete man" or "a complete woman." Thus, while sterilization is increasing in popularity, a great deal of resistance persists among those who hold fragile images of their own sexuality.

In the final analysis, the decision to have a sterilization is one that is made under conditions of uncertainty. The decision is likely to be made through the combination of evaluations and attitudes. These include confidence in one's desire for no additional children, hopes for reducing the fear of an unwanted pregnancy, the view of sterilization as enhancing sexual pleasure, and the notion that a sterilization would have no undesirable side-effect on one's sexual identity or sexual appetite. Through adding finality to their childbearing at an early age, it means that an increased number of years will be available for men and women after their childrearing responsibilities have been completed. As childrearing plays a declining role within the life course of individuals, new cultural blueprints are likely to be drawn as innovative sources of meaning for couples in the middle and later years of life.

Discussion

The linkages between the fields of popular culture and demography have not been recognized either by demographers or by the students of popular culture. Yet, there are several aspects of reality construction by young adults that shape such demographic aspects of a society as premarital pregnancy rates, marital postponement, voluntary childlessness, declining fertility, and contraceptive practices. Recent changes in these demographic variables are altering the size and the composition of the population of the United States and will have significant effects on future developments in American culture.

Claims for a linkage between popular culture and demography are based on a broad, rather than a narrow, conception of popular culture. In our view, popular culture includes not only the formal aspects of movies, television, novels, popular entertainment and the news media, but also the reality constructions that grow out of informal social relationships and the symbolic constructions that occur at the individual level.

The key to popular culture lies in the symbolic constructions by people-in-general as they attempt to make sense out of the world around them. The task of understanding the options available has become more difficult as a result of the expanded scope of popular culture over the course of the 20th century. Universal cultural blueprints have lost their hold over individual conduct, and an increasing variety of social scripts are being elaborated. The heritage from the past is no longer accepted as having a self-evident validity. As a result, individual men and women are required to reflect on their own values and on what they want to achieve out of life.

The linkages between popular culture and demography must be based on the recognition that two individuals are involved in the reproductive process. For this reason, the knowledge and values that are held by one individual must be aligned with the knowledge and values that are held by another. For example, the decision to have a child or an additional child require alignments of the hopes and aspirations of both wives and husbands. In achieving such alignments, individuals are required not only to examine their own desires and preferences but also to line up their personal conduct with the cultural blueprints available to them.[8]

In the final analysis, increases or decreases in population for the nation as a whole are shaped by the aggregate decisions that are made by individuals acting as individuals. In making decisions related to sexuality, marriage, fertility, and contraception, a great deal of false information is held. A wide gap exists between the world outside and the pictures that men and women carry around in their heads. In part, the false information about sex and reproduction stems from the view of sex as a taboo topic in our culture. Yet, people act on the basis of the information they have at their disposal, however incomplete or inadequate that information may be.

It seems reasonable to hypothesize that popular culture occupies an important place in the decision-making process. Teenagers are likely to respond to the many images provided by the mass media as they decide for themselves whether to be sexually active or to remain sexually inactive. Young adults are likely to draw upon messages from popular culture as they evaluate the advantages of getting married relative to remaining single. And, married couples are likely to draw on public stereotypes as they reject the single-child family as the desired family size for themselves. Systematic inquiry into potential linkages between the themes of popular culture and decision making at the individual and couple levels offers a great deal of promise for a better understanding of the family formation process.

Notes

[1] Landon Jones, *Great Expectations: America and the Baby Boom.* New York: Coward, McCann and Geoghegan, 1980.

[2] Sandra L. Hofferth and Cheryl D. Hayes, editors. *Risking the Future: Adolescent Sexuality, Pregnancy, and Childbearing.* Washington, D.C.: National Academy Press, 1987.

[3] This section is drawn from H. Theodore Groat, Jerry W. Wicks, and Arthur G. Neal, *Differential Consequences of Having Been an Only Versus a Sibling Child.* Final Report submitted to the Center for Population Research, NIH, Bethesda, Maryland, 1980.

[4] Kenneth W. Terhune, *A Review of the Actual and Expected Consequences of Family Size,* Washington, D.C.: Government Printing Office, 1974. U.S. Department of HEW, Public Health Service, National Institutes of Health, Publication No. (NIH) 76-779.

[5] Arthur G. Neal, H. Theodore Groat, and Jerry W. Wicks, *Family Formation and Fertility Control in the Early Years of Marriage.* Final Report submitted to the Center for Population Research, NIH, Bethesda, Maryland, 1981.

[6] See Kathy Merlock Jackson, *Images of Children in American Film: A Socio-Cultural Analysis.* Ph.D. Dissertation, Bowling Green State University, 1984.

[7] For a recent empirical study, see H. Theodore Groat, Arthur G. Neal, and Jerry W. Wicks, *Psychosocial Aspects of Contraceptive Sterilization.* Final Report submitted to the Center for Population Research, NIH, Bethesda, Maryland, 1987.

[8] For a discussion of aligning personal actions with cultural values, see Randall Stokes and John P. Hewitt, "Aligning Actions," American Sociological Review, Vol. 41 (1976), pp. 838-849.

Philosophical Reflections on Popular Culture

Diane Raymond

> And the first rude sketch that the world
> has seen was joy to his mighty heart,
> Till the Devil whispered behind the leaves:
> It's pretty, but is it art?
>
> Rudyard Kipling

It is ironic for a philosopher to be writing on the issue of popular culture, for philosophers have tended traditionally to be *anything but* popular. Socrates, that exemplar of philosophical method, was executed for his unpopular beliefs, and Aristotle, we are told, fled his city-state rather than have the same fate befall him. One can fairly easily think of other philosophers—Spinoza, Kant, Kierkegaard, Nietzsche, and Peirce come to mind almost immediately—who, though escaping such dire consequences, nonetheless lived in isolation from mainstream society. This is not to suggest that there are no exceptions to this generalization: John Dewey in the United States was internationally known for his philosophical ideas, his views on education, and his social activism; Bertrand Russell in England was philosopher, mathematician, and social reformer who ran for Parliament three times and was occasionally jailed for his pacifist views; and, in France, existentialist Jean-Paul Sartre wrote fiction as well as philosophy for both popular and scholarly audiences and continued even up to the end of his life to immerse himself in the political and social climate of his time.[1]

Despite these exceptions, though, philosophers have generally enjoyed little favor in mainstream society. Often their works are ignored by popular audiences; when those works are read, they are frequently reviled by the public: Spinoza was excommunicated, Kierkegaard was painfully ridiculed, Russell was not allowed to teach at City College in New York. This "unpopularity" is more than a response by laypersons to a discipline that has traditionally been highly abstract and bound by its own peculiar conventions. If such were the case, then all academic specializations (which are almost always inaccessible to non-practitioners) would probably meet with the same fate. But while stereotypes about philosophers abound in some of the same ways as they do for any elite academic discipline, philosophy seems to fall into special disfavor. More specifically, popular audiences tend to react to philosophy either with outright animosity or just plain bewilderment. Today, one never hears of philosophers being executed, but this fact alone may reveal just how little actual social power and prestige philosophers enjoy. Yet philosophers have rarely given such issues any serious attention. Indeed, instead of exploring what this dynamic means, philosophers have developed an almost glib self-righteousness about their invisibility. "We are misunderstood," philosophers moan, "but genius is never truly understood in its own time." Or, philosophers complain, "we are undervalued," adding "but one always wants to kill the messenger." And, it should be noted, philosophers have tended to have as much (if not more) disdain for the public as the public has had for them. As a result, the dialogue between popular culture and philosophy which could ultimately enrich both areas of study fails to emerge.

Philosophers have tended to cultivate a detachment from social life in order to be better able to serve as social critics. It was Socrates, for example, who described his role as that of a gadfly, as one who annoys and irritates by making others aware of how truly ignorant they are. Most people, he maintained, dwell in the world of shadows, and only the true philosopher can move them from shadow to light to attain truth; the light of truth may, though, be blinding to those accustomed for so long to living in darkness. Since the days of Socrates, philosophy continues to question and criticize the assumptions which most of us customarily take for granted. Urging others to embark on the perilous journey of abandoning presuppositions for some uncertain end is hardly likely to win one great favor.

Further, philosophers have tended to be contemptuous of the masses. Plato was vehemently antidemocratic. Nietzsche wrote of the "herd mentality" of most individuals. Many philosophers contrast "mere opinion" (or "common sense") with real knowledge. Kierkegaard's view of the public is especially condemnatory, but not out of line with this tradition:

Yes, the larger the crowd, the more probable that that which it praises is folly, and the more improbable that it is truth, and the most improbably at all that it is any eternal truth.... The truth is not such that it at once pleases the frivolous crowd— and at bottom it never does....(p. 191)

Finally, philosophers have consistently extolled the virtues of a life of reflection. For Aristotle, the life of contemplation was the ideal form of existence. Since the essence of being human for most philosophers lies in our rational faculty, then other human faculties—emotion, sense perception, care, playfulness, and so/forth—are dismissed or devalued. One must, this view asserts, avoid immersion in the affairs of the everday world, for they can only serve as distractions from the pursuit of *sophia,* wisdom. Even the fact that we are "imprisoned" in a physical body is a disadvantage with which one must reckon; the body is the source not only of personal "sin" but also of intellectual error.[2] Seen in this context, those individuals Heidegger calls "das Man" or "the they" live in the world of the everyday, the world of distractions; consequently, such groups fail to promote authentic behavior. It is not much of a logical jump to move from here to the claim that ALL group culture is inauthentic.

Thus, there are good reasons why philosophers are not popular and popular culture is not taken seriously by philosophers. Philosophers have almost without exception disparaged popular culture and the masses themselves. At times philosophers employ examples of popular culture to illustrate a point in question, but this usually occurs only in the context of "serious" philosophical analysis. Popular culture theorists, though, have not done much better toward philosophy. For example, the *Journal of Popular Culture* has published "in-depth" sections which focus on specific disciplines including "popular culture and history" (Volume 11, #1), "popular culture and cultural geography" (Volume 11, #4), and "popular culture and sociology" (Volume 11, #2), but there has yet to be a volume which explores intersections between philosophy and popular culture. Issues that concern specific cultural groups (e.g. Chicano perspectives on popular culture) or time periods (e.g. popular culture before print) or themes (e.g. amusement parks or sports) or geographical areas (e.g. the South and popular culture or Latin American Popular Culture) largely ignore the contributions of philosophers past and present.

This is not to suggest that critical approaches to popular culture have not been philosophical; indeed, they often are. But it *is* to suggest that they are generally not acknowledged as such. In this essay I want to suggest some of the ways in which this gap between popular culture and philosophy might be bridged. Though there have been theorists who have attempted to develop intersections between the two disciplines, this potential for connection is largely uncharted territory. My aims, then, are necessarily modest. My emphasis will be primarily methodological, outlining approaches rather than analyzing specific content areas. But I will employ some concrete examples which I hope will highlight these points and perhaps even be suggestive of future directions philosophers of popular culture might take.

The information card on "popular culture" in the catalog of my school library reads:

Here are entered work on literature, art and music produced for the general public, i.e. mass consumption. Works on traditional ("high") culture are entered under *Intellectual Life*.

This brief statement makes clear its underlying assumption that popular culture cannot be "high" or even intellectual. Traditional philosophy has contributed to the evolution of this dichotomy in a way that has, as I have suggested, reflected the presuppositions of the discipline. Thus, philosophy's "elitism" has not been merely idiosyncratic but rather is consistent with its own methodological biases. Let's look at one classic example of such an approach and its implications for popular culture.

Rene Descartes, sometimes referred to as the "father of modern philosophy," used the "method of doubt" in order to discover a solid foundation for knowledge. What he sought was some indubitable belief as the ground for system-building. Adopting a radical skepticism, he doubted all that he could: his own body, God, the reality of an external world. Certainly we are not strangers to the countless possibilities for deception inherent in sense perception.

Perhaps I am dreaming, he argued, or deceived by some malevolent demon. What he arrived at was a statement he could not doubt, a statement whose certainty was beyond question: *cogito ergo sum*. From this statement he derived his notion that truth depends on clear and distinct ideas, and using what he viewed as deductive method, proved that God exists and returned the external world to us. I have no wish here to rehash all the powerful criticisms levelled at Cartesian philosophy. Rather, I want to explore the implications of this system and to suggest what all this might have to do with our study of popular culture.

John Dewey has characterized philosophy as a "quest for certainty" and Descartes, not unlike Plato, sought to develop a philosophical system whose conclusions followed logically from its premises. Such a system would necessarily be true, and hence objective, universal, and immutable. For Descartes, who struggled with the conflict between science and religion that was so much a part of the modern period, this almost mathematical model promised a secure ground for metaphysical speculation and religious faith. But what emerges from the Cartesian system is a profound dualism not only of mind and body but also of self and other. If the *Cogito* is what is certain, then all other facets of human being are uncertain, changeable, and suspect. Indeed, error cannot come from intellect but only from abuses stemming from what Descartes calls the will. Sense perception, even the existence of my own physical body, can be doubted. What is spiritual or immaterial thus has more reality than what is not.

This immaterial world, then, provides the ground for my knowledge of the world. In this way, the essence of all beings—their essential "what-ness"— is what is truly real. All other characteristics of entities in the world become "accidental" insofar as they are not related to the essential "what-ness" of the object. Such "accidental" or "secondary" qualities are then less real or are unreal or are perhaps in the beholder and not in the object at all. Empirical studies, since they do not deal with essences and are linked to specific temporal periods (remember, time is change and change is unreal), fail to reveal Truth to us.

It is not a very big jump from this view to statements like that of idealist F.H. Bradley that "the real is not rational and the rational is not real." Not only are mind and body separate, but so is one self from others. Since I can only know directly and with certainty the contents of my own soul, I cannot be sure that you too are a *Cogito* as opposed to, for example, a sophisticated machine. This solipsism makes all feeling private to the individual feeler. This view is hardly the common sense view, but we must acknowledge that "common sense" (even if we could determine what it is) is frequently in error.

Many of the current discussions of popular culture smack of this Cartesian dualism. For example, there have tended to be two differing critical approaches to the literature, one of which is directed at the cultural forms themselves, the other of which stems from a critique of the audience without specific reference to or regardless of the expressions of culture. These prongs of attack are quite different, as the former contends that there are qualities inherent in the production of popular culture that keep it from being real art, while the latter maintains that there is something about large groups that prevents what is popular from qualifying as real art. But this presupposed dualism assumes that a distinction between the two is a sensible one. What can philosophy contribute to this discussion?

There have been several schools within philosophy itself which have sought to challenge the assumptions of the canon and to urge new paradigms to replace those of classical philosophy. These non-traditional approaches have begun to pave the way for richer connections between philosophy and popular culture. For example, feminist philosophy has argued that women and other traditionally excluded groups must be brought into discussions of philosophy. One cannot claim to build a "crystal palace" (as Kierkegaard described Hegel's philosophy) if some individuals are not allowed residence inside it. One cannot write of ethics and rationality without putting those concepts into a context in which women and people of color have been denied access to education and then assumed to be incapable of rationality. Similarly, Marxist philosophy has critiqued the essentialist position that "the good" or "the true" exists independently of our concrete historical and material circumstances. In particular, Marxism has charged philosophy with a failure of vision, that is, that philosophy has tended to be a reactionary tool defending bourgeois culture and values. The philosophy of pragmatism in this country argued against essentialism and the view of knowledge as certainty. For pragmatists, scientific method is the basis of rationality, and knowledge is a dynamic process rather than a static "idea" that we find. Indeed, for pragmatists, it is far better to speak of "truth value," that is, how ideas "work," rather than "truth itself." Finally, existentialism and phenomenology have led to a reexamination of many of the assumptions of traditional philosophy. Phenomenology's slogan "to the things themselves" is a mandate to explore being as it reveals itself to us without bias and presuppositions about "how it ought to be." Phenomenological investigations have provided rich and insightful analyses of some of the more basic, more everyday aspects of human experience, including, for example, play, sexuality, and loneliness. Phenomenologists, rather than doubt the reality of the world, have "bracketed" that issue and instead looked at how we see or feel or taste or experience desire. Analyses of popular culture can presumably provide similar insights. Existentialists have likewise rejected the notion of transcendent values and substituted the concreteness and subjectivity of human experience. In Camus's classic work *The Stranger*, for example, the protagonist Mersault confronts a priest who is attempting to offer him assurances of eternal life. Mersault finally chooses the concrete over the absolute as he realizes that none of the priest's certainties, none of his theories, was worth even "a strand of a woman's hair."

Finally, all four of these views have tended to be both interdisciplinary and somewhat empirical. Since these theories tend to be antiessentialist, they must refocus their eyes away from the heavens back to the "ordinary", the everyday, the concrete. And since philosophy has no inside track in that regard, there has been a healthy blurring of disciplines.

This is not to imply that these four schools swallow all that popular culture has to offer without any critical analysis. Indeed, each has offered serious critiques of mass culture. Feminist philosophers have pointed out the oppressive ways in which women are portrayed in much of popular media. Marxists have argued that popular culture may not even be "popular" at all but rather a tool of the powerful to manipulate the masses. They also focus on the historical and economic bases of popular culture. Existentialists have opposed popular culture when it dehumanizes and is inauthentic. But this *is* to imply that these frameworks allow for consideration of the forms of popular culture without presupposing that the notion of "popular culture" is itself contradictory. They reject the notion of objective and eternal truths and so reject any *a priori* categories which would preclude by definition certain forms. Further, each view rejects the dichotomy which pervades much of traditional philosophy between objectivity and subjectivity. Thus, they do not trivialize (at least not in principle) what is subjective, temporal, historical, personal, actual, singular, or, finally, popular.

Is there any way that the view that anything popular must necessarily be inferior is more than mere snobbism? Spanish philosopher Ortega y Gasset contends that "the masses not only vulgarize and dehumanize but actually destroy art," and other critics like Dwight McDonald maintain that popular culture lacks even the theoretical possibility of being good. How might one defend such a view? Irving Howe maintains that to apprehend as meaningful the "aesthetic and intellectual values of high culture" certain conditions are necessary, including time (and patience), inclination, discipline, focus, guidance, and an environment in which style can be experienced. Is there something about the nature of large groups that precludes the possibility of those conditions being met? Many of these conditions, for example, emerge from certain kinds of education as well as the ability to have leisure time. Is this then a reflection of class bias? Surely we know that large numbers of upper-class individuals are not necessarily guaranteed the possession of "good taste." And obviously there is much mediocre art that is produced by elite classes. Whence come these standards?

Philosophy has since its beginnings been concerned with standards, and critics of popular culture have often been sloppy in their presuppositions that such standards are obvious and objective. Ernest van den Haag, for example, maintains that even training and formal preparation are insufficient to teach one to "experience a work of art as meaningful." (p. 528) Thus, the fact that more and more of us are college-educated does not necessarily reflect any superior appreciation of culture. But if this capacity is not related to class origin *or* education, how does one develop "good taste"? And why is it that masses cannot have it? The critics of popular culture like van den Haag and Howe seem to presuppose an essentialist position, that is, a view that certain aesthetic standards are objective and immutable and need only to be discovered by those with privileged access to truth. Yet when we explore the arguments more thoroughly, they appear to be guilty of circularity.

Ironically, the conservative and radical critics of popular culture agree on the criticism, but where the conservative finds the problem in the masses the radical maintains that the problem is in the hegemonic culture which seeks to manipulate and exploit the masses. "At its worst, mass culture threatens not merely to cretinize our taste, but to brutalize our senses while paving the way to totalitarianism." (Rosenberg, 1957, p. 9). And to defenders of popular culture who maintain that it provides us with freedom, Rosenberg argues: "There can be no doubt that the mass media present a major threat to man's autonomy. To know that they might also contain some small seeds of freedom only makes a bad situation nearly desperate." (p. 5) One can certainly agree that freedom does not inevitably lead to goodness *or* good taste, but this view seems overly simplistic. It makes the "public" a passive receptacle of media and culture. For example, some critics argue that the mindless and alienating nature of work has robbed humans of imagination. Though we may have more leisure time, we have become deadened by work and so the best we can manage is "mindless" excitement. This view too, though, seems to oversimplify. Further, it seems to make of "culture" a monolithic structure developed by those in power with the intent to exploit and manipulate others. Though one cannot deny that this is true much of the time, it seems not to be true in all cases. And, most importantly, it is too easy. In simply dismissing all group-culture as non-culture, it fails to answer the difficult question how one distinguishes what is of aesthetic value from what is not.

The second strand of criticism relates to the issue of culture itself. Plato, for example, criticized art which did not lead us to the form to The Good. Since most of us live in the shadows, fiction can only be a "shadow of a shadow" leading us away from truth. Fiction could not be edifying. Similarly, today, one often hears the complaint that popular culture is homogenized, created to suit the masses and so it takes no risks but rather adopts a "least common denominator approach." There has probably always been popular culture, but industrialization creates for the first time the possibility for popular culture to become mass culture. With this "massification" Plato's critique is reincarnated. "Its morality sinks to that of its most brutal and primitive members, its taste to that of the least sensitive and most ignorant." (Macdonald, p. 70) It is very soon that the "formula" in mass culture becomes hardened, cliched. Most disheartening, it cannot possibly get better, critics claim, but only worse. And, following Gresham's law, it drives out what little *is* good. This view is an exceedingly popular one. Raymond Williams, for example, has pointed out how easy it has been for researchers to receive funding for "impact studies" on television or film, the assumption being that anything "mass" corrupts the viewer.

Rosenberg, for example, adopts the same traditional view of contemplation described above when he writes of the "real artist."

The artist is basically an anarchist who should have as much solitude and tranquility and as much withdrawal from commercial or political clamor as society can provide. (1971, p. 11)

Yet this assertion seems to be empirically false, as many artists past and present have been immersed in social life. Also, this statement commits the fallacy of bifurcation, that is, it assumes falsely that one must choose either a life of solitude or the clamor of society.

What relevance is the production process to something's aesthetic value? Is *A Midsummer Night's Dream* popular culture (and therefore of no or little value) when televised because millions more people are able to view it than would have had it appeared in a theatre? If so, is this about the audience or the medium? Is this true of all television programming, no matter what its content? If so, then what about film? Bernard Rosenberg, for example, writes, "tyranny plus technology is the formula for totalitarianism" (1971, p. 8), yet it seems that technology is neither a necessary nor a sufficient cause of tyranny and that popular culture must not be assumed to be tyrannical. Before one can make such assertions, relevant differences must be shown; there is a tendency in much of the literature not just to assume that such differences exist (which seems obvious) but also that they are morally, aesthetically, and politically relevant.

These sorts of arguments tend to be consequentialist in character, that is, they attack the issue from the point of view of the alleged negative results. In mass culture, where quantity replaces quality, they argue, the results can only be negative. "Popular art says *relax*; private art says stretch," writes Marshall Fishwick (1974, p. 2). At times this criticism focuses on the intent of popular culture, namely that it is designed to manipulate. William Gass, for example, has argued that "no mind is paid to the intrinsic nature of its objects; they lack finish, complexity, stasis, individuality, coherence, depth, and endurance." (quoted in Browne and Madden, 1972, p. 15) Thus, he claims, the products of popular culture have "no more esthetic quality than a brick in the street." Some writers argue that high culture must be sought, whereas popular culture seeks us. Or, they maintain, mass culture alienates us from each other.

All mass media in the end alienate people from personal experience and, though appearing to offset it, intensify their moral isolation from each other, from reality and from themselves. One may turn to the mass media when lonely or bored. But mass media, once they become a habit, impair the capacity for meaningful experience. Though more diffuse and not as gripping, the habit feeds on itself, establishing a vicious circle as addictions do. (van den Haag, p. 529)

Rather than whet our appetites for more and better culture, instead popular culture spoils us through its oversimplification and makes us incapable of appreciating what is truly of cultural value, much the way sugar destroys one's appetite.

To spare us trouble, to save our time for more important things (like commercials) these works are cut, condensed, simplified, and rewritten until all possibilities of unfamiliar or aesthetic experience are strained out and plot and action become meaningless thrills...(Howe, pp. 524-525)

Some even attack popular culture on the grounds that it overstimulates our senses, gives pleasure, or serves a utilitarian function.

These views, though, conflate certain results of popular culture with inherent qualities of popular culture itself. And ultimately these arguments are circular. Howe, for example, argues that even if the Book of the Month Club sends its members Proust, the result will still be "homogenization" and that the function of the work of art is changed as a result of its distribution and means of production. But doesn't this assume an essentialist bias that somehow works of art *have* a proper function? How does one know when this function is being distorted? Is art never utilitarian? What is the relation between aesthetic value and the pleasure one experiences in response to a work of art? Can pleasure edify? Is art never rhetorical? What about the works of Dickens or Tolstoy? When one probes more deeply into Howe's argument, his only defense is that such a use of "high culture" is "incongruous." But this only serves to beg the question. Why can't artifacts of "high culture" have positive effects on the "masses"? Did more people read Victor Hugo's *Les Miserables* after seeing the musical version? Is this bad? Should we assume that the reading was lost on them? Or that they wouldn't finish it?

This is not to suggest that the arguments of defenders of popular culture are unflawed. Indeed, many of these defenses tend to take for granted some of the same assumptions of the Cartesian world view I have outlined above. Thus, they tend to be defensive since they do not question many of those presuppositions. Some, for example, argue that popular culture is so much a part of our everyday existence and so powerful and unavoidable that it must be analyzed. But there are presumably many aspects of human experience which are powerful and even pervasive that are not necessarily analyzable from a scholarly perspective. Others maintain that popular culture is of value because it reflects cultural diversity. But are all expressions of diversity of value? And, even if we can show that they are (and this would take some doing), that is a separate issue from the aesthetic question of their value. My focus has been on the opponents of popular culture primarily because the tradition of classical philosophy has a natural affinity with the critical perspective on popular culture. But philosophical analysis can serve to enrich all sides of this complex issue.

Emile Durkheim has maintained that two conditions are necessary for the systematic enquiry of a given subject area: clear definition and comprehensive classification. Kroeber and Kluckhohn have discovered at least 164 different definitions of the word 'culture' alone, and theorists of popular culture, both defenders and opponents, are struggling with definitions. There is, as yet, no consensus on terminology, and a wide range of labels appears in the literature. Some speak of radicals and conservatives (Rosenberg, 1957); of providers, traditionalists, progressives, and radicals (Hall and Whannel); democratic and aristocratic (de Toqueville); popular and dominant (Gramsci); popular culture and genuine art (Lowenthal); elitist, optimist, and revisionist (Nye). And lists seems to proliferate with every new article. There is something to be said for this pluralism in approaches, but philosophers have much to contribute in the area of conceptual clarification. In particular, philosophical methodology can make clear when terms are used descriptively and when prescriptively. It becomes apparent after not much reading of this literature that implicit in the terminology is a normative bias. There is nothing wrong with such a bias, but it is essential that it be acknowledged and defended rather than concealed.

Finally, one must ask what is left if we reject objectivist ideologies which are based on *a priori* assumptions. Are we left with a rejection of all standards in the way that Plato feared? How does one defend a standard without some objective, external gauge by which one measures the item in question? If critics of popular culture are wrong, are we left with a naive and uncritical acceptance of all forms of "culture"? If one rejects the idea that the experience of pleasure precludes the possibility of enlightenment, must we argue, as Bentham did, that "poetry is as good as pushpin," or, in more contemporary terms, *L.A. Law* is as good as *Ulysses* or even that *Growing Pains* is as good as *L.A. Law*? Utilitarian John Stuart Mill tried to address this question by suggesting that there might be qualitative differences in certain kinds of pleasurable experiences. But when pushed to explain how one sorts out those differences, he was forced to resort to reliance on the opinions of "expert" judges. Such a solution is obviously unsatisfactory, for it either presupposes (once more) the very absolutism we sought to reject or it begs the question: what if *my* taste differs from that of the experts? These questions of evaluation are neither repressive nor capricious. And philosophy can begin to outline a framework within which those questions can be considered.

Note

[1] I believe that it is no coincidence that these three examples are all of the twentieth century, and my argument in this essay will make clear why that is so. But this is not to say that one could not find other examples in earlier centuries.

[2] It is perhaps not an *ad hominem* attack to point out in this regard that most philosophers have been not only male but also upper class, with the leisure time necessary for this "life of the intellect."

Works Cited

Benedict, Ruth, *Patterns of Culture*. Boston: Houghton Mifflin, 1934.

Bigsby, C.W.E., *Approaches to Popular Culture*. Bowling Green University Press, 1976.

Browne, Ray B., ed., *Popular Culture and the Expanding Consciousness*. New York: John Wiley, 1973.

Browne, Ray B., Larry Landrum, and William Bottorff, eds., *Challenges in American Culture*. Bowling Green University Press, 1970.

Browne, Ray B. and David Madden, *The Popular Culture Explosion*. William C. Brown, 1972.

Browne, Ray B., et al., eds., *Frontiers of American Culture*.

―――― "Popular Culture as the New Humanities," *Journal of Popular Culture* 17, 1 (Spring 1984), pp. 1-9.

Fishwick, Marshall, ed., *American Studies in Transition*. Philadelphia: University of Pennsylvania Press, 1964.

——— *Parameters of Popular Culture*. Bowling Green University Press, 1974.

Harper, Nancy, *Human Communication Theory: The History of a Paradigm*. Rochelle Park, N.J.: Hayden Book Co., Inc., 1979.

Kierkegaard, Soren, *Purity of Heart is to Will One Thing*. New York: Harper and Row, 1938.

Kroeber, A.L. and Clyde Kluckhohn, *Culture: A Critical Review of Concepts and Definitions*.

Lewis, George H. "Between Consciousness and Existence: Popular Culture and the Sociological Imagination." *Journal of Popular Culture* 15, 4 (Spring 1982), pp. 81-92.

Lowenthal, Leo, *Literature, Popular Culture and Society*. Palo Alto: Pacific Books, 1961.

Macdonald, Dwight, "A Theory of Mass Culture," in Rosenberg and White, eds., *Mass Culture*, pp. 59-73.

Macdonald, Dwight and Edmund Wilson, *Against the American Grain*.

McLuhan, Marshall, *Understanding Media*. New York: McGraw-Hill Book Co., 1964.

Nye, Russel B., ed., *New Dimensions in Popular Culture*. Bowling Green University Press, 1972.

Oswalt, Wendell H., *Understanding Our Culture*. New York: Holt, Rinehart, and Winston, 1970.

Real, Michael, *Mass-Mediated Culture*. Englewood Cliffs: Prentice-Hall, 1977.

Rosenberg, Bernard and David Manning White, eds., *Mass Culture Revisited*. New York: Van Nostrand, 1971.

——— *Mass Culture: The Popular Arts in America*. New York: Free Press, 1957.

Rourke, Constance, *The Roots of American Culture*. New York: Harcourt, Brace and World, 1942.

Schechter, Harold and Jonna Gormley Semeiks, *Patterns in Popular Culture*. New York: Harper and Row, 1980.

Van Den Haag, Ernest, "Of Happiness and of Despair We Have No Measure," in Rosenberg and White, eds., *Mass Culture*, pp. 504-536.

Voelker, Francis and Ludmila, *Mass Media: Forces In Our Society*. New York: Harcourt Brace, 1972.

White, David Manning, ed., *Popular Culture in America*. Chicago: Quadrangle Books, 1970.

Psychology and Popular Culture:
Psychological Reflections on *M*A*S*H*

Peter Homans

Introduction: Psychology and Popular Culture

Neither the study of popular culture nor the uses of psychology to further that study are new. But in the late 1950s the two, which until then seemed to bear no necessary relationship to each other, became prominent. At that time university-based intellectuals became interested in what they chose to call "mass culture," carefully separating it from "high culture." The impetus for much of this interest no doubt derived from a number of very different sources: the sense of relief and renewal which followed the second great war, the arrival of television as a new and exciting medium of communication and a fresh sense of the importance and attractiveness of higher education. These and other trends were consolidated in a single, widely read anthology, *Mass Culture*, edited by Bernard Rosenberg and David Manning White.[1]

The 1950s approach is notable on several counts. Critics spoke from many different disciplines but with hardly any sense of their complexities. Despite the presence of different disciplines, much of the criticism was on the whole psychological and the psychology was heavily reductionistic: mass culture was the dream of the masses and as such an enormous and very simple "escape mechanism." Nor was there in all this criticism much sense of the social context of popular art forms. And, the forms themselves were what I call "para-institutional," which is to say that they contained little interest in or concern for social and political issues.

As everyone knows, the cultural upheaval of the 1960s changed almost all of this. The firm distinction between high and mass culture weakened and the term "popular culture" appeared. Critics began self-consciously to view themselves along disciplinary lines: the literary approach, the sociological, the historical and so forth. Psychology for the most part dropped out of the picture, turning away from cultural interpretation to create important advances in clinical theory and practice. Perhaps most important of all, major segments of popular culture became explicitly oriented to social and political issues, a trend which continued on into and through the 1970s and, so it now seems, into the early 1980s as well.

In this article I develop a psychological analysis of one relatively new form of popular culture, what I call the "politically-toned situation comedy," chiefly *M*A*S*H* and its precursors, *All In The Family* and the *Mary Tyler*

Reprinted from *Journal of Popular Culture*, Winter 1983, Vol. 17, No. 3. Reprinted with permission.

Moore Show. In doing this I hope to accomplish several goals. First, I wish to revitalize the early psychological criticism which has been rightly neglected due, I think, to its reductionism and its claims to explain practically everything. There is irony here because I think that the legitimate power of psychological explanation comes most convincingly into play precisely at those moments when its limits are most explicitly recognized. So I deliberately limit the psychological approach, which does in fact continue to center upon a "dream dimension" or "dream aspect" of popular culture, by introducing literary and sociological concepts.

Second, I plan to lift out some of the central values, ideals and meanings which popular culture embodies. To be sure, popular culture clearly does give some form to strong emotional states and complex social attitudes; but it also "thinks" and I try to cull out and identify some of these thoughts. Psychology is useful in this approach, for it explores the implicit or "deep" structure of meanings which it assumes lies beneath the surface or conscious level of the text, thereby introducing in a fresh way complexity and nuance into the art of interpretation. Third, I propose that some historical continuity persists from one popular form to another alongside the more obvious discontinuities. So I make certain connections between the politically-toned situation comedy, a principal genre of the 1970s, and the western, a principal genre of the 1950s. But because these continuities are often shadowy and evanescent, I only suggest them at the end of the discussion, although I also allude to the western insofar as it shares certain structural commonalities with the politically-toned situation comedy.

Before turning to the analysis itself, however, it is necessary to establish, if only briefly, the central features of a psychological approach which is less ambitious but thereby more effective than the psychologizing of the 1950s.

II
Psychological Criticism of Popular Culture—What Is It?

One of the most interesting and important features of popular culture is the mode of participation which it almost always commends to the viewer, a mode I call "thinking with" popular culture. Unlike the reading of a great novel or the viewing of a fine painting or statue—but somewhat like the experience of a dream—the experience of viewing popular culture occurs without much inner, objective thoughtfulness. Particular episodes are rarely talked about, and if they are one usually remains, on such occasions, imaginatively "outside" the world of the form. And it is difficult, often impossible, to remember particular episodes which one may have viewed, even only days before. On the other hand, unlike a dream but like a great work of art, popular culture is public and social and clearly possesses a reality independent of our minds. My point is simple: popular culture stands mid-way between the private, pre-reflective and unconscious world of dreams and the public, conscious and objective world of everyday social reality.[2] This somewhat dream-like sensibility or sense of immersion which characterizes the viewing of popular culture, and which is so essential to its enjoyment, recalls what Robert Warshow, to my mind still one of the very best critics of popular culture, meant by his now famous phrase, "the immediate experience."

But the psychological critic uses a readiness to "think with" popular culture alongside other members of the audience as the medium through which to "think about it." "Thinking about" requires objective analytic reflection on one particular dimension of the form, its dream-like qualities. This dimension lies hidden or veiled in and beneath the surface of the text.

Unlike the 1950s writers who used psychology, however, current psychological criticism recognizes that dream-like meanings comprise only one of several dimensions in the form and therefore develops its analysis in conjunction with the analyses of others. In the case of the interpretation of *M*A*S*H* which follows I take from literary criticism, concerned with aesthetic structure and effects, the concept of genre; from the sociologist, concerned with attitudes and socialization, the concept of socialization from the family to institutions; and from the historian, concerned with chronologizing and contextualizing popular art forms, the notion of historical continuity between current and earlier forms. Each of these "moves" reduces somewhat the claims of the psychological approach but at the same time gives something substantial to it which it might otherwise not have.

But what does the psychological critic think about? The answer is, genres and the several elements of which genres are composed. It is a truism to say that any object in the sphere of high culture can serve as a text and that some texts group themselves into genres. But when this principle is transferred into the sphere of popular culture it becomes a rule: while in theory any single showing of any popular culture form can serve as a text, in practice it is the case that only a genre provides the critic with the sense of permanence and objectivity necessary for interpretation to take place. So it was that when popular culture critics first appeared on the scene they readily spoke of westerns, detective stories, science fiction, and the like.[3]

When considered psychologically, a genre can be broken down into its constitutive elements of setting, types or typical personages, plot or narrative and significant detail or primary images. These four elements blend together to create a cohesive form through such processes as transposition, fusion and transformation.[4] These processes are active both within and between showings and series, and also between audience and showings. From one showing to another within a series and from one series to another within a genre, this cohesive blend of the four elements continuously creates the impression of novelty and freshness; but at a deeper level the blend simply repeats set patterns endlessly. Psychological interpretation breaks down the genre into its constitutive elements by moving from surface to depth. An illustration from a study of westerns will clarify these clumsy terms which are in fact quite simple and straightforward. Precisely because it is now defunct and has been so overstudied, the western can be both easily and briefly discussed.

It is possible quickly to recognize in westerns a limited number of types: the hero, adversary, good girl, bad girl, debauched Easterners and so forth. The given characteristics of specific types (the type never appears in pure form in any one showing) generate through transposition, fusion and transformation the specific figures of any one episode. And endless numbers of westerns knit these types into endlessly varied plots, all of which nonetheless share a common pattern. Type and plot are in turn elaborated to include recognizable settings, and all these are punctuated with recurrent primary (or typical) images. Insofar as anyone can break these elements down, veiled or hidden meanings will emerge. One can reflect upon the manner in which the types and plots of westerns together canalize and organize violent urges, such that the hero's victory over his adversary is on the surface level a morally approved achievement but at a deeper level also appears to be an execution. One can imagine the transposition or splitting or displacement of sexuality from the wholly good girl to the wholly bad girl. In a more sociological vein, one can reflect on the tensions between Eastern and Western ways and why non-violence and controlled sexuality are also ways associated with the former. Many different analyses of the western have worked over these more obvious issues, which are only illustrative.[5]

While a psychological analysis of genres can be made to go a considerable distance in interpreting the western, with its epic and almost mythic shape, a sharper sociological reference is needed in the case of the politically-toned situation comedy, so representative of immediate and conventional every-day social experience. The key to this sociological dimension is the concept of the family, for the family is at the heart of all situation comedies, both politically-toned and pre-political. Any psychology of the situation comedy will have to be a psychology of the family, understood as a series of primary psychological processes set within the context of secondary socialization of the individual into institutional structures. These psychological-sociological processes will be represented (in the sense of a publically-shared visualization) by means of images and symbols in the shape of the situation comedy.

At the psychological heart of all family life is a paradox so obvious that its mere mention may well appear gratuitous; but this paradox, which is as profound in psychological resonance as it is simple, sometimes escapes unnoticed. I call this paradox "the psychodynamic core" of family life and also of the situation comedy. The family is the child's first social setting and in it occurs the life-long struggle between two fundamental modes of inner, psychological organization—autonomy and dependency. In modern industrialized societies at least, the child strives for a progressively higher degree of separateness, individuality and autonomous self-regulation. But this very autonomy requires a long period of dependency upon authorities and, until recently, upon the father. How autonomy can grow from its logical and psychological opposite, dependency, is of course the paradox, for that is precisely what does happen over and over and over again. To this formulation can be added two other notions, that autonomy and dependency exist best in a context of interdependence and that when interdependence breaks down, autonomy and dependency lapse into a third mode of psychological organization, one which has earned the fear and hatred of all so-called modern people, authoritarianism.

Situation comedies work over and play out this paradox again and again, re-presenting and disguising the psychodynamic core and its three primary modes of inner psychological organization in the form of types. Central figures are assigned definite positions. In the ensuing action they depart from these, creating tension in the plot and pleasure for the audience. At the end, tensions are resolved and interdependence once again supervenes. Two examples will suffice. The *I Love Lucy* show clearly begins in a state of interdependence, with Lucy as dependent and Ricky as autonomous, according to the conventions of the bourgeois family. Then Lucy becomes mischievous (abortive efforts at autonomy), Ricky becomes frustrated (loses his autonomy and becomes authoritarian). This mix of type and plot is transposed into Ethel and Fred who season the action with variations. Then in the end the paradox is resolved and the plot returns the types to interdependence—that is, the family so to speak "recovers" itself. A great deal more than this is of course going on in *I Love Lucy*, but the veiled outlines of a psychodynamic core are also evident.[6]

This psychodynamic core appears in almost pure culture in *The Honeymooners*. At the outset Ralph is autonomous and Alice dependent, again according to conventional bourgeois expectations. Their dyad is transposed onto Norton and Trixie and also onto Ralph and Norton, the second complicated by a reversal in gender. Then things go awry. Ralph loses his autonomy, becomes authoritarian and, as is psychologically necessary, also dependent. Previously dependent figures become autonomous to the surprise and pleasure of the audience and confront Ralph. He rages against this—that is, struggles abortively to regain his autonomy. This rage is forbidden in the modern families which watch *The Honeymooners* but it is permitted to enter into the consciousness of the audience via the social dream of this genre of popular culture. Our guilt and anxiety about rage are transformed by the "magic" of popular art— Ralph is simply funny. In the end the plot eliminates the extremes in order to restore interdependence.

I call these comedies "pre-political" or "politically innocent" shows because in them the psychological and sociological issues which make up their psychodynamic core are separated from any overt institutional context and because the psychological issues themselves are never discussed as such by the various types. For this second reason, one might also refer to them as "pre-psychological" or "psychologically innocent," at least as far as the surface content of the shows would suggest. But all this changes in the politically-toned situation comedies. Here the earlier and innocent "debates" between autonomy, dependency and authoritarianism are now cast in the context of a struggle between cold, encroaching institutional authority and individual liberty, and in terms of right, advantage, and so forth. And my choice of the word "debate" is well-taken because the types in the newer comedies explicitly and self-consciously make use of psychological language, ideas, values and reasoning. In short, the family in these shows has become politicized.

In order to interpret these newer shows correctly, it is necessary to take account of these two shifts. This can be done by expanding one's understanding of the psychodynamic core to include institutional reality and the secondary socialization which it commands, and by recognizing that by doing so a second paradox indirectly comes into play. Strictly speaking, the psychological quest for autonomy in modern industrialized societies occurs in relation to institutional authority, and when that quest breaks down one loses one's autonomy, not in a vacuum (as Ricky and Ralph do), but either by merging blindly with powerful institutional authority, thereby becoming authoritarian, or by simply becoming dependent upon the dictates of others. Like the first, the second paradox lies in the fact that, developmentally, the achievement of autonomy in relation to institutional authority requires some sort of dependence upon that authority. When the psychodynamic core (autonomy, dependency and authoritarianism) is placed within a political context, it in effect forms two basic cognitive attitudes which I call "psychological modernism" and "psychological traditionalism."[7] Clarifying these rounds out this already too-long but unavoidably necessary theoretical discussion, and makes actual interpretation possible.

Psychological modernism refers to the deeply wished-for ideal of autonomy as it occurs first in the family but then in the realm of social and historical life. As a cognitive attitude or orientation it signifies a mode of thinking about the every-day social world which is calculative and instrumental and which is characterized chiefly by the capacity to separate information from source of information.[8] The rational, conscious mind reasons its way, so to speak, into all preferred courses of action. Consequently, the psychological modernist moves away from or against institutional authority. On the other hand, psychological traditionalism signifies the often negatively-valued orientation of either dependency or authoritarianism as these are experienced first in the family and then later, under the press of secondary socialization, in relation to institutions. As a cognitive attitude it suggests a readiness to accept and internalize handed-down values and attitudes toward every-day issues, especially as these are proposed and approved by institutional or traditional authority. I link institutions with history and tradition because it is a social fact that institutions derive their awesome power over people by appealing to their sense of, or need for, a heritage of some sort—that is to say, to their socially-located dependency needs.

As readers will quickly recognize, these two orientations are found in an otherwise enormously diverse number of sociological works on the subject of contemporary culture, such as those of Karl Mannheim and Talcott Parsons. I am not, however, primarily concerned with a broad sociological analysis of the social context of popular culture but am instead chiefly interested in "the inner world" of the genre, which is to say the subjectively meaningful orientations which the genre unconsciously conveys to viewers, especially since viewing consists in part of dream-like immediate experience. Hence my source here is psychoanalysis rather than sociology, and especially Freud's famous distinction between ego, superego and id. Ego processes are represented by psychological modernism, super-ego processes by psychological traditionalism. Superego processes refer to a kind of thinking informed chiefly by the need for "organic ties," also colloquially referred to as "blood and soil." By the phrase "organic ties," I mean those pre-rational, taken-for-granted loyalties which are, psychologically speaking, anchored in deeply felt connections with communal existence.

Every show belonging to this genre displays the psychodynamic core and associated cognitive orientation, representing them in some sort of clashing interaction, and every show resolves these according to a typical pattern.

With these few literary and sociological ideas at hand, it is possible to ask the psychological critic's essential and only real question: what meanings do these comedies conceal or veil? The newer political shows express definite perceptions of the tension between psychological modernism and psychological traditionalism. Like a dream, they repeatedly work over and play out this tension, re-presenting it in endlessly different ways. Their focus is upon institutional authority, explicitly or implicitly present, and they conceal or disguise what I call "the suspicion of tradition," the view that traditional institutionally-grounded figures of authority are unreliable guides to satisfying behavior in contemporary life, and that these must accordingly be replaced by autonomous, modernistic and institution-free modes. Consequently, figures of tradition will always be represented in parodic, twisted and deformed ways. This orientation, the suspicion of tradition, is not actively present in the consciousness of the viewer during the viewing experience but is rather experienced unconsciously, just as an aggressive wish is present in disguise in a dream and is therefore not recognized as such.

At the deepest level, however, the newer political comedies actually perform the reverse and, by representing institutionally-grounded and traditionalistically-thinking authority figures in a bad light, make it possible for some viewers to entertain wishes for a sense of pre-rational communal connectedness, wishes which the socially-approved ethos of modernistic autonomy denies or censors. If such wishes are permitted representation, they will be allowed to appear only in disguised and degraded forms. In either case, the point is the same: the comedies work over and play out the ambivalences which modern audiences share with regard to the proper place of tradition in modern life.

In the following analysis, I do not speak for or against the values embodied in and commended by these shows, but instead attempt to lift them out for all to see. At the close of the discussion, however, I do distinguish my psychology—what I call the psychology of the critic—from the psychological values of the shows, the psychological ideas which the genre "thinks." Like the shows which the psychological critic interprets, the act of interpretation itself in this case contains a paradox all its own: shows which are themselves deeply psychological are submitted to a psychological critique. But the two are not the same, a point I return to at the end.

III

Psychological Reflections on M*A*S*H *and its Precursors*

All in the Family and *The Mary Tyler Moore Show* and their spin-offs made possible the politically-toned situation comedy, but *M*A*S*H* made it a reality all its own as a new genre. In the first case the dominant issue was race, in the second, feminism and gender; in the third, these persisted but were augmented by war, politics and psychiatry. In a very fundamental sense, *M*A*S*H* is the paradigm for all politically-toned situation comedies, bringing together as it does these five issues which are so essential to the genre. In every case, setting, type, plot and significant detail work over and play out the psychodynamic core and its associated, cognitive orientations, such that its veiled or hidden meanings are relatively easy to establish.

Mike embodies psychological autonomy in clashes with Archie, the authoritarian figure, after the age-old fashion of conflict between father and son. Edith and Gloria round out the picture as dependent types. But they also serve mediating functions in two senses. They are what I call "cue-in figures," relatively plausible but somewhat neutral persons with whom the audience can quickly, easily and safely identify and thereby become alternatively close to and distant from the dangerous and raging madnesses of the two men. Edith and Gloria also function as mediators within the show itself, softening and editorializing upon its raw anger.

Because genres work through a cumulative process, every single showing represents all the essentials of the genre in one way or another. But some showings, it seems, highlight the intentions of the genre more than others. In one, memorable for its sheer and appalling primitivity, the two men mount an argument about blood, transfusions and transplants. Archie does not object to transfusions per se, but he is concerned about who might receive his blood. He is afraid that, were he to make a donation, his blood could be given to a radical student who was shot by the police in a riot. An Orthodox Jew, he continues, would reject a Christian's heart and a man would reject a woman's heart, especially if she were a liberal (for Archie all men are, it seems clear, conservative), and so forth. Mike, on the other hand, takes the conventional medical and scientific view: blood is a question of chemistry and a question of source, that is, the body and person of the donor does not matter.

The figure of Mike represents psychological modernism. His cognitive approach or style of thinking is rational, calculative, autonomous and ego-oriented. He can therefore separate information from source of information and in this case blood from donor. Archie on the other hand is a figure of psychological traditionalism and he is simply unable to make such separations. Archie's cognitive style displays a yearning for what I have called organic ties or "blood and soil" (in the case of the former in this example, quite literally). His thinking makes the explicit assumption that all people have strong, taken-for-granted wishes or yearnings, pre-rational in character, for social ties rooted in a shared communal past or tradition. From a psychological point of view, Archie's mind is organized largely along the lines of unconscious superego processes, for that mental structure is the link with what Freud called "the cultural superego," the psychological source of values embedded in the heritage of the past.

At this point some of the meanings which the genre disguises—its hidden or veiled meanings—can be discerned. Mike simply cannot tolerate the thought that mental processes such as those which the figure of Archie represents exist in the human mind. Nor for that matter can the audience, who, by laughing at the silliness of Archie's thoughts, identify with Mike, at least at this point in the show. Such thoughts are too primitive, too irrational, too fear-laden for Mike. Accordingly, the show must represent Archie's thoughts in distorted form by means of the disguise of parody. His faulty information, his ignorance of the rationales of tradition, his malapropisms, and so forth all serve to represent in a veiled way the psychological yearning for a mode of existence grounded in organic ties in "blood and soil." At one level these strike the audience as simply amusing or ridiculous; at another they are considered thoroughly offensive, odious and even deserving of hatred.

While Mike cannot tolerate psychological traditionalism in his father-in-law (or at a more profound psychological level in himself) he can and does approve of it in others whom he admires and defends—blacks and women. For the Civil Rights Movement, "Black Power," Feminism and "Sisterhood" all derive their strength to a considerable degree from collective loyalties based upon what the sociologist Talcott Parsons called ascription rather than achievement. On the other hand Archie can tolerate such thinking in himself but not in others—blacks and women. This contrast opens up another point, to be heavily underscored later on, that autonomous figures in these shows (Mike, Mary, Hawkeye) never display strong group loyalties, whereas authoritarian figures always do (Archie has his pals at the plant, Lou his sport fans and Frank his patriotism).

The Mary Tyler Moore Show follows the same pattern exactly but in a more shallow and banal way. This show, it now seems in retrospect, served as a transition from *All In The Family* to *M*A*S*H*. The embodiment of personal, psychological autonomy, Mary moves smoothly, tolerantly and with great interpersonal skill from one social situation to another. Her opposite number is of course Lou Grant, whose peremptory manner generally (he is so much "the boss") but especially toward women, makes him the embodiment of the blind, encroaching authoritarianism of psychological traditionalism. Ted Baxter's insatiable demands for admiration and approval portray a convincing image of dependency. Murray serves as the cue-in figure, mediating first between the audience and the show's central conflict, but also between the three clashing psychological types themselves.

To recapitulate, then, and by way of preparation for interpreting *M*A*S*H:* in these two shows

1) the psychodynamic core (tensions arising within the contemporary family between autonomous, dependent and authoritarian modes of psychological organization) and its associated paradox which the shows disguise (autonomy is achieved only in relation to its opposite dependency)

2) energize the two broader, cognitive orientations (psychological modernism and psychological traditionalism).

3) such that both generate the necessary blend of type and plot to permit entrance into social awareness, but only in veiled form of

4) the modern audience's unconscious ambivalence toward traditionalistic modes of thinking about the world.

It is in this sense that *popular culture is social dream.* It is *dream* for it embodies and disguises unconscious processes; but it is also *social* for both the matrix out of which the shows are constructed and their manifest contents are shared by groups. But like a "good dream" good popular culture has a kind of normal and non-defensive function which permits us to work over and play out disturbing unconscious conflicts and contradictions, thereby making the empirical, wide-awake world of everyday life more manageable.[9]

In *M*A*S*H* the feeble beginnings of *All In The Family* and *The Mary Tyler Moore Show* achieve an almost archetypical fulfillment or completion. No longer are we simply faced with a troubled family arguing about race, or a newsroom ironing out women's rights—as if these were not enough— now whole nations are in disarray and it is our own nation which is held up as exhibit A. In twenty-six or so minutes *M*A*S*H* mixes race, sexuality, politics, war and psychiatry into a potpourri drawn from the many facets of contemporary American social life. In the beginning the natural, technological and social "ecology" of the 4077th is in a state of quiet balance, conveyed by the lilting theme song, the effortless movements of the approaching helicopters set against a mountain landscape and Radar's wistful gaze. Then everything is frustration, rage and craziness. The action quickly devolves to the principals, Frank and Hawkeye. The spokesmen for the madnesses of military life are allowed to speak and then put in their place, and order re-emerges. The simplicity of *M*A*S*H* is artful in the entire—because it is a highly complex and intricate show, it can easily fool the critic in the same way that it always fools the audience.

The setting itself is highly significant and invites comparison with the otherwise moribund western, for both make use of the illusion of distance. On the surface *M*A*S*H* is of course about a surgical unit close to the front lines during the Korean war—that is, it is ostensibly "about" action far away from the audience in time and place. The western is also about action remote in time and place: the "early frontier" days. But, just as there is some truth in the cliche, Marlboro Country is more a state of mind than a place, so I also wish to note that the western was written in the East, by Easterners, for Eastern reading. It was not about the West at all, but about the mind or consciousness of the East. *M*A*S*H* is of course about a war in the 1950s, 7,000 miles away; but it is also about us here and now, the audience, in not-so-remote, middle-class America. The illusion of distance is an important device in some good popular culture. Just as a dream is so often "about" people and places so different from the everyday social reality of the dreamer, the contents of popular culture, however seemingly remote, are always about the everyday consciousness of the viewer.

Type and plot follow the pattern already described except that the types in *M*A*S*H* are considerably more nuanced, complex and interesting and are refigured many more times. Hawkeye Pierce embodies personal and psychological autonomy. He does not depend upon nor does he identify with military, medical or any other kind of institutional authority, but is instead contemptuous of both. The strength of his hatred for political and military authority is as strong as his respect and support for the personal autonomy, individual dignity and in this sense the "rights" of others. He takes a tolerant and empathic approach to the surrounding Koreans, who introduce the issue of race into the show, and even enemy soldiers—"they bleed like us," he says—are respected. While he advocates autonomy for women, he combines this with a fondness for his own homespun Rabelaisian sexual remarks. When he is with a woman himself—which occurs only infrequently and is somewhat inappropriate to his total makeup—affection and tenderness do not come easily to him (more about Hawkeye's asceticism below).

Hawkeye is an excellent and dedicated surgeon, and this capacity to manipulate the technological and biological worlds is vaguely associated with his capacity for personal autonomy, perhaps because the latter is achieved by means of the ability to break down and analyze one's own and others' emotions and thought processes "surgically"—that is, as if they were discrete objects in the sensible world. This unlikely condensation of surgical excellence and personal autonomy is also part-and-parcel of what is perhaps Hawkeye's most important attribute, namely his strong approval of and belief in the principles of modern dynamic psychiatry, symbolized effectively by his warm, admiring and collegial relationship with the 4077th's consulting (and psychoanalytically oriented) psychiatrist, Dr. Sidney Freedman.

Frank Burns enthusiastically embraces the blind and irrational authoritarianism which characterizes all military and political leadership in the show, forthrightly displaying deep collective loyalties. Without autonomy of his own he lapses again and again into moods which swing between snivelling dependency (usually on Margaret) and pugnacious authoritarianism, and consequently he is intolerant of the autonomy of others. Strong on in-group loyalty, he hates out-groups and speaks of the Koreans as "them." It is no surprise that he is a poor surgeon, a failure linked in some unspoken way to his adulation of militarism. His relationship to Margaret is entirely sensual and without tenderness, whereas his marriage is simple contractual (if he married Margaret, he would lose his wife's money). But he is capable of lust, a pleasure which for the most part eludes Hawkeye. And of course Frank has no use for psychiatry.[10] This may be the place to point out that generals in *M*A*S*H* are always overweight, entirely absorbed in their appetites and incapable of emphatically-toned interpersonal relationships.

The transposing or refiguring of types is frequent in *M*A*S*H* because, in part no doubt, of its longevity. Each character gives us the impression of being fresh and unique. Hawkeye is refigured in his friends, first Trapper and then B.J., who provide him with the opportunity to express his views, and in Dr. Sidney Freedman, already mentioned. Frank is refigured first in Major Charles Winchester, a snobbish, pedantic and egocentric upper-class Boston surgeon, whose shameless love of social status and money makes him a likely instance of the evils of psychological traditionalism, but also in Col. Flagg, an insane military espionage agent who constantly persecutes Hawkeye. Col. Flagg is the epitome of total loyalty to collectively-based military-institutional thinking (Frank admires him immensely) and according to the implicit, psychological values of the show, is psychotic (who could not diagnose this paranoid schizophrenic?).

The old maxim that sin is more interesting than grace applies in the case of *M*A*S*H:* the madnesses of Winchester and Flagg are more powerful and amusing than the sober, psychological ethics of Hawkeye and B.J. The same can be said for the dependent types: Radar, Klinger and Father Mulcahey. Incapable of coping with the sinister forces of the authoritarian military-political institutional ethos, yet unable to achieve freedom from it, each portrays a variant of simple dependency. Radar's low rank, his deference to officers (he often refers to them as "You Sirs"), his teddy bears and animals all project a childlike dependency. Klinger actively rebels but his protests only draw him further into the mire of more flamboyant outfits. Father Mulcahey withdraws into the mysteries of his priesthood which the secular military and medical world does not wish to understand.[11] Each of the dependent types exudes the timeless charm of childhood narcissism and thereby heightens the viewer's sense of contrast between Hawkeye and Frank.

The remaining two principals, Col. Potter (and Col. Henry Blake) and Margaret both perform mediating functions, but in very different ways. Potter, the Commanding Officer, is a senior career military man with service in previous wars. He is fully committed to and integrated into the collective irrationalities of military ways. But he is also sympathetic to Hawkeye and quietly contemptuous of Frank, Winchester and others like him. He is respectful of generals but he also shares Hawkeye's psychiatric values: he always welcomes the psychiatrist, Dr. Freedman, and knows well that Col. Flagg is "loco." Therefore, Potter mediates between the two polarities which constitute the essential tension in *M*A*S*H,* blind authoritarianism versus the quest for personal autonomy. But Potter also mediates between the audience and the principles by serving as a cue-in figure. We can attach ourselves psychologically to this plausible figure and from there cautiously enter the arena of madness inhabited by Hawkeye and Frank.

These characteristics of Col. Potter make him the only likely candidate for speculation about the socially-based perceptions of "fatherliness" which the show represents. He is the only father figure without hatred or lust who is nevertheless in the midst of the action. Col. Potter could be described as a "good father," that is someone who is both powerful *and* just. Indeed he is. But we must ask why the narrative so carefully distances him from the action, confers upon him semi-retired status, and calls attention to his disgust with everything and his yearning to spend his final days alone with his wife.

The society which created M*A*S*H entertains the thought of a good father only with considerable anxiety. Thoughts about a good father will have to be greatly reduced in intensity and their visual representation in popular culture greatly modified, if only because any such good father will valorize group loyalties. Such loyalties are, as I have attempted to show, inconsistent with personal autonomy. The image of Col. Potter therefore represents an attenuated "nostalgia for the father" rather than an attempt to reinstate such an image.[12]

Margaret mediates in far more complex fashion by fusing many diverse and otherwise contradictory attitudes. She manages to condense two of the show's major tensions, sexuality and politics. On the one hand, she portrays conventional feminity by yearning affectionately for her husband, Donald, stationed in Tokyo. But she seemingly reverses this through her cynical and purely physical sexual relationship with Frank, of whom she is at the same time contemptuous. Her ambiguous sexuality is shaped by the show's central dynamic: Margaret is strongly committed to the institutionally-grounded ways of military life. She freely associates herself with Frank, admires all authoritarian military figures, and despises dependency in the figures of Radar and Klinger. But she is also an independent woman with a career, seeking personal autonomy, which accounts for her secret admiration for Hawkeye, although that too is largely colored by the masterful authority which she accords to his surgical skills. The capacity of the image of Margaret to condense so many different conflicting attitudes makes this figure a valuable, cohesive force throughout the show's many episodes. And for this reason Margaret is perhaps the most interesting type of all.

These several types interact to generate a narrative line, which is very simple: an initial conflict is established between figures representing institutional loyalty and personal autonomy; the conflict has its ups and downs, its ins and outs, its peripeteia; then, in the closing moments, the psychologically autonomous point of view wins the day and authortarianism receives its just rewards. But the deeper psychological meaning of this plausible resolution is that unabashed enthusiasm—the show almost represents it at times as a mania—for communal ties is a state of mind which must be banished—all the losers (Frank, Winchester and Flagg) have strong group loyalties and believe they owe such groups devotion in exchange for their support. And all the winners (Hawkeye, B.J.) eschew such loyalties. The dependents (Radar, Klinger and Father Mulcahey) remain attached to the group but only reluctantly.

Because all the major issues with which M*A*S*H deals (race, sexuality, war, politics and psychiatry) are polarized around the central—though unconscious—tension between psychological modernism and psychological traditionalism, and because both type and plot are constantly condensing and displacing in ever-new ways many and sometimes all of these issues, no single episode need overtly portray all the issues, plots or types. Instead, many episodes can and do dwell upon seemingly trivial events (for example, everyone sitting around in the tent complaining about the extreme cold—or the extreme heat) or center upon one rather than another type. But such episodes still create that total effect which is *M*A*S*H*. This smooth interlocking of narratives and types around a central tension is the essence of effective popular culture.

Still it is correct to say, perhaps for this very reason, that some showings of a popular culture genre are more representative than others and that such showings will be especially instructive. I have already pointed out that Hawkeye's personal autonomy, closely linked as it is to a psychological view of the world, constitutes the core of values and meanings which the show projects, disguises and commends. And, despite the absence of technical, psychological terminology, psychiatry (understood as the science of applied psychology) is very much present in *M*A*S*H*. Authoritarian figures tend to suffer regularly from psychiatric distress: Frank's departure from the 4077 was due to a mental breakdown; in one episode, Winchester recklessly takes "uppers" in order to appear more superior to everyone and only Hawkeye and B.J. have the skill to diagnose and then provide therapy for his difficulty; I have already mentioned the psychotic Col. Flagg; in another episode Radar poignantly asks Dr. Freedman if he is crazy; and Hawkeye enjoys the kind of immediate sense of rapport with Dr. Freedman which can only derive from an awareness of shared values. In fact, Dr. Freedman often remarks that in his medical-psychiatric view Hawkeye is the most sane man he has ever seen in Korea.

This rapport and all that it implies form the basis for one of the most interesting and in my opinion most representative showings of the series, centering as it does upon the mental breakdown of that paragon of mental health, Hawkeye himself. This showing in effect creates a test or trial for all that Hawkeye represents.

As the establishment shots unfold, Hawkeye begins to behave in a bizarre fashion. He has frequent nightmares from which he awakens screaming; he plays an imaginary game of basketball outside his tent late at night; he acquires minor automatisms; he telephones boyhood friends back in the States, fearing that they have been harmed. Everyone becomes alarmed and Dr. Freedman is summoned. The doctor (who incorporates every virtue one would like to have in his psychiatrist: gentleness, patience, tolerance, firmness, and above all good hard-nosed psychodiagnostic knowledge) at first approaches his patient warily, but then rapport deepens and Hawkeye begins to talk.

The nightmares are about childhood friendships in his hometown of Crabapple Cove, Maine. One relationship had more hostility to it than Hawkeye ever imagined. And Hawkeye has been even more depressed than usual about the carnage of the war—all those "boys" wounded and dying. Gradually, Dr. Freedman (and we the audience) get the picture. Hawkeye talks some more. The automatism and fear of nightmares disappear. Hawkeye becomes his old self, and the episode ends. Good psychological thinking, it would seem, leads to personal autonomy and the strength to live apart from the madnesses and passions of collective life. In such fashion does popular culture embody meanings and values—in such fashion does popular culture "think."

By this time it should be clear that what I think popular culture thinks bears some resemblance to Philip Rieff's sociological analysis of the contemporary ethos.[13] Hawkeye is indeed a species of "psychological man," one who uses psychoanalytic ideas to liberate the mind from social restraint and to thereby repudiate commitment to community and tradition. Like psychological man, Hawkeye lives in what Rieff calls "a hospital culture," wherein everyday social relations are judged according to rules of mental health rather than those of traditional morality. But the "real" hospital is not the "O.R." of the 4077th nor is it the 4077th itself. While each is indeed a madness in its own right, the real hospital culture is the shared social consciousness of middle-class America in the 1970s and early '80s. More recently, the historian Christopher Lasch has carried forward Rieff's theory into the "culture of narcissism" by emphasizing the supportive role which theories of psychotherapy play in the natural appeal of the so-called "awareness movements."[14]

But my analysis also differs from Rieff's and Lasch's in important ways. Rieff analyzed high culture texts such as the writings of Carl Jung, Wilhelm Reich and D.H. Lawrence and Lasch discussed self-help books and journalistic advice. Both of these are consciously elaborated in print. My analysis has emphasized unconsciously elaborated, visually represented and socially shared symbols which capture the immediate experiencing of large segments of an entire culture. While I share with Rieff and Lasch a debt to Freud, I also in effect join his work to that of two writers in the tradition of sociology begun by Durkheim, Maurice Halbwachs and Erving Goffman.[15]

Sweeping analyses of contemporary culture such as those of Rieff and Lasch also emphasize the decline of traditional values and ideals as a decisive factor in the formation of our current ethos. In the following section, I align myself to this point of view—except that my estimate of the resourcefulness of psychology is far greater than theirs—and explore the possible relationships between *M*A*S*H* and the politically-toned situation comedy and earlier popular art forms, in particular the western. In this I do not claim direct continuity but only that certain elements persist from one to the other and I try to identify these elements. In so doing I attempt to enrich the preceding psychological, literary and sociological discussions with a few historical considerations.

IV

M*A*S*H, *The Western and the Persistence*
of Tradition in the Figure of Hawkeye

When placed alongside the above analysis, my remark that *M*A*S*H* may in some ways resemble the western seems far-fetched indeed. The close social relationships, the articulate, stinging psychologically-informed repartee, the concern with the themes of race, sexuality, war, politics and psychiatry and the ever-present military and medical technology—all these contrast sharply with the remote pre-industrial and well-nigh pre-social, distance-infused and more explicitly mythic world of the western. Still, when one genre of popular culture fades and another surges forward, a total break is unlikely. This is especially so if we look at the two genres psychologically, in which case the western appears to capture many of the values of psychological traditionalism and the western hero is a superego figure.

This central feature of the western hero is perhaps best seen in his reluctance to give any account of his actions. He does not need to, because he knows who he is—he possesses identity, depth and interiority. He is a profoundly ascetic figure who conveys a strong sense of moral clarity and the capacity to be alone. He is then, as I have said, a figure in whom the superego is especially prominent. These features together convey a vague sense of vocation which in turn is anchored in an even more vague sense of heritage: while it is true that in the simplest westerns (often the best indicators of what the genre is really all about) the hero always emerges "out of the past," it is also true that the western hero's connection to his past is very loose. That past is of course the Puritan culture of the American eastern establishment with its fading Christian aura.

In all this the western seems worlds apart from *M*A*S*H*, but if we look for a moment at the decline of the western, especially that "interim genre", the anti-western, linkage appears. In making such films as *The Wild Bunch* and *Little Big Man*, for example, directors like Sam Peckinpah and Arthur Penn sought to unmask what they perceived to be the irrational and blind violence in westerns. In doing so these directors in effect criticized the values and ideals of westerns from the perspective of what I have called psychological modernism, with its heavy emphasis upon ego processes and personal autonomy. As such their work represents a transitional phase between the western, with its superego orientation, and comedies such as M*A*S*H, committed as these are to a more explicitly egological-psychological viewpoint. The efforts of such directors are expressions in the sphere of movie-making of what the psychoanalyst Allen Wheelis described some years ago as "the decline of the superego"—a psychological and sociological process in which deeply internalized values erode and give way to the release of strong emotions, a weaker sense of identity and a yearning for the lost and stable past.[16]

Linkage between the western and comedies like *M*A*S*H* also appears if we set aside the latter's social criticism and contrast the western hero with Hawkeye, remembering all the while that the dream dimension of popular culture is one in which social images follow the rules of transposition and transformation similar to, but not identical with, those found in dreams. The logic of dream interpretation simply asserts that things are not what they seem. Social dreams can also be interpreted, decoded or destructured so long as interpretation does not simply reduce their images to replications of infantile developmental processes.

Hawkeye's social awareness, his distrust of institutions and his sexual freedom suggest the culmination of modern, liberal, rational and self-fulfilling personal autonomy. He is all of this. But alongside these there exist other, not-so-modern traits. His name, Benjamin Franklin Pierce, sets the tone for another view, that he is an essentially ascetic figure. Despite his sexual openness, sexual experience does not move him. He has no permanent commitments to women, nor does he wish them; in fact, he has no commitments to anyone (except his friend B.J.) or anything beyond his work, to which he is totally dedicated. In this he displays a definite sense of calling or vocation. He is the only member of the *M*A*S*H* team (with the exception of Father Mulcahey) who does not yearn for home. Hawkeye muses nostalgically about his boyhood in Crabapple Cove, Maine; but he is more psychologically detached from it than are the others who speak frequently and longingly of their eventual return. Hawkeye is in some sense reconciled to a state of homelessness. And, he is confidently anti-intellectual. In these several important though very different aspects, something of the western hero—a residue of some sort—persists into the central figure of *M*A*S*H*.

In fact, *M*A*S*H* as a whole may bear some lingering likeness to the western. Hawkeye's surgical skills, which require split-second timing in the manipulation of technologically-derived objects, may be a transposition from the western hero's awesome skill in the handling of guns, the only piece of technology in the otherwise pre-industrial western. Perhaps the train could be considered a second item of technology in the western, but these trains are always an instrument of corrupt Eastern businessmen and therefore are not part of the hero's self image or of our consolidated sense of him. The gunfight of the western is transposed into a drawn-out but no less climactic verbal duel in which Hawkeye defeats Frank, Winchester, Flagg or numerous generals.[17]

The good girl and the bad girl, so essential to westerns, are fused into the single figure of Margaret who at times resembles the chaste schoolmarm while at other times the sexually free female saloon owner. Dependent figures— Radar, Klinger and Father Mulcahey—bear some similarity to "the boys," those ever-present neutrals who gather about in westerns to watch the gunfight. Col. Potter may have been more successful than Col. Henry Blake as the C.O. because Potter's career goes back to service in the cavalry—in one showing Radar makes him weep with gratitude by presenting him with a horse for his birthday. And so forth.[18]

Conclusion: The Moral Psychology of M*A*S*H

Because I have used psychology to interpret a genre which is itself in its manifest content heavily psychological—it "thinks" psychological thoughts— it is important to clarify the relationship between the two, lest my interpretive efforts appear to be simply a vague and confusing kind of solipsism in which the critic sees only what he already knows. This also raises other fundamental questions, such as the relation between high culture (from which the interpretive tools and techniques of the psychological critic are drawn) and popular culture, between the ideas of the academy and of the intellectual and the ideas of the people or masses or what have you. Many of the thoughts set forth implicitly by the politically-toned situation comedy are systematically and self-consciously articulated in the current social science literature on modernization and secularization, as I have already suggested. While this is not the place to explore this issue, it is possible to cast one ray of light upon it, at the point of psychology.

For the psychological-interpretive approach advanced here is not the same as the psychology which $M*A*S*H$ proposes.

Hawkeye speaks for the Freud people know best, the Freud of popular psychology, the schematic and conventional Freud who champions liberation of the individual mind from group-oriented taboos against sexual and aggressive drives. This "popular Freud" is also an ideological Freud, Freudianism in the service of striving for social advantage. And it is of course true that Freud did attempt to unmask the cruel and psychologically damaging effects of blind institutions with a cunning all his own, as does Hawkeye.

But there is another, less-known Freud, the Freud who attempted to teach the modern world how deeply and inextricably intertwined were personality and communal life, both social and historical. It is a lesson which some current social scientists have learned well. The heart of this lesson is the mandate to deliberate reflection, not only upon natural urges but also upon the ways in which all persons carry within them deeply felt, unconscious wishes for social ties supervised, so to speak, by institutional authorities. The purpose of such reflection (perhaps it should be called "recollection") is not to enable the individual to overthrow institutions but to recognize the heretofore unrecognizable. Only under such circumstances does ethical action become truly rational, for such recognition requires that leaders and led alike each recognize the other in themselves. Freud's psychology does not dissolve group ties, although it does reduce their crippling hold upon the individual.

The point can be made in another way by returning to the concept of the psychodynamic core of the family and of social life and their double paradox. Although the goal of psychological development is personal autonomy, any such autonomy necessarily emerges from dependency—first in the family and then, under the auspices of secondary socialization, from dependency upon social groups and institutions. Freud's psychology forces the recognition of the depth-psychological issues in both of these paradoxes. At one level the politically-toned situation comedies deny this recognition. And at a deeper level these shows express it, although first disguising it beyond recognition.

Some may think that I have labored the word "paradox," asking of it more than it can carry. But in point of fact, it cannot be used often enough in this sort of discussion. For the notion of a paradox captures well the single most important feature of the psychological approach to popular culture: the view that the contents of popular culture at one and the same time give expression to and yet disguise deeply felt but also deeply feared personal and social forces.

Notes

[1]*Mass Culture: The Popular Arts in America*, ed. Bernard Rosenberg and David Manning White, Glencoe, IL: The Free Press, 1957.

[2]This point draws upon Alfred Schutz's phenomenology of the social world and Sigmund Freud's view of "reality" as the set of necessary social and historical conditions to which the ego must adapt. Schutz's phenomenology includes the world of dreams and Freud's psychology assumes an every-day social world. See Alfred Schutz, *Collected*

Papers, Vol. II: *Studies in Social Theory*. The Hague: Martin Nijhoff, 1964, and Sigmund Freud, "Introductory Lectures on Psychoanalysis," *The Standard Edition of the Complete Psychological Works of Sigmund Freud*, Vol. 15, London: The Hogarth Press, 1969, Parts I and II.

[3]Genre has a psychological component akin to the anxiety-reducing function of form of which Norman Holland speaks. Like form, genre belongs to a group of devices which structure and communicate expressive content. See Norman Holland, *The Dynamic of Literary Response*. New York: Oxford University Press, 1968, p. 106. Genres, I would add, focus and organize consciousness to keep it from "wandering," which is to say, to keep it from engaging personal feelings which are best organized by the imaginative productions of society—such as, in this case, the forms of popular culture.

[4]These three processes or functions are intended to wed Freud's famous trio of displacement, condensation and secondary elaboration to literary devices such as metonymy, metaphor and followability or narrative intelligibility. Freud's functions are of course unconscious whereas the literary ones are not.

[5]See for example, Peter Homans, "Puritanism Revisited: An Analysis of the Contemporary Screen-Image Western," in *Studies in Public Communication*, No. 3, 1961. Many of the points there introduced have been further elaborated by John Cawelti in his *The Six-Gun Mystique*, Bowling Green, Ohio: Bowling Green University Popular Press.

[6]Horace Newcomb's excellent discussion of the *I Love Lucy* show brings out its aesthetic features. Horace Newcomb, TV: *The Most Popular Art*. Garden City, New York: Anchor-Doubleday, 1974, ch. 2.

[7]I am indebted to the psychologist Stanley Stark for developing these two categories in relation to popular culture. Stanley Stark, "Toward an Anthropology of Dogmatism: II. Traditionalism, Modernism, Existentialism and the Counter Culture: All in the Family," *Psychological Reports*, 1971, 29, 819-830.

[8]A time-honored example of the failure of psychological-modernistic thinking is that of the king who orders his messenger killed for having brought bad news, in lieu of directing royal rage to its true object.

[9]I derive the concept of "a good dream" from psychoanalytic theory, especially from Erik Erikson's ideas about "dreaming well" and "good sleep" which he develops in the course of a discussion of Freud's dreams in "Psychological Reality and Historical Actuality," in *Insight and Responsibility*, New York: Norton, 1964.

[10]Frank's dislike of psychiatry (and Hawkeye's approval of it) in the TV series, when the TV and film versions of *M*A*S*H* are compared, signals the omission of an issue about which contemporary culture thinks and feels strongly and with some dread: the competition between psychiatry and religion as sources of morality. The original film version portrayed a Frank Burns deeply committed to fundamentalist Christianity (thereby further accentuating his traditionalistic thinking) but did not highlight psychiatry at all. The TV series on the other hand omitted references to Frank's religion but introduced psychiatry and associated it with Hawkeye. It may be too much to bring religion and psychiatry together in the same show.

[11]That a Catholic priest should be so misrepresented illustrates further the way *M*A*S*H*, understood as a social dream, works. Pious Catholic viewers can laugh with a clear conscience at Father Mulcahey's inept adolescent tentativeness whereas such thoughts would be too painful were they to be directed toward their own priests in the clear light of ordinary every-day life. On the other hand, Father Mulcahey's boyish inability to "fit in" to the highly specialized and efficient world of the 4077th probably also expresses many viewers' perception of the essential backwardness and irrelevance of the tradition-laden Catholic church.

[12]For a useful and well-argued discussion of the decline of the father in today's world, see Alexander Mitscherlich, *Society Without the Father*, New York: Schocken

Books, 1970.

[13]Philip Rieff, *The Triumph of the Therapeutic*. New York: Harper's, 1966.

[14]Christopher Lascsh, *The Culture of Narcissism*. New York: Norton, 1979.

[15]See Maurice Halbwachs, *The Collective Memory*. New York: Harper's (Colophon Books), 1980, and Erving Goffman, *The Representation of Self in Everyday Life*, Garden City, N.Y.: Doubleday-Anchor, 1959.

[16]See Allen Wheelis, *The Quest for Identity*, New York: Norton, 1958.

[17]The western hero's convincing natural affinity for gun-play symbolizes a trait essential to the American character, great manual skill with machines. And so does surgery. Interestingly, in the hands of the two respective heroes these devices (the gun and the scalpel) both protect the community from death. At a deeper level these two images may express the heretofore buoyant American confidence in technology and science and the hope that both can reduce anxieties formerly allayed by religion.

[18]In the two-hour so-called "farewell" showing of *M*A*S*H*, Col. Potter departed from the 4077th by "riding off" (presumably "into the sunset") on a horse. Like Hawkeye's mental breakdown in the same showing, this scene raises an important question: Do writers self-consciously elaborate the plots of popular culture, giving the public, as it so often says, "what it wants"? Or are they simply channels for the articulation of the unconscious values and conflicts of their culture? It is enough to note here that Potter's mode of departure is true to the personal style which the show as a whole had already established for him.

Communication and Popular Culture

Marshall W. Fishwick

"We are all linked together in a single chain."

Cicero

So pervasive and persuasive was the union of communication and popular culture in the late twentieth century that some considered them Siamese twins. Significantly, the most popular American president, Ronald Reagan, was often called "The Great Communicator."

Communication makes us human. What would popular (or any other) culture be without words—spoken, written, recorded; taped, faked, and filmed? Communication's four greatest revolutions have been speech, alphabet, print, and electronics. They are the basic pillars on which both communication and popular culture stand.[1]

Today "communication" brings to mind computers, satellites, television—changes from Morse to McLuhan.[2] We must go much further back, in order to understand either communication or popular culture: how they work and intertwine.

Consider the word *communication: comm* (with) *uni* (one) *catus* (past participle of care). Communication means sharing or relating with one another; imparting and interchanging. This makes society (and hence popular culture) possible. All other "disciplines" derive from communication. Involved are not only all the symbols of the mind, but also the means of conveying them through space and preserving them in time.[3]

"Communication" refers to a social process—the flow of information, the circulation of knowledge, the external and internal flow of thoughts—not just to linguistics and media.[4] *Logos* is far more than a static word: it is word, thought, and consequence, all moving at the speed of sound and light. In this basic sense, communication is the root of our civilization, our very humanity.

There can be no philosophy without communications, and vice versa. To be morally and intellectually informed about the world around us is the basis on which communication takes place. Society is a sum of humane relationships in which information is exchanged.

Humane: marked by compassion, sympathy, consideration for other human beings; the branch of learning tending to refine. Education has always had this great goal: to understand, teach, and broaden the horizons of humane communication.

The task is difficult, if not impossible. History was still blind when man began communicating. Scholars suggest possible origins: (1) the "bow-wow" theory—words came into being through the imitation of natural sounds; (2) the "poo poo" theory—speech grows out of involuntary expression of emotions; (3) the "yuk yuk" theory—words arose from chance sounds that happened to be associated with events of special importance or excitement; (4) the "sing-song" theory—words grew out of primitive and wordless chants, celebrating special events; (5) the "yo-heave ho" theory—words developed from grunts and sounds of physical exertion.[5]

Who knows which one (if any) is closest to the truth—the facts are buried too deep in the past. Somehow, language *did* grow; we got *logos*. Today there are more than 3,000 spoken languages extant, and no one can even estimate how many words. If language is a miracle and mystery, so is writing. Only man has been known to draw unaided a picture of his environment, using petroglyphs, hieroglyphs, alphabets.

Communication, like all Gaul, can be divided into three parts: beginning, middle, end (sender, message, receiver). Messages exist in three distinct realms; intrapersonal (inside the sender—dreams, for example); interpersonal (between two or more people, within eyeshot and earshot); and mass (largely dispersed by electronic devices to an anonymous audience).

English—the words we are using here—form a mass medium, as does every language. That point is clear when we deal with *logos*. What is less obvious is the new mass media (film, radio, television) are new languages, with new *logos*. Each codifies reality differently—each conceals a unique metaphysics.[6]

No two media work the same way—so no *logos* means the same in different media. Writing didn't just record oral sounds; it was a new language which the spoken word came to imitate. Oral languages tend to be polysynthetic, in which images are fused and forced like tight knots; written languages tend to be linear, using little words in chronological order. Subject became distinct from verb, actor from action, essence from form. Spoken words are temporary, on the tip of the tongue; printed words are permanent: truth embalmed for posterity.

How the newer languages (film, radio, television) create new syntax and meaning we are still finding out.[7] Evidence so far indicates that all old languages (including print) have profited enormously from the development of new media and languages. "The more the arts develop," E. M. Forster writes, "the more they depend on each other for definition."[8] This much seems certain: POPULAR CULTURE IS POPULAR COMMUNICATION.

Popular culture is also humane communication. Why not look to the findings in the area of communication (as well as in literature, history, art, or sociology, which is usually the case) for new answers? Why try to see words only as products, when they are in fact also processes? *Logos* is multi-faceted. No word, no meaning, no culture (popular or otherwise) exists in a vacuum. Communication is circular, irreversible, and unrepeatable. *Logos*—a word, a sound that has meaning. We hope for precise meanings, written down in a word-book (dictionary). But as early as the eighth century, an unknown Chinese poet warned us not to count on it:

That art is best which to the soul's range gives no bound.
Something beyond the form, something beyond the sound.

Words have no "exact" meaning—in fact, never mean the same thing twice. The time, place, context, stress, inflection cannot be duplicated. The meaning of the *logos* is what the speaker intends to be understood by the listener. Words not only channel, but form and program thought.

When we think of "word," we usually think of print and records. The word's original home—and still its native habitat—is sound. Logos grew in an oral-aural culture, where there is no history in our modern sense of the term. "The past is indeed present," Walter Ong points out, "but in the speech and social institutions of the people, not in the more abstract forms in which modern history deals."[9] The human voice has been the great transmitter, the human ear the great receiver, for most of man's history. Following this lead, we could go now to an examination of voice, hearing, and perception; language and meaning; verbal behavior; language and culture; and linguistic propriety. We could become even more technical, and analyze phones, phone-types, phonemes, morphemes, and syntactical structure.[10] Where does all this confront the *demos*, and popular culture? On the stage, in church, at home, in the town square, at elections: as *rhetoric*.

The Greek root of *rhetoric* is *eiro*, "I say;" *rhetor* means orator. For many centuries what we now call history, poetry, and drama were all *heard* as oral discourse, and shaped by the rhetorical theory of the time. Invention, arrangement, style, delivery, and memory were all involved—and still are.[11]

Aristotle defined rhetoric as "the faculty of finding in any given case the available means of persuasion." The Greeks recognized the latent power in an advocate who, through logical and emotional appeals and the manipulation of language and symbols, could influence decisions and public opinion. In the 5th century B.C., Gorgias asked, "What is there greater than the word which persuades?" There can be no doubt that H. I. Marrou is correct when he says "Hellenistic culture was above all things a rhetorical culture;"[12] for over 2,000 years rhetoric held a central place in humanistic education.

Early Roman education emphasized rhetoric. Rhetoric formed one of the seven liberal arts in medieval European universities. The *trivium* consisted of grammar (to teach a man to speak correctly), logic (to teach a man to speak consistently), and rhetoric (to teach a man to speak effectively).

Over the years rhetoric lost its central position, and by the end of the nineteenth century generally meant oratory or elocution. A "rhetorical question" was not meant to elicit an answer but to cause an effect. Then new movements and theories revitalized rhetorical interest; today rhetoric is concerned with all the ways in which we influence thinking and behaving through the strategic use of symbols.[13]

Modern rhetorical studies also involve the description and analysis of public discourse. Akin to literary criticism, rhetorical criticism concerns itself with the values, assumptions, and language style in oral communication events. Most importantly, it looks at the *effects* of messages on audiences, to discover why and how messages persuade or fail to persuade.

Similar to much historical investigation, rhetorical studies are by their very nature essentially descriptive and analytical, attempting to explain the causes and effects of speech acts in human affairs rather than to generate "new knowledge" or theoretical insights.

One possible way to pursue the *logos* in our day would be to trace contributions by such rhetorical scholars as I. A. Richards, Chaim Perelman, Wayne Booth, and Kenneth Burke. This task, already well done, is not central to our needs.[14] We shall choose to go another route—the printed word—and to single out for close examination popular and influential links between print and popular culture.

Man spoke long before he wrote; but for many centuries—certainly since the printing press—print has been our Supreme Court; keeper of records, laws, and literature. From the printed birth announcement to the printed obituary, print daily dictates our fortunes and failures. Print is our medium of continuity. Phonetic writing translated man from the tribal to the civilized sphere. "Civilized" and "literate" are generally held to be synonymous.

To trace that process, matching *logos* and communication would take us back to clay, the stylus, and cuneiform script from the beginnings of civilization to Mesopotamia; papyrus, hieroglyphics, and hieratic to the Greco-Roman period; reed pen and alphabet to the forming and failing of the Roman Empire; on up through parchment, paper, brush, celluloid, plastics, and laser in our own century. There would be chapters on the Egyptians (who with abundant papyrus and skilled labor worked out an elaborate system of writing), the Babylonians (whose dependence on clay and the stylus developed an economical system of writing), the Phoenicians (who improved the alphabet so that separate consonants were isolated in relation to sounds), and the Greeks (who took over the alphabet and adapted it to the demands of a flexible oral tradition by the creation of words). We would stress the adoption of the Ionian alphabet in Athens (404-3 B.C.) and the emergence of Athens as the center of the city-state federation in 454 B.C. By 430, a reading public had emerged in Athens and Herodotus had turned his recitations into book form.[15]

It was not a Greek, but a Roman who brought Greek thought into the forefront during the Roman Era, who is the real hero of our story. Marcus Tullius Cicero (106 B.C.—43 B.C.) was the major transmitter of Greek thought to and through Rome; the shaper of civilized speech and the Founding Father of what we now call popular culture.

So great was his impact that we have no way of measuring it. "The glory of Cicero's rhetoric still remains," wrote Plutarch. "Cicero is the great popularizer, who brought philosophy within reach of the common man," observed Erasmus. In our own day, Michael Grant has summed the matter up in these words: "The influence of Cicero upon the history of European literature and ideas greatly exceeds that of any other prose writer in any language."[16]

Cicero believed in writing things down—unlike Plato who said doing so would destroy memory. What might they have said about mass culture in the electronic age? Walter Benjamin predicted that it might soon be hard (if not impossible) for us to find our way back to the "exacting silence" of a book.[17] Many other critics agree, bringing the merger of communication and popular culture into question. Robert Hughes thinks we may be insulating ourselves from reality itself, "turning everything into disposable spectacle: catastrophe, love, war, soap. Ours is the cult of the electronic fragment."[18]

The language itself, others argue, is being undermined and bombarded by overkill—polluted by media fallout. Many who teach language and literature would agree. Our schools have struggled to teach the written language, producing semi-literates, whose measured ability to read and write declines year after year. Millions of dollars and thousands of remedial programs have hardly dented the problem. How can this be—with our wonderful new media methods, and *techniques*?

Ortega Y. Gasset gave one possible answer over thirty years ago. "It has become impossible to do more than instruct the masses in the *technique* of modern life," he wrote in 1951. "It has been found impossible to educate them. They have been given tools for an intenser form of existence, but no feelings for their great historic duties."[19] T. S. Eliot agreed, pointing out that a technological society creates media and masses detached from tradition, alienated from religion, and susceptible to suggestions: in other words, a mob.[20] And it will be no less of a mob filled with fast foods and driving fast cars. An even more threatening thought is set forth in a 1981 report from the Foundation for National Progress: an homogenized culture is developing. Pre-figured in Nazi Germany and, less clearly and effectively, by Soviet Russia, its outlines are most perceptible in the United States. It is dominated and pervaded by technology.[21] "In progressive, scientific societies," Joseph Campbell writes, "every last vestige of the ancient human heritage of ritual, morality, and art is in full decay.... The conscious—unconscious zones of the human psyche have been cut: we have been split in two."[22]

But have we not *always* been split in two? Is the dilemma any worse today than it was when it confronted Thales, Plato, Marcus Aurelius, Augustine, Descartes, Freud, and Einstein? Is the "fallout" any worse in today's Washington than it was in Socrates' Athens, where the babbling Sophists drove him to drink? And is the prospect for Europeans facing Communism at the Berlin wall in 1988 A.D. any grimmer than it was when they faced Islam at Tours in 732 A.D.? *Plus ça change, c'est plus la même chose.*

Perhaps it is part of the human predicament to say with one of the major philosophers of our day, Woody Allen: "My only regret is that I am not someone else." But we are who and where we are: the media will be no better and no worse than we make them. Because Woody Allen has moved too easily from media to media, role to role—and because he is a genius whose appeal crosses "brow" lines and oceans with ease—let's look at him. A joke-writer in the 50s, a comedian in the 60s, a film director in the 70s, he has become a living embodiment of the best American talent in the 80s. Starting with *What's New Pussycat* and *Casino Royale* in 1965, he has given us some of the acknowledged film classics of our generation: *What's Up Tiger Lilly*, *The Front*, *Take the Money and Run*, *Bananas*, *Everything You Always Wanted to Know About Sex...Ask*, *Play It Again Sam*, *Sleeper*, *Love and Death*, *Annie Hall*, *Interiors*, *Manhattan*—milestones on the long journey to combine communication and popular culture, and invoke one of *homo sapiens'* greatest gifts: laughter.[23]

We have come a long way (from Menes and his hieroglyphics to 3300 B.C. to Woody Allen in 1988 A.D.) and passed through many media: stone, clay, tablets, papyrus, parchment, paper, film. But the basic problems remain the same. How can we make sense of the human condition; not only survive but thrive on our precious planet? How can we transform our lore, legend, values, and aspirations into a popular culture which embraces us all?

Each age is compulsively creative, transforming myth into history, history into belief, belief into iconic images. Sometimes they form a cluster to guide and inspire us: Plato's Ideas, Kant's Categories, Jung's Archetypes, McLuhan's Media. Are we at the point, as the twentieth century ends, when we can formulate the idea of a common culture?[24]

Defining and explaining "common" takes not only columns but pages in the authoritative *Oxford English Dictionary*. Even the origin of the word is disputed. One possibility is the Latin *com*, meaning together, and *munis*, meaning bound or under obligation. Things are common when they are bound together, and we are obligated to share them. This is where our fellow-feeling comes from—how life becomes symbolic, significant, and shared.

Shared, joint, united; belonging to all mankind alike; possessed by the human race. "Longing the common light again to share," wrote John Dryden in 1697. Two centuries later, Robert Browning spoke of "the higher attributes of our common humanity." That light, and those attributes, are central.

Begin with the sound of John Donne's bell, tolling not just for me but for thee. We need not ask for whom the bell tolls; we already know. *Common* sense tells us, for it is part of our common knowledge.

A host of other concepts link up with *common*. A common carrier, such as a bus or train, is obligated to transport all who solicit the service. The common denominator works with all numbers in the equation; common law applies to us all; the House of Commons, like the Book of Common Prayer, cuts through all class privileges. A common right is the property of every citizen, "Do me the common right," Shakespeare has a character say in *Measure for Measure*, "to let me see them."

To be common, anything must be accepted, normative, popular. For historical and linguistic reasons, we shall emphasize common culture, and keep referring back to it constantly in all that follows.

Standing just outside, but integrally connected to the concept, is community. By that we mean a social group, of any shape, size, or color who live together, sharing a common heritage. Such congealing is part of our nature: man, Aristotle pointed out centuries ago, is a social animal. We do not come together just to do things, but to be together. Community is the tangible evidence of the abstract idea of common. It is the word made flesh.

A commonly used set of words helps us understand. We think of a hamlet as a small group, a village as larger, town still larger, and a city as very large and complex. But contemporary scholars will not let us stop there. They point out that a metropolis can grow into a megalopolis (super-city), then into a tyrannopolis (city of tyranny) and finally a necropolis (city of death). No matter what the political or economic plight, any place which is inhabited is a seat of community.

People come together to share not only concepts but things: artifacts, objects, icons, physical contact. They depend on language, gestures, codes, symbols. But the most important "thing" they have in common escapes easy definition. Call it a workable community of will—what Rousseau termed the "general will," Herder the "volksgeist," Christian apologists the "holy spirit." Name it what you will: but cling to it with all your being, since it is the most precious thing you can ever have.

The sense of place is a variable of the sense of space: a factor which varies greatly and is often ignored by most historians. Primitive people were literally limited to the visible horizon; the thrust outward has always been the supreme human adventure. Ancient man was fascinated with environment, but never thought it was within his powers to alter it. Nature had purpose and design (to the Greeks, *telos*) which mankind must either accept or defy at a terrible peril. Centuries later, during the Renaissance, nature took on the guise of a framework of rationally contrived structures. Stability and ratio were deified. Natural change, though recognizable and measurable, was thought to be a superficial aspect of being. It did not alter fundamental structure, and the immutable laws which Isaac Newton would finally reduce to physical laws. Said Alexander Pope:

"Nature and nature's laws lay hid in night.
God said, 'Let Newton be,' and all was light."

"All who are included in a community," wrote Saint Thomas, "stand in relation to that community as parts to the whole." Centuries later Arnold Toynbee re-stated the idea in 20th century terms: "The true hallmark of the proletarian is neither poverty nor humble birth, but a consciousness of being disinherited from his ancestral place...being unwanted in a community which is his rightful home." Realizing this, institutions and governments have made huge efforts to "create" community. They have found that it cannot be done by committee meetings, publications, or official decrees. Only when there is a deep communal dedication to ideals will it grow: then its radiance will shine forth with blinding light. The true community respects the individual and his history; it is immediate and real. False community centers on groups or ideologies; it tends to be abstract, remote, and artificial. The end product of true community is concern; of false community, exploitation.

No one is born into a culture or community—he must learn about it, and work at it. Communities are complex things, with their own structure, codes, goals, traditions, and memories. They use not only a special language, but also a jargon. They define both orthodoxy and heresy, and translate these into rule and etiquette. One defies them at great risk.

Great scholars have distinguished between the organic community (*Gemeinschaften*) and atomistic (*Gesellschaft*). The organic is small and cozy— a band of brothers. The atomistic is large and much less personal—a group of office workers, or factory employees. The amount of the former shrinks, and the need for the latter grows. We leave the small town to live in the large city; the separate nation to live in the global village.

The transition is terrifying—as transition always has been. To survive we shall have to be creative, innovative, flexible. We shall depend (as we always have) on communication. Linked with the new electronic popular culture, might we indeed create a Brave New World?

Notes

[1]See Walter J. Ong, *The Presence of the Word* (New Haven: Yale University Press, 1967) and Bruce B. Wavell, *The Living Logos: A Philosophical-Religious Essay* (Washington, University Press of America, 1978). Wavell believes that language contains a natural wisdom of the greatest human significance. This wisdom pervades all aspects of popular culture.

[2]See Daniel Czitrom, *Media and the American Mind: From Morse to McLuhan* (Chapel Hill: University of North Carolina Press, 1982).

[3]Wilbur Schramm, *Men, Messages, and Media* (New York: Harper, 1973), chapter 1. In short, human communication is something people do. Of course, animals communicate—and did so for millions of years before any of them developed the ability to generalize on signals they had learned to give. This required *logos*. How did it start? Many different forms of both verbal and nonverbal communication, including kinesics (body and eye language), paralanguage (such as laughs, yawns, grunts), proxemics (human use and perception of space), smell, touch, etc. How did all this result in *logos*? We are only beginning to get some hints at answers.

[4]This idea is further explored by Y. V. Laskhmana Rao, *The Development of Communication* (Minneapolis: University of Minnesota Press, 1966). Looking at the subject from the viewpoint of his own "traditional" culture (India), he points out that communication in a "progressive" (Western) culture includes urbanization, industrialization, division of labor, mobility, literacy, media consumption—in short, wide-spread participation in nation-building activities.

[5]These particular designations are made by Wilbur Schramm, *Men, Messages, and Media* (New York: Harper and Row, 1973). Other labels abound in various studies.

[6]Edmund Carpenter, "The New Languages," in *Explorations in Communication*, chapter 1, (Boston: Beacon Press, 1960).

[7]For T.S. Eliot's comments on differences in realism when a play becomes a film, see George Hoellering and T.S. Eliot, *Film of Murder in the Cathedral* (New York: Harcourt, Brace & World, 1952); Bela Belazs, *Theory of Film* (London: Dennis Dobson, 1952); and Alan Casty, *Mass Media and Mass Man* (New York: Holt, Rinehart, and Winston, 1968).

[8]Alan Casty, *op. cit.*, p. 46.

[9]Walter Ong, *op. cit.*, p. 23. This brilliant book has been most helpful in sorting out my own thoughts on *logos*, as has been his *Rhetoric, Romance, and Technology: Studies in Interaction of Expression and Culture* (Ithaca: Cornell University Press, 1971.)

[10]An excellent source would be H.A. Gleason's *An Interpretation of Descriptive Linguistics* (New York: Holt, Rinehart, & Winston, 1961.) See also Theodore Clevenger, Jr., and Jack Matthews, *The Speech Communication Process* (Glenview: Scott, Foresman, 1971.)

[11]James L. Golden, Goodwin F. Berquist, and William E. Coleman, *The Rhetoric of Western Thought* (Dubuque: Kendall/Hunt, 1968). I am also indebted to an unpublished essay by my colleague Professor Elizabeth Fine, called "Introduction to Communication" (1982).

[12]H. I. Marrow, *A History of Education in Antiquity* (translated by George Lamb), (New York: New American Library, 1964), p. 269.

[13]Douglas Ehninger, *Contemporary Rhetoric* (London: Scott Foresman, 1972), p. 3.

[14]One might well begin with Kenneth Burke's "Rhetoric—Old and New," in *The Journal of General Education*, vol. V, April, 1951; and I. A. Richard, *The Philosophy of Rhetoric* (New York: Oxford University Press, 1965).

[15]Here I paraphrase Harold A. Inness, whose study of *The Bias of Communication* (Toronto: University of Toronto Press, 1964) is indispensable to our subject.

[16]There is of course a whole library by and about Cicero. I still find Gaston Boissier's *Ciceron et ses Amis* (Paris, 1857) the most satisfactory biography, although D. R. Shackleton Bailey's *Cicero* (London, 1969) and C. Stockton's Cicero, *A Political Biography* (New York, 1971) incorporate new findings and opinions.

[17]Quoted by Robert Hughes, *The Shock of the New* (New York: Random House, 1981). His own duality on these issues makes Hughes' work fascinating. He derides the "Myth of Pop," insisting that even in a culture split as disastrously and in so many ways as ours, the problems of choice, taste, and moral responsibility for images still remain. See also Malcolm Bradbury and James McFarlane, eds., *Modernism 1890-1930* (London: Penguin Books, 1978).

[18]Hughes, *op cit.*, p. 345.

[19]Ortega Y. Gasset, *The Revolt of the Masses* (London: Allen & Unwin, 1951), p. 65. His ideas are further expounded in *The Modern Theme* (New York: Harper & Row, 1961).

[20]T. S. Eliot, "Religion and Literature" in *Essays Ancient and Modern by T. S. Eliot,* (New York: Harpers, 1936). Duncan Williams uses and explores the ideas of both Gasset and Eliot in *To Be or Not To Be: A Question of Survival* (Oxford: Pergamon Press, 1974).

[21]Quoted by Joel Garreau, *The Nine Nations of North America* (Boston: Houghton Mifflin, 1981).

[22]Joseph Campbell, *The Hero With a Thousand Faces* (New York, Bollingen, 1949), p. 388.

[23]For more details consult the "Filmography" in Myles Palmer, *Woody Allen: An Illustrated Biography* (London and New York, Proteus, 1980).

[24]I have developed these thoughts in my book on *Common Culture and the Great Tradition* (Westport, Greenwood Press, 1983).

Systems-Theoretical Aspects of Popular Culture and Mass Communication

Linda K. Fuller

Introduction

The issue of the interrelatedness of popular culture and mass communication is a controversial one, as public and academic responses vary from thinking that the two are actually the same to thinking they are diametric opposites. This paper takes a stance somewhere in the middle, hoping to prove that not only are popular culture and mass communication interrelated, they are also interdependent. And the clearest way to consider this symbiosis is by means of the systems-theoretical perspective.

As can be seen in the following figure, popular culture and mass communication are influenced by, and share, many common variables:

Definitions, Descriptions, and Literature Reviews

Mass Communication

To the question, "What is mass communication?" Bittner (1980, p.1) responds:

> It is the deadline of the investigative journalist, the creative artistry of documentaries, the bustle of a network newsroom, the whir of a computer, the hit record capturing the imagination of millions, the radio disc jockey setting the pace of a morning show, and the advertising executive planning a campaign. It is radio, research, recordings, resonators, and ratings. It is television, talent, telephones, and tabloids. It is satellites, storyboards, systems, and segues. It is all these things and many more,

Severin and Tankard (1979) cite an unpublished paper by Professor F.E.X. Dance[1] of the University of Wisconsin at Milwaukee in which he compiled a list of 98 different scholarly definitions of communication. The authors then list some basic differences in the way it has been viewed: stressing sharing, intentional influence, or including any kind of influence or response (with or without intent.) Mass communication, they contend, is distinguished by three characteristics:

1. The audience is large.
2. The source is an institution or organization.

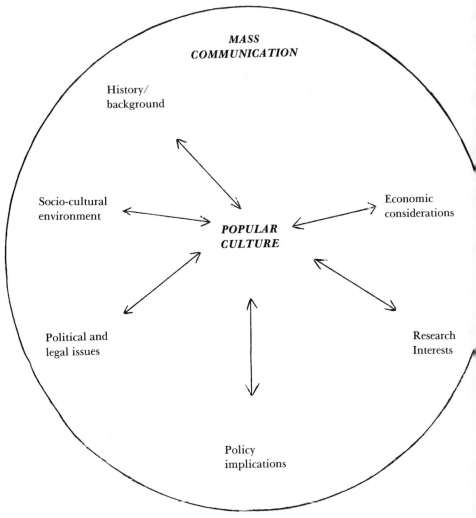

Figure 1. The Interrelatedness of Popular Culture and Mass Communication.

1. History/background—their roots

2. Economic considerations—institutions, audiences/consumers, products, prices and payments

3. Research interests—people, places, events, and items

4. Policy implications—what it all means, and what we should do and/or be doing about it

5. Political and legal issues—internal and external constraints

6. Socio-cultural environment—customs and concerns

3. Some kind of mechanism is used to reproduce messages.

Characteristics of mass communication, according to McQuail (1984, p. 33), are best understood if considered as part of the media institution: a distinct set of activities (sending and receiving messages), carried out by persons occupying certain roles (regulators, producers, distributors, audience members), according to certain rules and understandings (laws, professional codes and practices, audience expectations and habits.) He distinguishes the following as key features of mass media as an institution:

1. It is concerned with producing and distributing "knowledge"—information, ideas, culture.
2. It provides channels for relating certain people to other people—senders to receivers, audience members to other audience members, everyone to their society and to its other constituent institutions.
3. The media operate almost exclusively in the public sphere.
4. Participation in the institution as audience member is essentially voluntary, without compulsion or social obligation.
5. The institution is linked with industry and the market, through its dependence on work, technology and the need for finance.
6. The institution is invariably linked in some way with state power, through legal mechanisms and legitimating ideas which vary from one society to another.

Popular Culture

Ray B. Browne, Director of the Center for the Study of Popular Culture at Bowling Green University and editor of the *Journal of Popular Culture,* discusses the difficulty of defining "popular culture," then offers this umbrella-like one (1972, p. 11): "all those elements of life which are not narrowly intellectual or creatively elitist and which are generally though not necessarily disseminated through the mass media. Popular Culture consists of the spoken and printed word, sound, pictures, objects and artifacts." Later (1984, p. 1), Browne expands that definition:

By the terms 'popular culture' we generally mean all aspects of the world we inhabit: the way of life we inherit, practice and pass on to our descendants; what we do while we are awake, the dreams we dream while asleep. It is the everyday world around us: the mass media, entertainments, diversions, heroes, icons, rituals, psychology, religion— our total life picture. Although it need not necessarily be, it is generally disseminated by the mass media....Most important, the popular culture of a country is the voice of the people—their likes and dislikes, the lifeblood of daily existence, their way of life.

Citing a number of theoretical analyses, case studies, and historical treatments of it[2], Laba (1986, p. 107) states that popular culture has emerged "as a process that defines a particular mode of human activity, operates to organize individual and group knowledge and behavior in everyday life, and imparts both style and substance to the expressive dimension of culture." He speaks of this audience-oriented perspective as an "interface" between a particular mass medium and its interpretation of it by "human expressive behavior" (sic, popular culture.)

General themes concerning mass media and the popular arts, common issues and questions, include the following according to Rissover and Birch (1983, pp. 24-5):

1. Social values
2. Social roles
3. Standardization and diversity
4. Mass appeal versus specialization
5. Access and input
6. Control and regulation
7. Media-made events
8. Stars and media celebrities
9. The profit motive
10. Influences of media as media
11. Media interdynamics
12. Future directions

"Wide exposure to the public," say the authors (p.4), "is really what makes the popular arts popular. And wide exposure is possible only through the mass media." Yet, they continue, "When a type of advertising, journalism, fiction, music, or movie becomes popular, usually because of public concerns with a particular, and often well-crafted, hit captures the public fancy, other producers, writers, and performers rush in to capitalize upon the interest of the success."

And so comes interrelatedness, with mass communication popularizing the culture and popular culture creating development, demands, and distribution from its media. That phenomenon is best understood from the systems-theoretical perspective.

Systems Theory

An outgrowth of mathematics and engineering science, systems theory is a means for taking a broad overview of phenomena in an effort to understand its many configurations and implications. This multifaceted approach helps apply knowledge from other fields so that the dynamics between and through disciplines can be better understood. A reaction to overspecialization, systems theory is by nature interdisciplinary, asking not just Why, but How and Why components interact with one another.

The person most associated with systems theory is Ludwig Von Bertalanffy, whose General System Theory (Braziller, 1968) has been a landmark publication on the topic. Dating to his work on the "theory of the organism as an open system" in 1940, he considers it a general science of "wholeness," integrating both natural and social sciences.

Von Bertalanffy discusses intentions of his "paradigm" as an evolutionary theory, including:

1. Systems science—i.e., scientific exploration and theory of "systems" in the various sciences (e.g., physics, biology, psychology, social sciences), and general system theory as doctrine of principles applying to all (or defined sub-classes of) systems.

2. Systems technology—problems arising in modern technology and society, comprising both the "hardware" of computers, automation, self-regulating machinery, etc. and the "soft-ware" of new theoretical developments and disciplines.

3. Systems philosophy—i.e., the reorientation of thought and world view ensuing from the introduction of "system" as a new scientific paradigm (in contrast to the analytic, mechanistic, one-way causal paradigm of classical science).

a. Systems ontology—what is meant by "system," and how systems are realized at the various levels of the world by observation: real, conceptual, or abstracted.

b. Systems epistemology—see science as one of the "perspectives" man with his biological, cultural and linguistic endowment and bondage has created to deal with the universe he in "thrown in," or rather to which he is adapted owing to evolution and history.

c. "Values"—the humanistic concern of general system theory.

To return to the earlier model on the interrelatedness of popular culture and mass communication, it would be noted that regarding history/background between the two that inputs are normally stochastic, functions of time. Economic, political, and socio-cultural considerations exhibit generality and interchangeability. Research and policy are particularly applicable to the systems theory perspective in terms of its inherent capability of operational decision-making.

Pre-eminently, systems theory has been valuable for its role in assessing technological developments, and so it becomes an ideal tool for considering communications technologies vis-a-vis the wider culture within which they are developing.

Investigations of Interrelatedness

Newspapers

It took centuries after the invention of the printing press for the prototypical newspaper as we know it to develop. That history included an evolution from political commentary in the penny press to availability and acceptance in what is largely a mass/conglomerate newspaper today, dictated by popular taste.

Example: "Newspaper Managerial Involvement in Community Affairs: Economic and Ethical Implications"

An article written for the Press Concentration and Monopoly Research Project for the Association for Education in Journalism and Mass Communication[3], this was an investigation into the debate about journalists as newsmakers and/or newsmolders, and whether newspaper management should be involved in community affairs. Press credibility was the key issue in the study, which included a systematic random sample of 150 daily newspapers. A brief history of newspaper managerial involvement was discussed, then the economic-political concerns and socio-cultural ramifications; policy implications from the findings were critical.

Radio

Owing its existence to pre-existing technologies (telephone, telegraph, photography, sound recording), radio's 60 plus history began as a response to the need for rapid communication. Since the Radio Act of 1927, the underlying principle that "The airwaves belong to the people" has predominated.

Example" "International Propaganda Via Shortwave: The Dutch Example from an American Perspective"

Published in *World Communication*[4], this study first defined and discussed the term "propaganda" as an image-development tool, then applied it to Dutch broadcasting by way of example. Background information on domestic radio and television in the Netherlands was given, as it is pivotal to an understanding of the country's international thrust; history, philosophy/purpose, characteristics, economics, audience, and future are discussed. Then, from primary research sources and a monitoring of its shortwave system, a program analysis of Radio Nederland Wereldomroep is performed, with implications drawn regarding the Dutch example toward perpetuating its propaganda worldwide.

Television

An outgrowth of radio, television is an all-pervasive medium in American society. With 98% of all households owning at least one set, and with Nielsen data saying those households spend 6 1/2 hours/day watching, the power and popularity of television are unparalleled.

Example: "Constructing New Approaches to Cable Technology"

Cable television[5], as a representative medium of new communication technologies, provides an excellent example of the kind of approaches one can take both academically and/or professionally in terms of studying, researching, and working with these issues:

1. Historical development
2. Physical/technical characteristics—constraints and configurations; services
3. Legal considerations—roles of the government and the courts, special problems (such as copyright, compliance, censorship), First Amendment issues, and regulatory responsibility
4. Programming—the abundance of channels concerns issues such as regular vs. pay cable, types of programming content—and value-wise, experimentation, and competition
5. Corporate media—ownership considerations, superstations, teletext and videotex/interactive services
6. Franchising—the process, plus public access and local origination capabilities
7. Minorities—representation, ratings, and rights
8. International cable—global research and policy implications

Film

Beginning at the end of the 19th century as a technological novelty for entertainment, motion pictures have been characterized by great variations in popularity throughout their history, dependent on systematic relationships between audience tastes and demands, the financial composition of the industry, social climate of the times, and technological innovations.

Example: "The Changing Image of 'Family' in Film:
A Mirror of Reflection of Society?"

From a socio-cinematic perspective, a tracing of the image of "family"[6] provides some keen insights into the changing style and nature of film. Chronologically depicted through the Silent Era, talkies, the introduction of color, and on to contemporary times, family as a theme is seen to have been influenced by concomitant economic, political, and sociological concerns. Of research interest is the adaptability of this genre type to its times, the beginning of an answer to the perpetual question about film as a mirror or a reflection of society.

Implications

Predominantly, both mass communication and popular culture serve as socializing agents, providing us with images, ideals, and information that, depending upon their acceptance into the mainstream, help characterize our societies.

For studying contemporary American culture, according to Tosuner-Fikes (1982), it is best to analyze ideology, enculturation, ethnohistory, cultural ecology, and social structures, and their functions. Fuller (1983) argues that media usage helps not only in the socialization assimilation process but also in the development of individual identities.

Arguing for a functional model of mass media as a social system, DeFleur and Ball-Rokeach (1975) suggest a schematic means for analysis, including content, production, distribution, legislative bodies (official regulators and voluntary associations), financial backers (advertising agencies, market research and rating services), and external social and cultural conditions. Their dependency theory of audience-media-society relations has as its key the notion that "persons as members of media audiences encounter media messages with both constructed social realities and considerable dependency on media information resources." (p.278)

Chambers (1986), assessing the impact of urbanization and commerce on popular tastes, considers the value of popular culture as a key to understanding the everyday world. While Wilensky (1964) considers traditional theorists of mass society pessimistic in ideology and macroscopic in sociology, he makes the distinction between "high culture" and "mass culture"[7] in terms of the social context of production; pre-eminently, he finds, "for both intellectuals and the general population...the cultural atmosphere is permeated by the mass media."

Interrelatedness and interdependence, viewed from the systems-theoretic perspective—including history/background, economic considerations, political and legal issues, socio-cultural environment, research interests, and policy implications—characterize the relationship between mass communication and popular culture.

Notes

[1]F.E.X. Dance, "Some Definitions of Communication(s)," unpublished manuscript (February, 1970).

[2]Selected citations include publications by C.W.E. Bigsby, Tom Burns, James W. Carey and Albert L. Kreiling, John G. Cawelti, Simon Frith, Dick Hegdige, Herbert J. Gans, Martin Jay, Michael R. Real, Bernard Waites, Tony Bennett and Graham Martin.

[3]Chapter submission to the Press Concentration and Monopoly Research Project, Mass Communication and Society Division, Association for Education in Journalism and Mass Communication by Linda K. Fuller, 1985.

[4]Linda K. Fuller, "International Propaganda via Shortwave: The Dutch Example from an American Perspective," *World Communication*, Volume 15, #3 (Fall, 1986), pp. 143-154.

[5]"Constructing New Approaches to Cable Technology" was a workshop presented by Linda K. Fuller at "Infomania," a conference of the Communication Association of Massachusetts at Curry College, Milton, MA on April 10, 1987.

[6]Linda K. Fuller, "The Changing Image of 'Family' in Film: a Mirror or Reflection of Society," unpublished paper.

[7]Also, see Herbert J. Gans, *Popular Culture and High Culture: An Analysis and Evaluation of Tastes*, NY: Basic Books, 1974.

Works Cited

Bittner, John R. *Mass Communication: An Introduction.* 2nd ed. Englewood Cliffs, NJ: Prentice-Hall, Inc., 1980.

Browne, Ray B., "Popular Culture: Notes Toward a Definition," in Ray B. Browne and Ronald J. Ambrosetti (eds.) *Popular Culture and Curricula.* Bowling Green, OH: Bowling Green University Popular Press, 1972, pp. 1-11.

——, "Popular Culture as the New Humanities," *Journal of Popular Culture* 17: 4 (Spring, 1984), pp. 1-8.

Chambers, Iain. *Popular Culture: The Metropolitan Experience.* London: Methuen, Inc., 1986.

DeFleur, Melvin L. and Sandra Ball-Rokeach. *Theories of Mass Communication,* 3rd ed. NY: Longman, Inc., 1976

Fuller, Linda K. "Enculturation: An Axiomatic Theory of Mass Communication," paper presented at the Fifth International Conference on Culture and Communication, Philadelphia, PA, 1983.

Laba, Martin, "Making Sense: Expressiveness, Stylization and the Popular Culture Process," *Journal of Popular Culture* 19: 4 (Spring, 1986), pp. 107-117.

McQuail, Denis. *Mass Communication Theory: An Introduction.* Beverly Hills, CA: Sage Publications, 1984.

Rissover, Frederic and David C. Birch. *Mass Media and the Popular Arts*, 3rd ed. NY: McGraw-Hill Book Company, 1983.

Severin, Werner J. and James W. Tankard, Jr. *Communication Theories: Origins, Methods, Uses*. NY: Hastings House, Publishers, 1979.

Tosuner-Fikes, Lebriz, "A Guide for Anthropological Fieldwork on Contemporary American Culture," in Conrad Phillip Kottak (ed.), *Researching American Culture*. Ann Arbor, MI: The University of Michigan Press, 1982, pp. 10-35.

Von Bertalanffy, Ludwig. *General System Theory: Foundations, Development, Applications*. NY: George Braziller, 1968.

Wilensky, Harold L., "Mass Society and Mass Culture: Interdependence of Independence?" *American Sociological Review* 29 (April, 1964), pp. 173-96.

Marxism and Popular Culture: The Cutting Edge of Cultural Criticism

Michael Real

"People make history but in conditions not of their own making."

Stuart Hall (1985)

"Marxism, in general, and Marxist media analysis, in particular, have a great deal of appeal—especially to people with a strong sense of social justice and desires for a more egalitarian, more humane world....In its best forms, Marxism is a humanistic system of thought that seeks to make it possible for people to have productive, useful lives. However, Marxism is also an ideology that explains everything (or nearly everything) in the world on the basis of certain axioms or beliefs from which everything else follows. And that is its danger."

Arthur Asa Berger (1982)

To most unbiased observers it is obvious that Marxism has contributed a great deal to our understanding of popular culture: critical examinations of the power of ownership and commercialism, the problems of cultural domination and hegemony, the relation of culture to ideology and consciousness, the complexity of working class culture, and the conflicts between imperialism and liberation. These and numerous other issues and insights in the investigation of popular culture have originated from or found important expression within Marxist forms of discourse and analysis.

What may be less obvious to observers is that popular culture analysis has contributed significantly to Marxism as well. The peculiarities of human activity and expression generally grouped under the label "popular culture" have proven complex and illusive enough to have forced some of our best contemporary Marxist thinkers—Raymond Williams, Stuart Hall, Pierre Bourdieu, among many others—to move away from the doctrinaire danger mentioned by Berger above. Marxist critics who have seriously engaged in analysis of popular culture have seemed to emerge more subtle and sensitive in their definitions and distinctions. The elitist simplicity with which an earlier Marxist, T.W. Adorno (1941), approached popular music is replaced by the immensely richer, but no less Marxist, analysis of more recent rock critics such as Chapple and Garofalo (1977). In fact, one of the most noteworthy qualities of the present generation of Marxist scholars of popular culture and media is the degree to which they have moved beyond the more mechanical absoluteness of the original Frankfurt School—the paterfamilias of Marxist popular culture analysis—to a series of more complex, subtle, and sophisticated variations of Marxist analysis.

The summary which follows of groupings and issues in Marxist work on popular culture cannot pretend to exhaust this subject but simply points to certain central figures, trends, and concepts more or less representative of Western Marxism. At the same time, with limited resources and access, we must acknowledge the omission of many Marxist writings and possibilities, especially those generated from within the socialist world and which are not readily available in the English-speaking capitalist West.

"Marxism" is an incredibly difficult label in late twentieth century America. The legacy of McCarthyism and related variants of anti-Communism in the United States has made it virtually impossible for prudent scholars to accept a Marxist self-label, no matter how intellectually comfortable they may be with it. The ideological domination of modern U.S. history by anti-Communism has also created such negative connotations for everything associated with Marx's legacy that non-Marxist scholars are effectively chased away from even selectively and explicitly borrowing from Marxism the way they might. The general public in America, by residing within the capitalist camp in a world contextually divided along Cold War lines, is heir to a popular culture and ideology bent toward private enterprise and profit and away from socialist consciousness and culture. Within this larger anti-Marxist context, it becomes necessary to define Marxism, then, not so much formally as a specific intellectual system with its explicit self-acknowledged adherents, but rather as a general critical and political orientation with many varieties of partial and full contributors.

For our purposes here, "Marxism" is taken to refer to critical works which examine popular culture in reference to economic and political forces and the exercise of power, with attention given to social, historical, and ideological contexts. Marxist critiques of political-economic dominance and superficial epistemologies arise from a common ground of concern over the real world importance and consequences of the popular culture and a skeptical scrutiny of concentrations of power. This generic Marxism within capitalist countries is marked by a readiness to consider practical alternatives and structural change. Curran, Gurevitch, and Woollacott (1982) find the most prominent critical approaches today to be (1) cultural studies, (2) political economy, and (3) structuralist textual analysis. What are major recent contributions to these approaches and what do they tell us of our popular culture?

Cultural Studies

Cultural studies of popular media and culture have come to be especially associated with Stuart Hall (1980, 1982, 1984, 1985a, 1985b, 1985c) in England and James Carey (1967, 1975a, 1975b, 1979, 1981, 1982, 1985) in the United States. Their emphasis on cultural products and expressions as "text" has bypassed the methodological and epistemological narrowness of the dominant empirical approaches to media audience effects, a narrowness which cultural studies has been at pains to identify and diagnose. Instead of demanding measurable behavioral change as the task of media—a demand promoted by

American empiricism but inappropriate to many cultural subjects such as classical literature—cultural studies emphasizes reading the cultural expression as a text in the way that Clifford Geertz (1973) has pioneered in cultural anthropology. The interpreter reads the text "over the shoulder of the natives" and pitches his tent with them to understand its meaning. The text is composed of signs and codes, as semiotics teaches us, and arises through cultural myths and rituals, as anthropology emphasizes (Fiske, 1982).

In the work of Hall and Raymond Williams, the cultural studies approach becomes increasingly Marxist as it considers ideology, class-based decoding of texts, historical forms of consciousness, and the relation of base and superstructure in the institutional determination of popular culture. Whereas earlier Marxist analysis considered the last item somewhat mechanically—the ownership and control base directly dictates superstructural expressions—cultural studies retains the rejection of cultural practices as "autonomous" but relates specific practices to base context in more general ways through what Williams (1973) calls the "whole indissoluble practice," the totality of the dominant "structure of feeling" in a particular culture. Antonio Gramsci's notion of hegemony is central here in demonstrating how a dominant culture insinuates itself over alternatives.

The way multi-party political debates are conducted on television reveals, according to Hall, the interrelations among audience, message, and broadcast institutions. The conventional form of such a program is to have representatives of the main political parties and an "uncommitted" moderator examine the issue. Hall's analysis of the way the politicians share the broadcast time and the way the moderator treats them proposes that the real meaning of the program is not in the issue but in the form. The form suggests that representative democracy works and that the media demonstrate its working. The same analysis may apply to American presidential campaign debates. The structures of thought and feeling of the audience call for the format, the encoding structure of the broadcast message recreates it, and the structures of the broadcast institutions undergird and reinforce this form. For Hall there is a hidden but *determining* relationship among these forces of audience, message, broadcasting, and cultural context.

The way a photograph is cropped and framed for newspaper presentation also reveals this determining role of what Hall calls the "preferred reading" of the dominant system and *dominant code*. Fiske (1982) has illustrated this by placing side by side the uncropped photographs of two encounters in London between blacks and police. Both photos—one from the *Daily Mirror* in 1981 and the other from the *Observer* in 1976—reveal the way conventions of editing and expected audience interpretations dictate that the photographs be presented with an emphasis on conflict and drama but with care taken to protect the police image while giving little regard for supporting the black representations. Certain areas of the photo are eliminated and others emphasized, captions are selected, other photos and headlines are placed around the photo, all in such a way that the conventional, dominant, preferred reading will be maintained.

Such interpretations challenge the establishment assumption that news and public affairs are unbiased, elaborated codes of media and that they provide objective and universal standards of truth in their presentation. Instead, hidden conventions structure audiences, messages, and broadcasters into specific dominant meanings. This method of analysis by Hall, Fiske, Murdoch, and others links the negotiated meanings of a message with the social structure within which newsreporting, message and reader all operate. Cultural Studies insists that, alongside this dominant code, there exists a *subordinate code* which accepts the dominant values and structure but argues that one group's status may need improving. There also exists an *oppositional code* which rejects the dominant version and the social values that produced it. The oppositional code interprets the message in a meaning system radically opposed to the dominant system, for example, arguing that the photographs of blacks and police reveal the oppressive and distorting power of capitalist power in protecting its own interest through both the police and the media.

How the dominant system and preferred reading operate in America can be seen in the writings of Todd Gitlin. For one of his books, *Inside Prime Time* (1983), Gitlin interviewed hundreds of television industry people in order to identify the business calculations of the networks, the working methods of network television production, and the influence of politics on network decision-making. He found that the conventional expectations and themes of American network television result from the oligopolistic pressures to compete for the same general audience. This dominant code then provides America's version of itself as an impoverished recombinant culture, dull-edged and antipolitical. Douglas Kellner continues this line of analysis, with modifications, as described below.

Political Economy

If the cultural studies approach shows how audience, message, and media institutions incline toward dominant codes, political economy attempts to explain the arrangements of institutionalized power that dictate and structure that pressure toward dominant codes. Nowhere has Marxist popular culture analysis been more significant than in examining the configurations of ownership, economics, transnational markets, and concentrations of cultural industry power. The study of political economy was founded by Marx as a means of focusing on the combined power of intertwined political and economic institutions. Today the best political economists draw from tangible historical and economic data to uncover the size, organization, and influence of current monopolies and cartels in media and popular culture.

The historical and materialist thrust of Marxism is put to use by Nicholas Garnham (1985; also Preface to Mattelart, 1984) in explaining the political economy of popular media power today. He reasons that economic and technical factors determine cultural production in a world market dominated by multinational corporations. Cultural expression, for Garnham, always has an ideologico-political function and is increasingly used as a mechanism for social control. The symbolic and imaginary cannot be simply collapsed into the ideological or economic but are related to them. The tensions between centralization and deconcentration, between localism and internationalism, are controlled through economics and are the site of class struggle and resistance.

Political economists such as Herbert Schiller (1984), Cees Hamelink (1983b), and Armand Mattelart (1983) in recent years have raised high the twin issues of *privatisation* and *deregulation*. Privatisation takes mediated cultural expression, thought previously to have been intrinsically public in nature and publicly accountable, and instead declares these cultural products to be private property subject to no laws other than those of supply, demand, and profit. Privatisation of information, media, and cultural policies and products has taken power away from public bodies and further concentrated decision-making in transnational corporations and financial institutions. Legislatively and judicially, deregulation then serves to canonize this transfer of power.

The objection to these trends that most concerns political economists is that cultural industries do not serve all equally. The media not only serve dominant codes, they serve dominant groups. Rich nations can flood poor nations with media and cultural products; information rich groups can pay for and use controlling forms of information while the information poor are deprived of even the opportunity to know what is going on behind the scenes. Transnational banks and corporations gather extensive information about consumers and creditors while revealing very little of themselves and what they know to the public. Ironically, the traditional right to privacy is thus one of the values most threatened by privatisation of cultural power. If fewer powerful private entities control larger areas of cultural power, whether they be film companies, broadcasting conglomerates, newspaper publishers, or others, and if these private entities are less publicly regulated and accountable, Marxist political economists argue that the potential for widespread democratic participation in cultural expression and decision-making is diminished.

Political economists today, however, argue against monolithic absolutist interpretations of the nature and effects of concentrations of cultural power. First, in regard to concentration of power itself, as Mattelart insists, the dual demands of competition and consumption force transnationals to splinter their power and prevent a closed system. The search for competitive advantage works against completely totalitarian planning and creates cracks in the system. Second, in regard to the effects of concentrations of power, even within contexts of highly concentrated power, oppositional readings can arise and sustain themselves. Resistance individually and collectively is always at least theoretically possible. This more flexible interpretation of cultural power contrasts with the earlier Frankfurt School's tendency to speak about the automatic elimination of oppositional readings or alternatives by the sheer size and power of the dominant cultural system and institutions. No longer can one assume that a Marxist analysis will condemn out of hand all the expressions arising within a capitalist context or all the possibilities of cultural power present in that privately controlled, consumerist context.

Political economists and those who work in cultural studies generally support movements of opposition, resistance, and independence within capitalist societies. This flows from Marxist analysis of political economy and support for oppressed classes. However, this support arises not negatively out of pre-established commitments against capitalism so much as positively out of continuously renegotiated commitments to responsive participatory political, economic, and cultural institutions. In fact, while it does not appear as prevalently in the literature, many political economists have no more use for Soviet state socialism than for American capitalism. Mattelart (1983, 1984), for example, argues for increased "Latin audio-visual space" for Latin America and Latin Europe against the cultural space expanding from various other sources. Hamelink (1983a) argues for national information policies that dissociate from the pressures toward cultural synchronization and develop self-reliant cultural and information systems. Cultural imperialism and domination may come from East or West and only informed, conscious, and vigorous regional and national policies can protect against it. The McBride Commission of UNESCO (1980), which explored the debate on the call for a New World Information and Communication Order, raised questions of political economy and championed independent national cultural policies and practices. This worked especially against the self-serving American libertarian theory of free flow of information within a privatized and unprotected international sphere. The UNESCO debates on communication policy are generally credited with being a prime reason for United States withdrawal from UNESCO in December, 1984.

The special contribution of political economy to the study of popular culture is the emphasis on economic and international structures and on acknowledging large-scale patterns and priorities within our popular cultures and surrounding them. The tendency to treat phenomena of popular culture as if each case—Elvis Presley, Wheel of Fortune, Formula One racing, Steven Spielberg—had dropped from heaven and did not emerge from and reflect any historical context or economic institutions was an early curse on popular culturalists that limited the field's credibility with systematic thinkers whether from sociology, literature, or other disciplines. The addition of a recognition of the role of political economy in the shaping of all cultural products takes a long step toward curing that particular shortcoming.

Structuralist Textual Analysis

That marvelous cadre of German ex-patriots known as the Frankfurt School pioneered the close reading of popular cultural texts within a Marxist framework. Following those innovations in the first half of the twentieth century, a new generation in the Frankfurt tradition, featuring Philip Wander and Douglas Kellner among others, carries on this practice. But the tendency toward absolutism, which disallowed oppositions within the dominant system and which could not account for cultural modifications within capitalism, has been modified. Wander warns, "The underlying error in critical theory...lies in its inability to account for change." (1981, p. 509) Drawing from semiotics, structuralism, and psychoanalysis, the analysis of popular texts from a Marxist structuralist perspective allows for readings of the dominant code, the subordinate codes, and the oppositional codes in their dynamic interplay.

The film *Saturday Night Fever* illustrates how Wander (1981) reads a text structurally. That 1977 film, starring John Travolta as a paint store clerk who at night becomes the star of the glitzy local dance palace, both capitalized on and contributed to the wave of disco music and dance that threatened the rest of popular music in the late 1970s. Written by Norman Wexler and directed by John Badham, *Saturday Night Fever* showcased Travolta's dancing and the Bee Gees music through a Brooklyn-based story rich in social commentary. In Wander's reading, the dead end of working-class adult life stares Travolta and the other characters in the face as they struggle with their sexual and other passages to adulthood. Family life is miserable but demanding. Pregnancy and marriage are threats which would precipitate immediate immersion in the trap of job and family and mark the end of the briefly experienced freedom of adolescence. The Brooklyn Bridge symbolizes the difficult route away from these traps: for Tony's misfit buddy it is a negative route ending in suicide: for Tony it is a positive route to Manhattan with his new and more sophisticated dance partner.

This critique of working-class frustrations and mythology fits very well the text of the movie and evokes classic Marxist analysis. But that was not the "preferred reading" of the text if one looks back at the reception of that movie. Instead, the movie was taken as a celebration of music and dance, a romantic fantasy with just enough pseudo-realism to make it interesting. Wander notes this discrepancy. Why did it happen?

Drawing now from Hall's distinction of dominant, subordinate, and oppositional codes, we can see this was a subordinate code in comparison to the dominant code in America that generally ignores working-class problems and represents instead a seemingly universal middle-class lifestyle of equality and opportunity. The hard-edged working-class consciousness of *Saturday Night Fever* disagrees with the dominant code by proposing the inadequacy of one group's circumstances. This is subordinate but not oppositional. The latter would require more direct rejection and critique of the dominant code. But the dominant code is able to subsume and wash out most of the impact of even the subordinate code. The Hollywood film format, the advertising and marketing of the film as an entertainment event and a star vehicle, and the standardized expectations of audience members combine to bring to the foreground those elements of the film that fit the dominant code and push to the background those elements, however intrinsic they may have been in the film text itself, of a subordinate code.

In cultural studies and structuralist textural analysis, the meaning of the cultural experience does not reside in a self-evident message sent from A to B but in the negotiation of meaning that includes producer-reader (parallel tasks), message text, and cultural environment. (Fiske, 1982)

The "contradictory imperatives" built into American television have drawn from Douglas Kellner a series of close readings (1979, 1980, 1981, 1982a, 1982b) of numerous television programs in reference to the conflict between their power to manipulate and their potential to liberate. The demands of attracting an audience leads television producers to provide criticism of the dominant system, insofar as such criticism attracts an audience, even as their larger messages generally confirm the system. Kellner finds subordinate and even oppositional codes in detective shows, situation comedies, soap operas, and game shows as well as in political reports. He reminds us that even the most exploitive of the dominant code movies, *Rambo*, moves finally toward a sequence in which the Stallone character attacks also the Pentagon-style computer arrays as well as all that is Communist and/or foreign. The film seems to serve the militarist right in its dominant code but, even in its superficial mindlessness, suggests alternative codes bordering on anti-bureaucratic anarchy, as in Rambo's predecessor *First Blood*, rather than pro-establishment anti-Communist America-first absolutes. In a similar vein, Kellner sees anti-authoritarian detective shows, muckraking mini-series, and Norman Lear subversive comedy as containing potentially emancipatory messages within the dialectic resulting from their contradictory imperatives.

The testimony of Colonel Oliver North in the Iran-Contra hearings in the summer of 1987 provides another rich text for structural analysis as a problematic for Marxist cultural studies. North's testimony was in both substance and glamor the center of those hearings. His fervent patriotism and choir boy sincerity, wrapped in a military uniform and expressed with articulate, emotional pride, touched off a firestorm of popular reaction and counter-reaction in the country and the press. His actual role as negotiator and weapons source for Central America and the Middle East, was as a kind of privatized, deregulated blending of the roles supposedly played by the Departments of State and Defense. But his good-Marine style of injured innocence and international responsibility, not to mention rabid anti-Marxism, cast him in the role of American hero, a receptacle of what the dominant ideology of the American public wanted to believe in.

The first condition of North's popularity was the uniformity between his message and the dominant code in America. The mainstream official Americana of the Reagan era respected strong military action against deserving enemies; the line of heroic accountability ran from John Wayne and Clint Eastwood directly to Oliver North. This was no subordinate or oppositional code, but clearly the "preferred reading" of the incumbent who happened also to be North's superior.

The second condition of North's popularity was that his testimony spanned across often separated spheres of daily life. Within the dominant code, North's testimony ranged freely over his multiple roles as family man, religious believer, public servant, fervent patriot, secret agent, international negotiator, military officer, faithful husband, and so on. To explain the significance of this, it is revealing to turn to Raymond Williams' theory that a culture is characterized by a particular "structure of feeling" across that culture. Hall (1980) echoes Williams' phrasing to explain culture as an organized complex of relationships:

> It begins with 'the discovery of patterns of a characteristic kind.' One will discover them, not in the art, production, trading, politics, the raising of families, treated as separate activities, but through 'studying a general organization in a particular example.'

North fit this characteristic perfectly. The length of his six-day testimony and the blending of his public and private life in the testimony and in the popular reactions enabled North to represent a much broader cross-section of spheres of human activity than a "new" public figure usually represents.

The third condition was that North articulated his experiences and convictions with the style and principles of classic Cold War propaganda. This dimension of his testimony warrants closer examination.

North's ideology and rhetoric were pure *Cold War*. In his prepared statement, he spoke of "Moscow's surrogates in Havana and Managua." (Federal, 1967, p. 266) He warned in his testimony: "This nation cannot abide the communization of Central America. We cannot have Soviet bases on the mainland of this hemisphere." (p. 270) What is the difference between Nicaragua and Vietnam? He responded, "You're talking about the efforts of the Soviet Union, not on the other side of the Pacific Ocean, but right here in this hemisphere." (p.271) Fundamentally, to North the world is divided into Soviet Communism, what Reagan traditionally preached about as "the evil empire," on the one side and American defense of democracy and freedom on the other. Everything else international is explainable by this basic dichotomy. The code is classically structuralist, that is, divided into a fundamental binary opposition around which all other meaning revolves.

The cultural studies sense of ideology, following Williams and Hall, calls attention to the "structure of feeling" that characterizes a culture across art, politics, and family. In Colonel North's case, his religious convictions were thoroughly identified with his political convictions. One North observer who attended North's church said, "He had a born-again experience in 1978, and he's integrated his religious life with his political life. It adds an element of righteousness to his cause. Religion is very important to him." (*L.A. Times*, 1987) Religion, politics, family life, moral code, military career all blended in North into a striking reflection of a stereotypical superhero in the Rambo, Superman, and Rocky molds. Ideologically, North believes he has the world figured out and is "righteous" about it.

North's ideological presentation was also classically *propagandistic* in its signs, codes, and structure. The sharpest evidence of this was in his presentation of the narrative of the administration's slide show on Nicaragua, a fund-raising show that congressman refused to let be shown, so only verbal description and narration were presented. The style and sequence of the slide show recalls the World War II Frank Capra "Why We Fight" series, the Johnson administration's less successful "Why Vietnam" film, and such anti-communist classics of the 1950s as "Communist Blueprint for Conquest," the anti-

Communist documentary history of the Soviet Union called "Red Nightmare," and the Jack Webb-narrated fantasy "Nightmare in Red."

North begins by engaging in the standard propagandist practices of labelling and association. The Soviet global military threat opens the sequence and is immediately tied to Cuba and Nicaragua. Weaponry, threats by Communist officials, and the grouping of Nicaraguan Sandinista's with terrorists of every stripe, including Muammar Qaddafi of Libya, vividly identify the "enemy." Then the traditional bleeding maps and domino scenarios identify the near diabolical strategy and practices of the enemy. All this is succeeded by photographs which bring out the bravery and altruism of the Nicaraguan "freedom fighters," the "democratic resistance." Their cause is the noblest and they desperately need our support. North finally proclaims: "The conclusion of the briefing is, gentlemen, that we've got to offer them something more than the chance to die for their country and the freedoms we believe in. Thank you, sir." (p.680) Even without visuals and a sound track, the would-be slide show reveals itself as classically propagandistic in style, format, and content.

The dominant ideology and the dominant code, at least in the minds of North and Reagan, reveal themselves to be nothing less than a hegemonic cultural system in which individual and collective values and lifestyles are inextricably united with a specific (and demonstrably narrow) moral and ideological stance. The centrality of Cold War threats justifies resorting to covert operations which require what would otherwise be unacceptable means: lying, killing, arming nations, overthrowing governments, and similarly. In opposition to the North-Reagan hegemonistic ideology, the subordinate and oppositional ideologies in America resisted Cold War superficialities and caused North's fame in July, 1987, to be relatively short-lived, making his a Pyrrhic victory.

To summarize this discussion of an applied cultural studies case, we might figuratively ask: What if Stuart Hall met Fawn Hall? Stuart Hall, the British Marxist, brings to mind the ideological significance of Fawn Hall, North's secretary, fan, and fellow true-believer, in large terms: biased representation, hegemony, distorted consciousness and culture in the Cold War context.

Marxism and Popular Culture: The Emerging Agenda

Marxism assumes a series of both positive and negative tasks in regard to popular culture, whether American or other. Let us summarize some of these issues, accomplishments, and tasks.

Cultural studies has provided an epistemological and pragmatic critique of American behaviorism, a behaviorism that is important not just as a scientific methodology but as a component in a larger set of cultural practices that constitute a dominant code and ideology. Marxist works have also provided an alternative to the shallow and unproductive debate on popular culture between the conservatism of cultural elitists and the liberalism of consumer capitalists. Marxism has been essential in developing the Third World critique of cultural domination through popular culture. Neo-Marxist cultural studies also evaluate and reject Stalinist state centralism and authoritarianism as well as the automatic and vulgar Marxism that defended them.

Complementing the above negative tasks of critique, Marxism's positive role holds out for more genuine, democratic, participatory culture than current exploitive systems generate. Marxism today defends the people's culture, for example, in the form of the "Nueva Cancion" uniting music and political concern in Latin America. With Enzensberger and others, Marxism demands participatory structures and practices to counter the centrally controlled, unidirectional, politically disengaging culture of the dominant structures of popular media. The call for egalitarian political-economic structures leads to demands for structural revolution and for the creation of empowering-motivating images, narratives, and ideals to strengthen the subordinate and oppositional codes. Marxism should be in the vanguard of struggles toward a democratized popular culture which carries with it feminine liberation, racial justice, protection of minority rights, and demilitarization.

As we proceed to slouch toward utopia, Marxism's contribution is readily documentable in the past and promising for the future. Popular culture is a foremost part of the "contested terrain" of culture where Hall sees human activity taking place. For its part, Marxism will continue to learn from its complex encounters with popular culture. Looking from the other direction, popular culture analysis will in turn continue to benefit from Marxist terminology, insights, and methods in the form of cultural studies, political economy, and the structural analysis of texts. For now, let us simply appreciate that neither Marxism nor popular culture would be half so much fun without the other.

Works Cited

Adorno, T.W. (1941). "Popular Music". *Studies in Philosophy and Social Science, 9,* 17-35.

Becker, J., Hedebro, G., and Paldan, L. (1986). *Communication and Domination: Essays to Honor Herbert I. Schiller.* Norwood, NJ: Ablex Publishing Corporation.

Becker, S.L. (1985, Fall). Critical studies: a multidimensional movement, *Feedback, 27,* 24-27.

Benjamin, J. (1980, Spring). The Bonds of Love: Rational Violence and Erotic Domination. *Feminist Studies, 6,* 144-74.

Bennett, T., Boyd-Bowman, S., Mercer, C., and Woollacott, J. (Eds.) (1981). *Popular Television and Film.* London: British Film Institute.

Berger, A. (1982). *Media Analysis Techniques.* Beverly Hills: Sage Publications, Inc.

Budd, M., Craig, S., and Steinman, C. (1985). "Fantasy Island": Marketplace for Desire. In M. Gurevitch and M. Levy (Eds.), *Mass Communication Review Yearbook* (Vol. 5, pp. 321-336). Beverly Hills: Sage.

Carey, J. (1967, Spring). Harold Adams Innis and Marshall McLuhan. *Antioch Review,* pp. 5-39.

_____ (1975a). Communication and Culture. *Communication Research* 2:173-91.

———. (1975b). Canadian Communication Theory: Extensions and Interpretations of Harold Innis. In G. Robinson and D. Theall (Eds.), *Studies in Canadian Communications* (pp. 27-59). Toronto: McGill University.

———. (1979). The Roots of Modern Media Analysis: Lewis Mumford and Marshall McLuhan. Paper presented to the Association for Education in Journalism, Houston, TX.

———. (1981). Graduate Education in Mass Communication. *Communication Education, 28*, pp. 282-293.

———. (1982). The Mass Media and Critical Theory: An American View. In M. Burgoon (Ed.), *Communication Yearbook V* (pp. 18-33). New Brunswick, NJ: Transaction Books.

———. (1985). Overcoming Resistance to Cultural Studies. In M. Gurevitch and M. Levy (Eds.), *Mass Communication Review Yearbook* (Vol. 5, pp. 27-40). Beverly Hills: Sage.

Carey, J., & Christians, C. (1981). The Logic and Aims of Qualitative Research. In G. Stempel and B. Westley (Eds.), *Research Methods in Mass Communication*. Englewood Cliffs, NJ: Prentice-Hall.

Carey, J., & Kreiling, A. (1974). Popular Culture and Uses and Gratifications: Notes toward and Accommodation. In E. Katz and J. Blumler (Eds.), *The Uses of Mass Communication*. Beverly Hills: Sage, pp. 225-48.

Chapple, S., and Garofalo, R. (1977). *Rock 'n' Roll is Here to Pay*. Chicago, Nelson-Hall Inc.

Curran, J., Gurevitch, M., and Woollacott, J. (Eds.) (1977). *Mass Communication and Society*. Beverly Hills: Sage.

Curran, J., Gurevitch, M., and Woolacott, J. (1982). The study of the media: Theoretical Approaches. In Gurevitch, M., Bennet, T., Curran, J., and Woollacott, J. (Eds.), *Culture, Society and the Media*. London: Methuen.

Enzensberger, H. (1974). *The Consciousness Industry*. New York: Seabury Press.

Geertz, C. (1973). The interpretation of cultures. New York: Basic Books.

Gitlin, T. (1983). *Inside Prime Time*. New York: Pantheon.

———. (1978). Media Sociology: The Dominant Paradigm. *Theory & Society*, Vol. 6, No. 2.

———. (1980). *The Whole World is Watching: Mass Media in the Making and Unmaking of the New Left*. Berkeley: University of California Press.

Glasgow University Media Group (1976). *Bad News*. London: Routledge and Kegan Paul.

———. (1981). *More Bad News*. London: Routledge and Kegan Paul.

Grossberg, L. (1985). Presenting 'Stuart Hall'. Paper presented to plenary Theme Session on Beyond Polemics: Paradigm Dialogues. International Communication Association, Honolulu.

———. (1986). Stuart Hall on History and Politics. *The Journal of Communication Inquiry 10*.

Grossberg, L. and Slack, J. (1985, June). An Introduction to Stuart Hall's Essay. *Critical Studies in Mass Communication 2*, 87-90.

Guback, T,. (1969). *The International Film Industry: Western Europe and America Since 1945*. Bloomington: Indiana University Press.

———. (1974, Winter). Film as International Business. *Journal of Communication, 24*, 90-101.

———. (1979). Theatrical Film. In Compaine, B. (Ed.) *Who Owns the Media?* (pp. 179-249) White Plains, NY: Knowledge Industries.

Habermas, J. (1983). Translated by F. Lawrence. *Philosophical-Political Profiles.* Cambridge MA: MIT Press.

Hall, S. (1980). Cultural Studies: Two Paradigms. *Media, Culture and Society, 2,* pp. 57-72.

———— (1982). The rediscovery of 'ideology:' return of the repressed in media studies. In Gurevitch et al. (Eds.), *Culture, Society and the Media.* London: Methuen, 56-90.

———— (1984, January). The Culture Gap. *Marxism Today, 28,* 18-23.

———— (1985a). Authoritarian Populism: A Reply to Jessop et al. *New Left Review, 151,* 115-24.

———— (1985b). Address to the Plenary Session on Beyond Polemics: Paradigm Dialogues. International Communication Association, Honolulu, HA.

———— (1985c). Signification, Representation, Ideology: Althusser and the Post-Structuralist Debates. *Critical Studies in Mass Communication, 2,* 91-114.

Hall, S., Grossberg, L., and Slack, J. (forthcoming) *Cultural Studies.* Macmillan Press Ltd.

Hamelink, C. (Ed.) (1980). *Communication in the Eighties: A Reader on the McBride Report.* Rome: IDOC.

———— (1983a). *Cultural Autonomy in Global Communications: Planning National Information Policy.* New York: Longman.

———— (1983b). *Finance and Information: A Study of Converging Interests.* Norwood, NJ: Ablex.

Horkheimer, M. (1972). Translated by M. O'Connell and others. *Critical Theory* (pp. 188-243). New York: Seabury Press.

Jay, M. (1984). *Marxism and Totality.* Cambridge: Polity Press.

Johnson, P. (1984). *Marxist Aesthetics.* London: Routledge & Kegan Paul.

Kellner, D. (1979, May-June). TV, Ideology, and Emancipatory Popular Culture. *Socialist Review* 9, 13-53.

———— (1980). Television Images, Codes and Messages. *Televisions, 7,* 1-19.

———— (1981). Network Television and American Society: Introduction to a Critical Theory of Television. In (1981) *Theory & Society,* 10, 31-62. Also in E. Wartella and C. Whitney (Eds.) (1982), *Mass Communication Review Yearbook* (pp. 411-42). Beverly Hills: Sage. Also

———— (1982). Television, Mythology and Ritual. *Praxis* 6, 133-135.

———— (1984). *Herbert Marcuse and the Crisis of Marxism.* London: MacMillan.

Mattelart, A. (1983). *Transnationals and the Third World.* South Hadley MA: Bergin & Garvey.

Mattelart, A., & Cesta, Y. (1985). *Technology, Culture and Communication.* Amsterdam: Elsevier.

Mattelart, A., & Schmucler, H. (1985). *Communication and Information Technologies: Freedom of Choice for Latin America?* Norwood, NJ: Ablex Publishing Corporation.

Mattelart, A., & Siegelaub, S. (Eds.) (1979) *Communication and Class Struggle: 1, Capitalism, Imperialism.* New York: International General.

———— (Eds.) (1984) *Communication and Class Struggle: 2. Liberation, Socialism.* New York: International General.

Mattelart, A., Delcourt, X., & Mattelart, M. (1984). Translated by D. Buxton. Introduction by N. Garnham. *International Image Markets: In Search of an Alternative Perspective.* London: Comedia.

Mosco, V. (1979). *Broadcasting in the United States: Innovative Challenge and Organizational Control.* Norwood, NJ: Ablex.

———— (Forthcoming). Marxism and Communications Research in North America. In B. Ollman & E. Vernoff (Eds.), *The Left Academy, Vol. III.* New York: Praeger.

———— (1982). *Pushbutton Fantasies: Critical Perspectives on Videotex and Information Technology.* Norwood, NJ: Ablex.

Mosco, V., & Wasko, J. (1983). *The Critical Communications Review: Volume I Labor, the Working Class, and the Media.* Norwood NJ: Ablex Publishing Corporation.

———— (1984). *The Critical Communications Review: Volume 2 Changing Patterns of Communications Control* Norwood NJ: Ablex Publishing Corporation.

———— (1985). *The Critical Communications Review: Volume III Popular Culture and Media Events.* Norwood NJ: Ablex Publishing Corporation.

Real, M. (1984, Autumn). The Debate on Critical Theory and the Study of Communications. *Journal Of Communication* ("Ferment in the Field"), *34,* 72-80.

———— (1986, December). Demythologizing Media: Recent Writings in Critical and Institutional Theory. *Critical Studies in Mass Communication,* pp. 459-86.

Real, M. (Forthcoming). *Super Media: Cultural Studies and Transnational Life.* Newbury Park, CA: Sage Publications, Inc.

Schiller, H. (1969). *Mass Communication and American Empire.* Boston: Beacon Press.

———— (1973). *The Mind Managers.* Boston: Beacon Press.

———— (1976). *Communication and Cultural Domination.* White Plains, NY: International Arts and Sciences Press.

———— (1981). *Who Knows: Information in the Age of the Fortune 500.* Norwood, NJ: Ablex Publishing Corporation.

———— (1984). *Information and the Crisis Economy.* Norwood NJ: Ablex.

Smythe, D. (1981). *Dependency Road: Communications, Capitalism, Consciousness, and Canada.* Norwood NJ: Ablex.

Sparks, C. (1985). Western Marxism: A Critical Review. *Media, Culture and Society,* 7, 503-8.

UNESCO (1980). *Many Voices, One World.* London: Kogan Page Ltd.

Wander, P. (1981). Cultural Criticism. In D. Nimmo, & K. Sanders (1981). *The Handbook of Political Communication.* Beverly Hills: Sage.

———— (1983a). The Ideological Turn in Modern Criticism. *Central States Speech Journal,* 34, pp. 1-18.

———— (1983b). The Aesthetics of Fascism. *Journal of Communication, 33.*

———— (1984a). The Rhetoric of American Foreign Policy. *Quarterly Journal of Speech,* 70.

———— (1984b). The Third Persona: An Ideological Turn in Rhetorical Theory. *Central States Speech Journal,* 35, 197-216.

Wasko, J. (1982. *Movies and Money: Financing the American Film Industry.* Norwood, NJ: Ablex.

White, R. (1981). Administrative vs. critical research. *Communication Research Trends,* 2.

Post-Structuralism and Popular Culture

David R. Shumway

What is post-structuralism and why should people working in popular culture care? We can't answer these questions simply by stating a set of doctrines. This is not to say that post-structuralism has no doctrines, but that to list them here would be an ineffective illustration of the movement because it would be reductive of its diversity and conflict and because it would ignore the actual practice of post-structuralists. If we consider post-structuralism to constitute one of several ways of doing cultural studies today, we might consider each of these ways as analogous to a Kuhnian paradigm. Paradigms for Kuhn define a science during a given period of its history. A new paradigm comes into being in a scientific revolution, and Kuhn describes the two as "incommensurable," in that adherents to the new and old ways of doing things do not understand each other.[1]

The notion of the incommensurability of paradigms may help explain the difficulty that post-structuralists and scholars holding different theories have in comprehending each other's work. Kuhn argues that paradigms are defined not by abstract rules or sets of beliefs, but by concrete "exemplars," ground breaking pieces of work after which scholars model their own, and the actual practice of scholarship or criticism.[2] The point is not that the abstract theory can't be understood as such, but that work done under that theory makes sense only if one accepts its terms. Yet to describe, much less merely to cite, the exemplars of post-structuralist popular culture studies would not be any more successful since these texts are certainly more persuasive on their own behalf than I could be for them.[3] What I hope to do here instead is show the significance of post-structuralism by using it to explore the way popular culture has been constituted as an object of various academic discourses. In order to present this critique effectively, it will be necessary for me to first explain several of the most significant assumptions of post-structuralism. What the discussion of these assumptions will show is the background of the "theoretical turn" which post-structuralism has brought about in literary studies. The critique of the academic enterprise of popular culture is an illustration of what can result from this turn, and it will thus serve as an illustration of post-structuralist practice.

In the United States post-structuralism is most strongly identified with literary studies and especially literary theory, yet of the four most significant post-structuralist thinkers—Jacques Derrida, Michel Foucault, Jacques Lacan,

160

Roland Barthes—only Barthes was primarily a literary critic. Foucault and Derrida were trained as philosophers and Lacan was a psychoanalyst. These disparate beginnings have been acknowledged by a new use of the term "theory" without "literary" meant to imply an intellectual project that goes far beyond determining how literary works should be interpreted. Furthermore, "theory" itself does not refer merely to work done by these four and their followers, but to a variety of projects including Marxism, feminism, psychoanalysis, and others. Although these projects remain distinct, they all have been influenced by post-structuralism and it is post-structuralism which has created the theoretical turn which allowed them to come to the fore.

As the name "post-structuralism" suggests, the movement is defined by its relationship to another set of ideas, structuralism. In its broadest sense, post-structuralism is simply what came after structuralism and developed under its influence, first in French and then in English and American intellectual circles. Post-structuralism is not anti-structuralism, but rather a revision of structuralism or perhaps part of an argument within structuralism. What it shares with structuralism is its grounding in the linguistics of Ferdinand de Saussure.[4] Saussure describes languages as systems of pure difference, composed of signs which are only arbitrarily related to the non-linguistic objects they name—what we are used to calling "the world" or "reality." The arbitrary character of linguistic signs is something everyone concedes about most language, onomatopoetic words such as "meow" being the only possible exceptions. No one believes today that there is any connection between the sounds designated by d-o-g, and the black dog on the mat or all of members of the species *Canis familiaris* also called *"chien"* in French or *"hund"* in German. But Saussure argues that a sign is based on the relation, not of d-o-g to a dog or all dogs in the world, but on the relation of d-o-g, a *signifier* or sound image, to a *signified* or concept, "dog," a relation which is equally arbitrary but which excludes "reality" altogether. Language functions, according to Saussure, because we distinguish the sound of a word from the sound of other words. Thus we recognize the sound "d-o-g" by its difference from "h-o-g" or "d-o-t," and we understand the concept "dog" by its difference from the concepts "wolf" or "cat" or "beast." In this description, language lacks positive terms. It is a closed system of interdependent parts.

Structuralism takes Saussure's account of language as a model by which other aspects of human life can be understood. So, for example, Claude Lévi-Strauss considers the patterns of kinship or the culinary habits of a culture as being structured like language. Post-structuralism begins with the assumption that the world is always already represented by language, but proceeds to destabilize that representation. Where structuralism focused on the power of convention to link signifier and signified, post-structuralism focuses on the inherently unstable character of this relationship. Instead of finding each word clearly linked to a single concept, we find that words usually designate many concepts, some of which are likely to overlap. Thus post-structuralists speak of the tendency of the signifier to slip or float over the stream of signifies, and so to be ever-shifting in its meaning.

The theoretical turn which post-structuralism gives to work done under its influence results from this vision of language as both radically unstable and the very stuff of our knowledge. It is this theoretical turn which has been the greatest influence of post-structuralism on literary studies, and it is also what post-structuralism has to offer popular culture studies. In order to understand the significance of this, we must distinguish theory from some things which are similar to it, method and approach. Structuralism or post-structuralism can be any one of these three things, but the latter two imply either a stable project or goal (method) or a stable object of investigation (approach). Prior to post-structuralism, literary studies used ideas such as structuralism or psychoanalysis mainly as methods or approaches. It was assumed that there were one or more ways to achieve the goal of determining the meaning of the text, and various means were used to reach this end. What wasn't questioned was the stability of the text's meaning or the value of the project of discovering such a meaning. But because post-structuralism questions the stability not only of the text, but of the self, and therefore of writers and readers, it makes business as usual difficult for literary studies.

Post-structuralism itself has not provided literary studies with a ready-made method, and cannot offer such to popular culture studies either. American, or Yale-school, deconstruction as practiced by such critics as J. Hillis Miller, Geoffrey Hartmann, or Paul de Man is one manifestation of the post-structuralist movement, one which has received unfortunate prominence so as to seem to stand for post-structuralist practice, but it must be distinguished from post-structuralism in the larger sense. The Yale critics have managed to turn the work of Derrida into a method, and the result has been virtuoso readings which show in intricate detail how literary works affirm nothing, a position which has been familiar since the Renaissance.[5] But simultaneous with the development of American deconstruction, there developed in England and the United States a renewed interest in psychoanalytic, Marxist, feminist, and reader-oriented theory and criticism. These theories were not taken up as alternatives to post-structuralism but under the impetus of it so that we can no longer speak of these theories without also speaking of post-structuralism, and this for two reasons. First, by undermining the stability of texts, readers, writers and the relations among them, post-structuralism allowed theory to become the focal point of the practice of literary studies. Suddenly the issues were bigger than "what is the meaning of *Moby Dick*?" Post-structuralism provided an opening for theories such as Marxism and feminism capable of explaining the connections between text and culture, reader and society. Secondly, post-structuralism undermined the claims of these theories to certainty and totality by replacing the mechanistic foundation they had inherited from the nineteenth century with its own theories of discourse and representation. Post-structuralism put language in between nature (e.g., instinctual drives, the history of modes of production) and the cultural artifact, but also between nature and the critic, and between the artifact and the critic. The result is a shift in emphasis from what the text means to the way it participates in ideology.

Post-structuralism maintains that we can never escape ideology. Its treatment of the concept derives from the Marxist use of the term, but post-structuralism offers none of solace of Marxism's claims to science. Marx held ideology to be the false consciousness that arises because the ruling ideas of any given era will be the ideas of the ruling class. Barthes adds the sense that ideology works not only by directly affirming ruling class ideas, but by depoliticizing reality.[6] Thus Barthes in *Mythologies* shows how popular narratives often pose a genuine social or political problem, but then depoliticize it by telling a story in which another, apolitical problem is solved. In other words, Barthes work assumes that the conventions of popular forms are more significant than the ideas which a particular work might express.

Barthes' elaboration on the concept of ideology was followed by an even greater development of that idea in the work of Louis Althusser who combined Marxism with the post-structural psychoanalysis of Lacan.[7] What Althusser learned from Lacan is that the subject, the very consciousness that earlier Marxist thought had promised to enlighten, is itself constituted by language and hence ideology. The result of this insight for Marxist theory was that the simple opposition of bourgeois false consciousness and Marxist science became untenable since Marxism itself could not be free of ideology. For Althusser, ideology is an unconscious system, reinforced by the state apparatus—education, for example—but also repeated and reenacted over and over in cultural life. Since ideology is unconscious, we can only get at it via its "symptoms" in cultural artifacts or texts by looking for what is unthought or unsaid, i.e., what in a particular ideological system is repressed. Thus a frequent strategy of post-structuralist interpretations is to identify what is significantly absent from the text.[8]

Ideology has not been the only way post-structuralism has dealt with the linguistic construction of reality. Foucault's work has focused on conscious discourses: sciences, disciplines, fields of knowledge. By investigating the histories of fields such as psychiatry, medicine, penology, and biology, Foucault shows that academic disciplines cannot be conceived as stable, progressing inquiries into naturally existing subject matters.[9] Thus the science of "natural history" during the Classical Age, which was concerned with classifying beings on the basis of external appearance, cannot be conceived as biology in an earlier stage since biology depends on the internal anatomy of beings and on a concept of "life" lacking in the earlier field.[10] What we can conclude from Foucault is that each academic field constitutes its own object of study. This idealized object contains only the features and attributes of interest to the discipline, but it appears to practitioners in the field and usually to everyone else as a natural object.[11] In the next section, we will look at the different ways in which popular culture has been constituted as the object of an academic field.

According to post-structuralism, any study of popular culture would involve ideologies present in the culture at large, and to the extent that such study is part of an academic enterprise, it must also be limited by the discourse of that field. We cannot explore here all of the conditions which determine the character of popular culture studies. For example, such studies have particular relations to other fields within the university. At present popular culture remains what Raymond Williams would call an emergent field. Although many objects that we would readily classify as being a part of popular culture are studied today in the university, most of this work is done in the context of more or less traditional disciplinary formations: popular music is studied in music departments, detective fiction is interpreted by professors of English, and films are treated in the growing discipline of cinema studies. On the other hand, the Popular Culture Association, *The Journal of Popular Culture*, and departments of Popular Culture such as the one at Bowling Green all reflect what is a different means of organizing the study of popular culture. Our focus here cannot be on the institutional and historical conditions of popular culture study. Rather we will look at the terms in which different discourses have constituted popular culture as an object of investigation.

We might begin by looking at what is being claimed by the name "popular culture." Both of these terms are floating signifiers, *par excellence*. In the name "popular culture," "popular" seems to claim two contradictory things. These claims are both entailed in a single definition of the term "of or pertaining to the common people, or the people as a whole as distinguished from any particular class" (OED). One claim is that the culture it names is democratically chosen; it is culture not only for the majority of the people, but also by and of them. On the other hand, "popular" names a particular group of people, the common people, as opposed to an elite. This designation invites a further difference within the word popular: it can signify something undistinguished and inferior to the culture of the elite, or a culture which is better than the elite culture but which is unfairly denigrated by that culture.

There are also two contradictory meanings for the word "culture," which do not exactly correspond to the meanings of "popular." In one sense, "culture" is synonymous with "high culture," or, to use Matthew Arnold's phrase, the best that has been thought and said. Arnold's theory of culture is at root of the importance that has been increasingly accorded to literature by schools and universities since the late nineteenth century, and its contemporary influence should not be dismissed. Education Secretary William Bennett is Arnoldian in his understanding of role of the humanities. In Arnold's terms, "popular culture" is an oxymoron unless it names the adoption of high culture by the majority. Perhaps the dominant meaning of the word "culture" derives from anthropology and other social sciences: the particular way of life of a group or of an historical period. This meaning conflicts with the Arnoldian one, since culture here is a relative term while for Arnold it is an evaluative one. The anthropological definition is not excluded from popular culture studies. A glance at an issue of *JPC* or at the program of a PCA Convention will reveal papers using social science methods on subjects ranging from television and movies, to chili festivals and barbecues, to back yard decks and family rooms, etc. However, the dominant meaning of the construction "popular culture" combines the positive, democratic meaning of "popular" with the Arnoldian meaning of "culture" so that the study of popular culture is understood to be the study of works of art enjoyed by the majority of the population.

In examining the ways in which the words "popular" and "culture" differ from themselves, we discover that the dominant meaning of each term in the name "popular culture" contradicts the dominant meaning of the other. We will not be surprised, then, to find that strategies used to legitimate the study of popular culture also conflict with each other. Popular culture has claimed that the materials it studies are valuable because they are what most people like. On the other hand, many who study popular materials seek to distinguish on aesthetic grounds among various artifacts within a popular genre or art form, and they have usually relied on standards of judgment borrowed from the criticism of high cultural forms. Colin McCabe observes, for example, that the French critics of the *Cahiers du Cinéma* who invented the *auteur* theory and rescued Hollywood film from aesthetic oblivion, did so in terms of "a concept of the artist drawn from traditional aesthetics. The popular culture of Hollywood was transformed to reveal the high art of the *Cahiers*-selected *auteur*."[12] The *auteur* approach has been so successful in redescribing the work of Hitchcock or Wells in high cultural terms, that it no longer clearly falls into the category of popular culture. Nevertheless, popular culture as a movement has continued to offer aesthetic judgments which create hierarchies of artists and works. This has especially been true of studies of objects most like high cultural forms, such as science fiction or detective fiction.

But it is not necessary to claim elite status for a popular work in order to use elite values to justify its importance. Dana Polan has pointed out a strategy which attributes such values to the popular itself. He argues that while elite critics have scapegoated popular culture as the Other which can be blamed for a host of social ills, "the euphoric sort of celebration of popular culture to be found in *The Journal of Popular Culture*...really does no more than reiterate the same scapegoating mechanism, exalting cases of popular culture only when the mythic, spiritual, transcendental values usually attributed to high culture can also be projected onto them."[13] This strategy thus tries to show that popular culture serves the same noble ends as high culture, and it thus fails to show what is different or potentially subversive of dominant values in popular forms. This may be inevitable when popular culture is constituted in populist terms and not as representing any class or subculture. The claims of popular culture to deal with what is popular, what the majority choose to like, doom it to always rediscovering what is dominant in popular works. The problem of legitimizing popular culture, whether that means either the study of objects not recognized as art or the whole field of products popularly consumed, determines that dominant values or aesthetic standards will not be abandoned since it is those who hold these values to whom the case for legitimacy must be made.

There is a third way of legitimating the study of popular culture which does not rely on the Arnoldian conception of culture as the repository of value. In this strategy, popular cultural materials are deemed worthy of study on the same grounds as any other objects, that they are there. But here nothing can be said about the aesthetic or moral value of the materials studied, although their *effects* may be evaluated. The social scientists who adopt this strategy rely on the prestige of science to overcome the low status of popular culture. From a post-structuralist perspective, what is valuable about this strategy is that it doesn't depend upon the value of the objects it studies. What is pernicious about it, however, is its claim to being outside of ideology, and its consequent inability to be openly critical of its objects. Post-structuralism does not offer grounds for rejecting empirical studies when they are possible, but it does call into question claims for objectivity which usually accompany those studies. Far from being genuinely disinterested, what empirical studies often do is simply assume the correctness of dominant values and then try to examine whether popular works will cause people to run astray. Once again, the popular is articulated in the terms of the dominant.

So far we have seen how the opposition of popular and high culture is not what it seems. The object of the academic field of popular culture explicitly valorizes the popular over the high while covertly assuming the superiority of the latter. Popular culture is not the only object, however, that has been constituted by academic discourse concerned with the materials popular culturists study. Mass culture names most of the same products and activities as popular culture, but it characterizes them in an altogether different way.[14] While "popular" is a term which gives a positive value to its materials, "mass culture" almost always implies a negative judgment. We have already described the way the term "popular" itself implies the positive meaning of "people's choice." The idea of mass culture is almost a complete reversal of this meaning of "popular." In the first place, the current meaning of "Mass Culture" denies the element of choice. Mass culture is the product of a culture industry which floods the market with commodities passive consumers simply absorb without judgment. This critique is most familiar in its left wing form, especially as articulated by Horkheimer and Adorno in *The Dialectic of Enlightenment*, where the culture industry is seen not only as disseminating the ideology of the ruling class, but of offering a vision of the world that makes thought itself impossible.[15] But the concept of mass culture also implies a specific set of negative characteristics associated with the objects themselves. Since the Roman satirist Juvenal complained about the public being bribed with bread and circuses, mass culture has been associated with barbarism, social decay, and the portent of apocalypse.[16] The most familiar example of this treatment of a popular form is the claim that television is responsible for problems that range from crime, to the decline of the family, to illiteracy. Like the concept of popular culture, the concept of mass culture assumes the superiority of high cultural values, but it finds the opposites of these values in the objects it names.

High or elite culture is the Other for popular culturists, just as popular culture is scapegoated by high culturists. By continually opposing the popular and the high, we tend to forget that it leaves us as academics out of the picture entirely. If we take our own position seriously, we recognize that while we readily deny an affiliation with high culture we cannot claim an identity with popular culture. From this perspective mass and popular culture become virtually identical, and are opposed to academic culture or avant-garde culture. From a "popular" point of view, these maybe understood as versions of high culture, but in fact avant-garde culture sees itself in opposition to received traditions and canonical texts just as popular culture does. And all of the people who study culture, whether high, popular, mass, or avant-garde, are participants in an academic culture which is not identical with any of the cultures they study. Although academic culture can become an object of the scrutiny of academics—as it is in this essay and has increasingly become under post-structuralism's influence—such self-study is often regarded as navel-contemplation or an obstacle to "real work." Both of these charges can be true, but unless we take into account both the way we represent ourselves and the effects of our discourse in representing others, we will have no way to get at the ideological blindnesses from which we like everyone else suffer. In representing ourselves as part of academic culture, and therefore as different from the popular or mass culture we study, we constitute another hierarchy. Our superiority here may be understood as a matter of taste and perception, or it may be put in terms of the ability to escape the ideology which mass culture purveys but which we can see through. On the other hand, if we identify ourselves with the popular objects we study, we are likely to assume that our criticism or scholarly research into them is itself "popular" or free from the elitism or exclusivity which characterizes academic culture. In fact, however, the study of popular culture is always a part of a specialized professional discourse. While the specialized language of post-structuralism often draws charges of exclusivity and elitism from members of the academy who do not use this language, their own language is just as likely to be perceived as exclusive by a non-academic audience.[17]

Academic discourses about the materials called variously popular or mass culture have the effect of limiting what can be said. When the field is constituted as popular culture it is difficult for the reality of the industrial production of its materials and their role in the maintenance of ideology to be taken seriously. If the field is constituted as mass culture, it becomes hard to assert that there can be anything genuinely hopeful or empowering to be found in these products. And the pleasure which people may take in them becomes as suspect as any derived from drugs. A deconstruction of the opposition of popular culture and mass culture can help us to imagine a new conception of the field of contemporary culture. What is needed is a conception of the field which is critical but does not depict its subject as an ideological monolith. What both the "mass" and the "popular" conceptions of contemporary culture share is the assumption of similarity of tastes, fashions, and practices among most people in America, if not the world. The objects constituted by current discourses about contemporary culture are deficient in the same way that the object constituted by Arnoldian theory of culture is deficient: they fail to take into account the diversity of cultural products and experience. An adequate conception of contemporary culture must take account of this diversity. Such a conception must also involve the paradox that contemporary culture is both a site of pleasure and a site of struggle. It is a realm of competing libidinal investments and competing ideological interests. Contemporary culture is neither the people's choice nor their opiate but always both, and hence it is one of the places where the struggle for genuine democracy must be waged. Post-structuralism has helped us to understand the conditions of this struggle.

Notes

¹Thomas S. Kuhn, *The Structure of Scientific Revolutions*, 2nd ed. (Chicago: Univ. of Chicago Press, 1970), p. 4.

²Ibid., pp. 187-191.

³Of the exemplars of post-structuralist analysis of popular culture, Roland Barthes, *Mythologies*, trans. Annette Lavers from the French *Mythologies* (1957), (New York: Hill and Wang, 1972), is certainly the earliest. While *Mythologies* is usually considered a structuralist work, it shares with Barthes' entire corpus the theme of the conventionality of all forms of representation. Barthes deals with materials so mundane or disreputable that no one could accuse him of attempting to find new examples of high art: professional wrestling, a Citroën automobile, striptease, etc. For an example of Barthian criticism in America see William Kelly, "More than a Woman: Myth and Mediation in *Saturday Night Fever, JAC* 2 (Summer 1979), pp. 235-247.

⁴Ferdinand de Saussure, *Course in General Linguistics*, Trans. Wade Baskin (New York: McGraw-Hill, 1966).

⁵I am thinking of Phillip Sidney's assertion in "An Apology for Poetry" that "the poet. . .nothing affirms."

⁶Barthes, p. 142.

⁷The two most often cited of Althusser's works are: "Ideology and the Ideological State Apparatuses (Notes towards an Investigation)," *Lenin and Philosophy and Other Essays*, trans. by Ben Brewster (New York: Monthly Review Press, 1972); Althusser and Etienne Balibar, *Reading Capital*, trans. Ben Brewster (London: New Left Books, 1970). For studies of popular culture, Althusserian theory has led to a great deal of productive work on the ways in which various forms interpolate their audiences into ideology. The most influential of these studies were published in the British journal *Screen*. Laura Mulvey's "Visual Pleasure and Narrative Cinema," *Screen* 16 (Autumn 1975), pp. 6-18, rpt. in *Art After Modernism: Rethinking Representation* (Boston: David Godine, 1984), pp. 361-373, for example, argues that filmic pleasure derives from its repetition of "pre-existing patterns of fascination already at work within the individual subject" (361). The major pattern here is scopophilia, the pleasure of a controlling gaze characteristic of voyeurism and, Mulvey argues, of most Hollywood cinema. In film as in the culture in general, the one who is gazing is presumed to be male and the object of his gaze, female. Mulvey's article has become an exemplar of feminist film studies. Another important article is Stephen Heath's "On Suture," *Screen* vol. 18 no. 4 (Winter 1977/8), pp. 48-76, rpt. in Heath, *Questions of Cinema* (Bloomington: Indiana Univ. Press, 1981). For a discussion of its impact and of the theory of suture in film studies see Kaja Silverman, *The Subject of Semiotics* (New York: Oxford Univ. Press, 1983), pp. 194-236.

⁸For a particularly lucid example of this sort of interpretation, see Catherine Belsey's reading of the absence of female sexuality in Sherlock Holmes stories, *Critical Practice* (London: Methuen, 1980), pp. 109-117.

⁹See especially "The Discourse on Language," trans. Rupert Swyer, *The Archaeology of Knowledge* (New York: Random House, 1972), pp. 215-237; *Discipline and Punish: The Birth of the Prison*, trans. Alan Sheridan, (New York: Random House, 1978); *The*

Order of Things: An Archaeology of the Human Sciences, trans. Alan Sheridan (New York: Random House, 1970).

[10]Foucault, *The Order of Things,* pp. 125-162, 263-279.

[11]For a fuller explanation of this point, see David R. Shumway, "The Profession of a Discipline and the Discipline of a Profession," *North Dakota Quarterly* vol. 55 no. 3 (Summer 1987), pp. 57-61.

[12]Colin McCabe, *Tracking the Signifier: Theoretical Essays: Film, Linguistics, Literature* (Minneapolis: Univ. of Minnesota Press, 1985), p. 5.

[13]Dana Polan, "Brief Encounters: Mass Culture and the Evacuation of Sense," *Studies in Entertainment: Critical Approaches to Mass Culture,* ed. Tania Modleski (Bloomington: Indiana Univ. Press, 1986), p. 169.

[14]My thinking about "mass" and "popular" culture has profited from many of the essays in Modleski's *Studies in Entertainment.* Her introduction, pp. ix-xix, a good statement of the "mass" position, is too quick to dismiss theories that have found possible empowerment in mass produced materials. In an interview conducted by Stephen Heath and Gillian Skirrow, pp. 3-17, Raymond Williams draws somewhat different distinctions between "mass" and "popular" which may be a reflection of the differences between British and American contexts.

[15]Max Horkheimer and Theodor W. Adorno, *The Dialectic of Enlightenment* (New York: Continuum, 1982).

[16]Patrick Brantlinger, *Bread & Circuses: Theories of Mass Culture as Social Decay* (Ithaca: Cornell Univ. Press, 1983).

[17]Gerald Graff makes a similar point with regard to literary studies in "The University and the Prevention of Culture," *Criticism in the University,* ed. Graff and Reginald Gibbons (Evanston: Northwestern Univ. Press, 1985), p. 64.

Material Culture in a Popular Vein: Perspectives on Studying Artifacts of Mass Culture

Beverly Gordon

Students of popular culture have for the most part been cognizant of the important resource that objects provide for cultural interpretation. Objects, or things, are the tangible, physical expression of the people and societies that produce them, and when properly "read" or decoded, yield information and insights about those people and societies. Since we in the twentieth century live our lives amidst a dense population of material goods, it is appropriate that we turn our attention to those goods and examine what they have to say for and about us. The study of "material culture" is thus particularly germane and pivotal to the study of popular culture.

There have been a number of insightful in-depth studies of material phenomena of mass culture, including, in the last year alone, such books as Thomas Hines' *Populuxe*, a treatment of the exuberant consumer goods of the post-war era; Philip Langdon's *Orange Roofs, Golden Arches*, a consideration of the architecture and interiors of McDonald's and other fast food restaurants; and Marsh and Collett's *Driving Passion*, an examination of the meanings of Model T's, hot rods, hood ornaments, and everything else having to do with the car-as-object.[1] These studies have emerged from different quarters and from people wearing very different hats—architectural historians, psychologists, and newspaper critics are represented in this sample—but relatively few serious students of contemporary popular culture have come from the ranks of those who specifically refer to themselves as material culturists. This chapter will offer an explanation for this apparent anomaly, and will explore the particular material culture perspectives that are called for in studies of objects that operate in a mass or popular culture context.

In his seminal essay, "Material Culture Studies in America, 1876-1976," Thomas Schlereth lists the major disciplines or fields of inquiry usually included under the material culture studies umbrella (archeology, anthropology, art history, cultural geography, history of technology, social history, and folklife studies), and delineates three major historiographical configurations he feels material culture scholarship follows. These configurations consider the object or artifact: 1) as an object of art created by an artiste; 2) as primarily the result of a mental and manual process called craftsmanship; and 3) as a manifestation

170

of the economic and social status of an individual in society.[2] Schlereth's analysis helps clarify the dearth of material culture studies that focus on popular, mass-produced objects. In the first place, scholars in most of the disciplines he mentions are concerned with a time or place other than our own, or with the evolution and retention of culture and tradition over periods of time; they are unlikely by their very training and area of interest to be concerned with contemporary fads or consumer products. Secondly and even more critically, all three historiographical configurations approach objects primarily through a consideration of their *makers* or *producers*. Serious students of popular culture, on the other hand, must consider the circumstances of object production, but must also shift their primary attention to a consideration of object *users* or *consumers.*[3]

In large part because of the predispositions that Schlereth indicates, many of the important material culture methodological models developed to date have largely ignored object users or consumers. Studies with such titles as "Style as Evidence," "Workmanship as Evidence," and "Mind in Matter" focus almost exclusively on the "cultural fingerprints" left behind by object makers; discussion of chairs, silver tea sets and the like proceed with little or no attention to the people who sat in them or drank from them. A lengthy and much-touted material culture study of Virginia folk housing looks not at residents' interactions with their homes, but at the way the house structures reflect the mental constructs or unconscious thought patterns of the people who built them.[4] The single most influential and comprehensive material culture methodology, posited by E. McClung Fleming in 1974, does ask for a consideration of who the object was made for and why, and for an analysis of the uses and roles the object plays in its culture. Even Fleming's model offers few specific guidelines to how these roles might be determined, however, and its underlying premise and operating assumption is still that the object is craftsman-made and from an earlier time period.[5]

Elements of all these methodologies can and should be extrapolated and appropriated by the popular culturist, and Fleming's model in particular should be used as a starting point for analysis of popular artifacts, but other avenues of investigation must also be explored. These include *analysis of use patterns and user or consumer demographics; analysis of the presentation or marketing strategy used to sell the objects,* including a content analysis of recurring advertisements; and where applicable, *analysis of the object as a popular reference or sign for another time, place or subculture.* The latter analysis is based on the premise that much of popular culture is a kind of formulaic representation or codification of what was formerly or is elsewhere experienced on a more direct, traditional or folk culture level.

To exemplify this type of extended investigation or analysis, a particular type of contemporary, popular culture artifact, denim blue jeans and related garments manufactured by Georges Marciano under the Guess label, will be discussed. These jeans, jeans jackets, shirts and other items have recently become enormously popular (company profits have increased almost 2000% in four years and overall volume stood at $100 million in 1985)[6], and are commonly seen in every city in the United States and much of the rest of the world. The Guess line of denimwear is far from unique, but it, more than any of its competitors, has recently captured the popular imagination, and can reasonably be treated as representative of its class.

If we were to follow the structuralist, workmanship, or stylistic model of material culture analysis, we would for the most part limit our consideration to the garments themselves. We would gather a sample of the Guess products, and observe and describe their physical and stylistic characteristics. We would see a group of worn-looking cotton denim jeans, for example, with a somewhat uneven, faded appearance. We would notice that the original dark blue color is most discernible at the seams, where there is a double layer of cloth, and most bleached out at the beginning-to-be-frayed edges. Some of the jeans are ripped or have holes at the knees. We would also see cotton shirts with sleeves that appear to have been quickly cut short with a scissors, and faded denim jackets with curling, worn pocket flaps and cuffs. All the garments look as if they have been washed many times. They have even, machine stitching, triangular cloth trademark labels, and metal buttons and rivets with Guess imprints. They come in a range of graded sizes, and are predominantly cut so as to be form-fitting or body-hugging, with no excess cloth or added trim or decoration.

Based on these observations we would draw a number of conclusions. We would determine that these are commercially manufactured, mass-produced garments. Because the denim fabric is strong and reinforced with sturdy metal buttons and rivets, because there is no surplus cloth that would impede movement, and because there is no decorative excess, we might surmise that they were intended to be used for hard work, and had possibly been manufactured for and marketed to people who were engaged in physical labor. If we had happened upon the garments with no contextual information—if we found them some years hence among piles of sheets in an old trunk, perhaps, or preserved in an old landfill—we would notice the frayed edges, the much-worn fabric and the ripped knees, and would most likely conclude that they had been used for years, and had been subjected to hard wear, including much bending, stooping, and kneeling. These conjectures would seem to further corroborate the hypothesis that the garments were used for hard physical work.

These hypotheses would, of course, be quite wrong. The physical "evidence" of the objects is in and of itself misleading, for the garments were painstakingly subjected to a brutal laundering treatment for ten to twelve hours; they were purposely aged, frayed, bleached and torn before they were ever sent to market.[7] The garments were designed to imply hard use, in other words, but might not have ever been used at all. At the time we found them, they might have been quite new.

Over 150 Guess styles have come out in each of the last few seasons, and though jeans make up the bulk of the line, overalls, jackets, and minidresses are also popular. Guess customers are largely female, young, and upwardly mobile. The range of products includes styles for men, women and children, but junior sizes account for seventy percent of sales, and teenagers are, according to major retailers of the product, the "mainstay" customers.[8]

The Marciano brothers, who run the Guess company as a family business, are well aware of their customer base and what it wants. They consciously determined that their line should look rugged, comfortable, and worn, for they intuited that it would appeal to their particular target population. Heavy laundering and breaking-in treatments are not so much reflections of their (the manufacturer/designer's) unconscious patterns of thought or of the inherent capabilities of the tools (machines) of their craft as they are responses to the unconscious longings and whims of their market.

The worn, hard-working image is sold to these young, leisured consumers through a carefully contrived advertising campaign and marketing environment. Advertisements are largely confined to upscale magazines. Full-page or double-page black and white "vignettes" appear regularly in fashion-oriented publications such as *Harper's Bazaar, Glamour, Vogue, Gentleman's Quarterly,* and *Elle,* and in other glossy magazines that include fashion features, such as *Seventeen* and *Esquire.* The 1986 budget for magazine advertising was fourteen million dollars, and the figure continues to accelerate rapidly.[9]

The advertisements all consist of rather mysterious images that have a similar mood or "feel" (all are credited to photographer Wayne Maser and are conceptualized and controlled by Paul Marciano), and a consistent underlying message comes through, though the specific images are keyed to a certain extent to the target audiences of the respective magazines. The vignettes usually include two or more characters who wear the Guess clothing and reflect the readers they are pegged to. The fall 1986 spread in *Esquire,* for example, features two men in a duck hunting scene; the *Seventeen* vignette features pubescent girls.

The images are ambiguous and intriguing, and raise more questions than they answer. In many, the characters face completely away from the camera or have their faces totally or partially obscured by unkempt long blond hair, battered hats, or leather-gloved hands. Where the faces are visible, their expressions are indecipherable: dreamy or petulant, perhaps, or something else, something that cannot be quite articulated. The backgrounds are also obscure, or are deliberately evocative of someplace rugged (a truck stop, a rodeo, a ranch) or exotic. The garments are not specifically stressed; on the contrary, they too are sometimes obscured, and are made to seem so much a part of the characters that they are simply an extension of them. The viewer is led to feel that the characters could take the clothing off and it would still hold their shape, their feel, and their smell. In many of the images, in fact, the clothing is not completely on: buttons are open, belts are unbuckled and left dangling, and jackets are draped over the shoulder. Cuffs are always rolled up rather than buttoned or fastened. All the images imply a sense of familiarity, comfort, self confidence, and a kind of easy, natural sexuality.

Sexuality or sensuality is sometimes explicit—there are glimpses of lacy, tantalizing underwear under the unbuttoned denim jackets in some of the spreads in women's fashion magazines—but in all cases, bodies are positioned suggestively, leaning, stretching or slouching with studied ease. "Our ads are definitely sensual," says Paul Marciano. "The look is dramatic and voluptuous."[10] The voluptuousness is also comfortable and natural, however, and implies ease and self assurance.

The confident but enigmatic image is also part of the marketing environment at the company-controlled Guess boutiques housed in large department stores in California and elsewhere. The advertisement photographs are blown up to wall-size murals that dominate the room, and the mood they create spreads to everything and everyone who enters the space. The rugged image is echoed in natural wood shelving units and wall panels in the boutiques, and in the sheer preponderance of the denim stock.

The $100 million sales figure clearly indicates the Guess product image and marketing formula is striking a responsive chord. What is it about these aged-looking garments and the insouciant characters shown to be wearing them that has such appeal? Why do hundreds of thousands of young girls flock to stores and exchange up to $50 for an already old-looking, even ripped item of clothing? The obvious hypothesis is that the young people are seeking the very easy naturalness and confidence the Guess characters seem to convey. They are at a time in their lives that is full of uncertainty and new and rather frightening endeavors, and the garments represent familiarity and sureness. The young people are also trying to come to terms with their own sexuality and sense of self, and are attracted to the free, comfortable sensuality that Guess epitomizes. The very ambiguity of the advertising vignettes is helpful in this regard, for the stories can be interpreted according to individual fantasies and wishes. The faces in the vignettes are probably obscured for just this reason; potential customers can easily project themselves and put their own faces into the scene and onto the characters.

The researcher of popular material culture might at this point conduct actual field or market research to test interpretive hypotheses of this kind. Guess customers could be asked to respond to questions about the advertisements ("What do you think is the relationship between the people pictured here?" "Select from the following list the adjectives you feel best characterize the people in this illustration," etc.) and about the garments themselves. Since this kind of study or survey can be carefully designed and executed, it lends itself to sophisticated statistical analysis, and to verifiable conclusions. Tools and methodologies that have been developed in the fields of market research and consumer behavior can be adopted or adapted. The VALS system of psychographic classification developed by the Stamford Research Institute[11] could for example be applied to consumer profiles.

The final level of analysis suggested here is once again hypothetical or conjectural, but is based on a careful "reading" of both the actual object and the marketing or sales strategy through which it is presented to the consumer. It is akin to the methodological operation Fleming calls "interpretation," but is in a sense a reversal of that operation. Fleming's interpretation focuses on the meaning and significance of the artifact in relation to our contemporary culture. It follows or is complementary to another operation, "cultural analysis," which focuses on the relationship between the artifact and its own culture.[12] Since popular culturists are concerned primarily with current-day rather than historic artifacts (Guess jeans certainly fall in this category; the whole product line has existed for less than a decade), they must look to the past rather than the present for comparisons. As stated above, I contend that much of popular, mass, or consumer culture is a formulaic representation or evocation of a more personal, "traditional" culture—of a culture based, in fact, on the producer rather than the consumer, or on the participant rather than the observer. The Disneyland version of Main Street, U.S.A. is based, however romantically, on a real prototype of the past, a place where everything and everyone was familiar. The Davy Crockett coonskin cap sold in Disney's Frontierland is an iconic representation of a functional garment once actually worn in the backwoods of Appalachia. Other popular artifacts, such as a Holly Hobby or Sunbonnet Sue doll dressed in calico, or a miniaturized rubber tomahawk also stand for or evoke indigenous or folk cultures of other, earlier times and places. In all these cases, the consumer or popular-level object serves as a reminder (or in the semiotic sense, a sign) of those times and their quintessential experience.

If we return to the artificially aged and battered Guess-brand jeans, what can we say is the indigenous, "folk" prototype they evoke or represent? What is the essence of the past that this apparel symbolizes or signifies on a popular level? My conclusion, based on the reading of the objects, the demographic profile of the consumers, and the strategy by which they are marketed, is that the Guess line evokes both the rapidly fading reality of day-to-day physical labor (particularly in an outdoor setting) and the counterculture experience of the 1960's and early 1970's. The Guess characters, as stated, are uniformly young, free, strong, and confidently sexual. Like the youth movement or counterculture prototypes of the past, they have wild, unruly long hair (it is portrayed more in the style of the late 1960's than the 1980's), and appear to eschew all make-up and other accoutrements of the tailored, establishment culture. They are at ease on the land or the earth, and are comfortable with "big" men who handle large animals or machines. At the same time, they embody softness, dreaminess and sensitivity.

The young people who are the primary purchasers of these garments are not likely to work at rodeos or truck stops—they are not likely to physically work at all—and they have not had these counterculture experiences; they have probably not yet even been far from home. They have not "gone back to the land," and in an age fraught with AIDS and cynicism about relationships, they have not had much experience with an easy sexuality. They cannot have lived or experienced more than they have, but they can step into clothing that makes them feel as if they have. These garments have been "through it;" *they* have lived and seen it all, and they hold the promise of experience and comfort. The garments, the material goods that are an integral part of consumer culture, are an embodiment of a desired experience. On a symbolic level, they serve as signs or references to a fantasized reality and to an imagined time or place where experience is direct, personal and exciting.

Artifacts or objects that are as pervasive and ubiquitous as the denim blue jean have, in sum, a great deal to say about our culture. Some of this silent, non-verbal message is encoded in the objects themselves, but the message can only be completely and correctly understood in the context of the consumer landscape of which it is a part. Artifacts of popular culture must be analyzed in a unique and multifaceted manner, as both the producer and consumer must be considered simultaneously. Material culture perspectives and methodologies must be combined with perspectives and methodologies borrowed from marketing and consumer research, and with iconographic content analysis of marketing strategies. Because they function on a symbolic as well as an actual level, popular artifacts must also be compared to similar prototypes that exist in other cultural contexts, and interpreted as a reflection of those prototypes. Such multifaceted analysis is demanding and complex, but well worth the effort. Contemporary culture is often characterized by its plethora of consumer goods, and it stands to reason that the culture can be understood in part through those goods. I hope this essay will pave the way for further discussion about this far-reaching and important topic.

Notes

[1]Philip Langdon, *Orange Roofs, Golden Arches: The Architecture of America's Chain Restaurants* (New York: Knopf, 1986); Thomas Hine, *Populuxe* (New York: Knopf, 1986); Peter Marsh and Peter Collett, *Driving Passion: The Psychology of the Car* (Boston: Faber and Faber, 1986).

[2]Thomas Schlereth, "Material Culture Studies in America, 1876-1976," in *Material Culture Studies in America*, Thomas Schlereth, ed. (Nashville: American Association of State and Local History, 1982) p. 4, p. 39.

[3]This idea has been previously expressed in another context by R. Serge Denisoff in a critique of *auteur*-oriented analysis of popular literature and mass media. See "Content Analysis: The Achilles Heel of Popular Culture?" in *Journal of Popular Culture* 14:2 (Fall 1975), pp. 456-460.

[4]Jules David Prown, "Style as Evidence," *Winterthur Portfolio* 15:3 (Fall 1980), pp. 197-210; and "Mind in Matter: An Introduction to Material Culture Theory and Method," *Winterthur Portfolio* 17:1 (Spring 1982), pp. 1-19; Philip D. Zimmerman, "Workmanship as Evidence: A Model for Object Study," *Winterthur Portfolio* 16:4 (Winter 1981), pp. 283-307; Henry H. Glassie, *Folk Housing in Middle Virginia: A Structural Analysis of Historic Artifacts* (Knoxville: University of Tennessee Press, 1975).

[5]E. McClung Fleming, "Artifact Study: A Proposed Model," *Winterthur Portfolio* 9:2 (June 1974), pp. 153-173. The article is also reprinted in an abridged form in Schlereth, *Material Culture Studies in America*, pp. 162-173.

[6]Steve Ginsburg, "Despite a Feud, Marcianos Make Guesswork Pay," *Woman's Wear Daily*, November 25, 1986, p. 4.

[7]Ginsburg, p. 5.

[8]Ginsburg, p. 4.

[9]Ginsburg, p. 4.

[10]Ginsburg, p. 5.

[11]See Arnold Mitchell, *The Nine American Lifestyles: Who We Are and Where We Are Going* (New York: Macmillan, 1983).

[12]Fleming, pp. 154, 157-158.

Where Architecture
and
Popular Culture Diverge

Dennis Alan Mann

Introduction

All physical forms have two fundamental characteristics. They have objective characteristics—that is, characteristics which describe the structure or form of the object; and they have subjective characteristics—that is, characteristics that are "seen" by the perceiving human being. The objective characteristics or the formal structures are brought about by an intentional process called *composition*. Composition is simply a putting together of the discrete pieces or elements in order to create a higher order whole. This process originates with the designer who, in the case of this essay, is the architect. Methods for composing form are drawn from a rich repertoire whose basis exists in history but whose techniques are constantly growing. Subjective characteristics, on the other hand, resonate between the object and the perceiving human being. What one person sees in an object and what another person sees in the same object are more than likely to be different. Subjective characteristics, or *meaning* as it is often called, can be highly personal or they can be a broadly based result of a cultural consensus. As we know, any object or event can have one meaning for one person and an entirely different meaning for someone else.

Formal structure or syntax is to a large extent knowable. Moreover, it is also learnable. Syntax can be discovered by studying existing structures or by inventing systems for the generation of new structures. The syntax of a structure never changes, although it is conceivable that a complex of syntactical structures can be uncovered within the same form. Generally speaking, forms remain constant as do the syntactical structures that have generated them. Meaning or, more accurately, meanings are constantly changing. The same form undergoes a myriad of meaning changes and interpretations during the course of its lifetime. It is precisely at the juncture between form and meaning, between that which the architect composes and that which the perceiver interprets, that the theme for this paper exists. For it is at this juncture that the paradigms of architecture and the paradigms of popular culture diverge.

177

The paradigms of architecture surround the idea that the only knowledge that architecture can claim to belong *solely* to architecture is that knowledge which is "about composition." The basis for this knowledge about composition lies in the history of the development of architecture as a discipline independent of other disciplines, one that has a knowledge which is singularly unique and nongeneralizable. The paradigms of popular culture, on the other hand, demand equal access to all knowledge. With Do-It-Yourself manuals, Everyman is a builder; with home computers, Everyman is a writer and publisher; and with Pop-psychology, Everyman is his own analyst. There are no longer any secrets. Secrets are suspect; secrets are subversive; secrets are anti-democratic. Popular-culture paradigms insist that all knowledge should be made public and accessible. Here, then, lies the dilemma. While the basis of architecture lies in the knowledge of architecture—the knowledge of formal composition—the basis of culture lies in shared and transmitted patterns of human belief—the knowledge of meaning and interpretation. These two factors are what scientists would call *independent variables*.

In this essay I will explore the paradigms of architecture, especially those "secrets of composition" which are maintained by the literature of architecture and by the primary methodology for teaching designing—the studio. I will suggest that the paradigms of architecture, notwithstanding its various idiosyncratic and individualistic theories, are endemic to the traditions of architecture, to the very act of composing itself. This factor, coupled with the architect's privileged access to those who make decisions about building, the wealthy and the powerful, has given them free rein to compose according to this specialized knowledge—that of composition. In contrast, the forces of democratization work counter to privileged knowledge and ultimate authority. In a democratic and pluralistic society, beauty *is* in the eye of the beholder; and meaning is constructed by each person. All a reader need do is peruse the editorial pages of any newspaper when a controversial work of art has been made public to grasp this point. Given this distinction, one might easily conclude that architecture and popular culture will slip by one another like two ships navigating through the fog shrouded dawn.

Object/Content or Form/Meaning

All architects eventually must address the process of composition since every object that we construct must be composed. In *The Secrets of Ancient Geometry*, author Tones Brunes has connected the founding of the craft of architecture with religious ceremonies and with the uses of occult geometry.[1] For thousands of years geometry was seen as a picture of the universe and it was believed to be a manifestation of the all-knowing, all-powerful Creator. The logic of those early times advanced the theory that if all things that man constructed were based on the same laws of geometry that man had discovered in natural forms, forms that were originally designed by the one Creator, then these forms, too, would be perfect. For thousands of years, it was believed that only one force could create and only that force could be called the Creator. Mortals merely realized the Creator's will. Ancient geometry, as Brunes has shown, was employed by architects at least since the constructions of early Egypt. The secrets of ancient geometry that were used then were embedded in the construction of early Temples and passed on from one Temple culture to the next Temple culture as trade secrets. In one form or another (Figure 1), these secrets survived into Medieval times where they formed the basis for the development and maintenance of small societies of guilds. These secrets were the basis of the science, (or scientia), of building and formed a rational theory of architecture based on geometry. These theories of composition are similar to what would be called industrial secrets today. Although clothed in an esoteric language, they are merely the trade secrets, techniques, and collected-over- time intuitive knowledge that is passed from master to apprentice. But knowledge is power. Therefore, by holding on to and protecting this knowledge architects were able to maintain a superiority in the building crafts over others who lacked the trade secrets.

The architect was, in a manner, the man in the middle. That is, he existed between these secrets and those whom the secrets would benefit: the Monarchy, the Church, or the Burgher. This combination of powers, both the internal powers of the knowledge of composition and the external powers of having made strong political connections, gave the architect an authority which on the one hand was mysterious, magical and mythical and on the other hand was political and pragmatic. If knowledge is power and if that knowledge can be kept as a trade secret from the powerful and from the public, then the architect, like the witch doctor and the alchemist, the priest and the scientist, had carved out a place for himself as a specialist within the structure of society. As long as he could protect that knowledge *and* maintain the respect and awe of those in power, then he alone would be commissioned to build the most important and culturally significant buildings—the Temples and Cathedrals; the Palaces and their Gardens; the Capital Cities; the Ramparts and the City Walls; the City of the Dead; and, later, the City Halls and Courthouses; the Universities, Music Halls, and the Palaces of Commerce.

Still there is the fundamental question of object composition versus meaning construction. Eventually all architects must develop a strategy for addressing this question. One such strategy was proposed by Umberto Eco as a result of his research in semiotics.[2] In this research into semiotics as it is applied to architecture, Eco studied the relationships between form and meaning. Meaning, he determined, has two functions. Its primary function, or denoted meaning as he called it, is its utilitarian and conventional usage. For instance, the traditional American single-family house denotes habitation. The secondary function, or the connoted meaning, is ideological and symbolic. The same house in the example above connotes family, status, and relative wealth.

But over time, as Eco continues to point out, there occurs a disassociation between form and meaning. Often not only does the primary function of a form change but also its secondary functions change as well. Moreover, there is seldom a cause-and-effect relationship between one or the other changing. The primary function might vary, but the secondary function could remain constant. For example, when an old manor is turned into an exclusive restaurant,

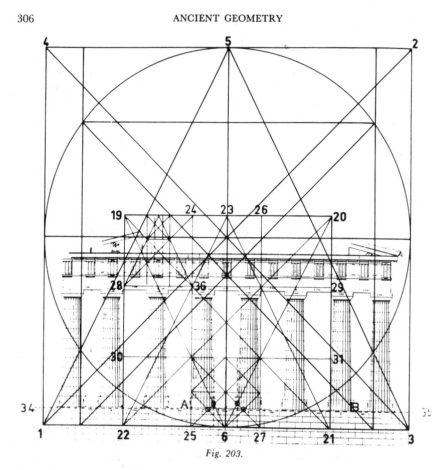

Fig. 203.

Figure 1 Elevation of the Parthenon
Source: *The Secrets of Ancient Geometry and its Use.*
Tones Brunes, p. 306.

the primary function has been altered; but the status and wealth that were attached to it remain. This realization caused Eco to come to the conclusion that over the life span of a building, its meanings might shift dramatically. This then leads Eco to recommend an appropriate design strategy. He suggests that the architect should ". . .design for variable primary function and 'open' secondary function."[3] But this strategy makes little sense on two counts.

First, to design for a variable primary function is to design for no function at all; and to design for open secondary functions suggests that the building has no rhetorical garb, so to speak. Second, it is interesting to note that none of the buildings that we regard with reverence, like the Taj Mahal, Hagia Sophia, the Paris Opera House or any of the Pre-Hispanic cities in Central America, was designed with variable primary function and open secondary functions.

While Eco's strategy for design seems off the mark, his recognition of the lack of a consistent relationship between form and meaning is not. That the relationship is volatile should be an accepted fact. That architects proceed primarily from formal or syntactical considerations while everyone else like critics, historians, and ordinary people make interpretations should also be self-evident. Composing is an immediate process that is bound to a time and a place. Interpretation is not. Interpretation and reinterpretations constantly occur, sometimes even after the building itself has disappeared and all that remains are accountings of the building, descriptions that might be written or visual. How often have interpretations been made of Solomon's Temple or the Globe Theatre or of Pliny's Laurentian Villa? Although form may carry with it a set of associations that exist in the present, there are no guarantees that any single meaning will remain attached to a form for all time.

But if we turn our attention to the history of formal development and the history of interpretations, and in the course of this survey we are especially alert for technological advancements or for major cultural or social shifts, we might learn that in most every case *form preceded interpretation*. That is, if we do not view the world through a "rear-view mirror," as Marshall McLuhan often accused us of doing, then we would realize that for whatever the reasons, formal changes happened prior to the fixing of meaning.

Frits Staal has pointed out that there are other fields where this same phenomenon occurs. In "The Search for Meaning: Mathematics, Music and Ritual"[4] Staal has investigated the hypothesis of "form as abstract and meaning as attached and variable" from a number of different perspectives. Although he discusses mathematics and music as well as ritual, ritual is most pertinent here since ritual, like architecture, is a direct manifestation of culture and is closely bound to social actions. In his extensive research, Staal has concentrated on uncovering the relationship between form and meaning in Vedic ritual. Most scholars who had studied ritual in the past had concluded that ritual was the symbolic transformation of beliefs, myths, ideas, ethics, and historical experiences. Since most rituals were originally connected to religion and since belief is the core of religion, these scholars felt that belief held primacy over the form of ritual.[5] And since ritual is embedded in culture, most anthropologists who studied ritual believed that it had clear meanings which were transmitted from generation to generation with little or no change. But few anthropologists were able to study the same ritual over a long period of time. Therefore, it was natural to accept the fact that a fixed relationship between ritual form and ritual belief existed. Asian civilizations, Asian rituals, and particularly Vedic rituals, because they have such an extensive history, can be studied not only from a symbolic perspective (meaning) but also from a syntactic perspective (form and composition). In his study of Vedic ritual, Staal discovered that while the form of the ritual remained the same, the meaning had changed over the centuries. In addition, he observed that when rituals are taught or transmitted from generation to generation, exclusive attention is paid to teaching the structure of the ritual while the meaning of the ritual or the meaning of its component ceremonial elements is seldom mentioned.[6] Although it could be assumed that the process of transmitting meaning is tacit, as it turns out Staal's research shows that when Vedic ritual meaning is studied over a long period of time, the same ritual form has had different meanings.

One of Staal's conclusions is so significant it is worth quoting in full.

All the evidence we have considered points clearly in only one direction: ritual and music have no meaning or content, and can be provided accordingly with any number of different meanings or interpretations. Suum cuique: to everyone his thing. The preponderant and enduring characteristics of music and ritual are that they consist of formal structures of sounds and acts, respectively, that can be studied most effectively and fruitfully by adopting a syntactic approach.[7]

That Staal also analyzes music and comes to the same conclusion is extremely significant; for while music may contain no meaning at all, it, like architecture, is also composed. And like architecture, interpretations of music are constantly being made.

As Eco had noted above, during the life of any object it is subject to a variety of readings regarding both its primary function and its secondary function. Juan Pablo Bonta reached a similar conclusion vis-a-vis meaning in his text analysis of the Barcelona Pavilion.[8] In this study, he described the process of interpretation by those who have constructed written texts of the pavilion. He summarized this process as consisting of a series of stages which over the life of all the writings include: (1) initial blindness; (2) precanonical responses; (3) canonical interpretation; (4) canon formation; (5) authoritative interpretation; (6) classification, followed by a (7) long period of silence before (8) reinterpretations begin to surface. That is, after a building is first constructed, little or no attention is paid to it by the press, by critics or by historians. In time the first writings share very few common positions. Slowly, though, there begins to emerge a common thread of interpretation until nearly all writers are interpreting the building in the same way. Finally, writers lose interest and no new literature appears. In the end, Bonta arrives at a conclusion similar to Eco and Staal. He says:

Attributing meaning to a work of architecture or art has been considered throughout this study as an operation solely performed by the critic. Designers were seen as playing a rather modest role in the process of meaning formation. *They create objects,* (italics by this author) but it is up to the interpreters to classify them—to read them—one way or the other.[9]

But here is where Bonta's conclusion diverges from that of Eco's and Staal's. Bonta is interested in the process of interpretation and meaning generation, not in the process of composition. Thus, he concludes that "the repercussion of a building would depend more on how it was interpreted than on how it was designed."[10] Here again we find the distinction made between the issues of culture, i.e. meaning, and the issues of architecture, i.e. composition.

To recapitulate: Using semiotics as a basis, Eco has shown that there is a dynamic relationship between form and meaning. Text analysis studies by Bonta substantiate this relationship. Studies of Vedic ritual by Staal indicate an independent relationship between the form of a ritual and the meaning of a ritual. Staal's conclusion, that ritual can be served most fruitfully by adopting a syntactic approach, is a significant milepost and will serve as the thesis for this essay.

Ritual and Architecture

Although ritual and architecture differ[11] in many aspects, they do share two important characteristics: first, both lack a fixed connection between form and meaning; and second, both ritual and architecture can be studied by taking a purely syntactic approach. Staal has studied ritual in a syntactic and abstract manner. Like the rules of grammar in language, the elements of ritual exist in fixed and knowable patterns. As Noam Chomsky has demonstrated about grammar, "Colorful green ideas sleep furiously" is *well formed* grammatically but makes no common sense from the standpoint of meaning; likewise for rituals. One of the major characteristics of a ritual is its strict adherence to a given structure. Following this structure is believed to be *intrinsically* worthwhile. Therefore, to understand ritual a full knowledge of the structure of its form is mandatory.

A simple example, common to Western religious ritual is illustrative. The sermon is a critically placed ritual element in many Judeo-Christian services. It exists at a critical point within the entire ceremony, delivering specific ethical, moral or scriptural interpretations aimed at making a distinct connection between a prescribed system of belief and everyday life. If the sermon were to be given at the beginning of the service, it would still make semantic sense but make little sense as part of a sequence of formal ritual actions which set it in place. Likewise, if placed at the end of the service, the sermon would lose its critical position of balance and thus would not be cemented into the minds and hearts of the congregation by the concluding ritual elements. The sermon not only has an important place within the service but, in a sense, it has been designed to occupy a very particular space.

The idea of a specific ritual element designed into a particular pattern of elements within an overall ritual structure helps to make the entire ritual knowable to all who participate in it. We come to understand the structure of our environment in a similar manner. Space schemata are slowly constructed over time, but for the perceiving human being, similar patterns are recognizable. Landmarks, edges, districts, paths, and nodes are the elements that we use in constructing our space schemata. Recognizing these patterns at any scale helps us to survive in the environment, to find our way about, and ultimately to make the environment knowable. Note that I have said "helps"; I do not mean to imply that it makes the environment fully understandable.

To return then to the hub of the argument would suggest that the trouble with understanding the results of the process of design or with designing itself might be similar to the criticism that Staal makes of current studies of ritual. The results of the design process, call them compositions, have seldom been subjected to the same rigorous and systematic syntactical analyses as Staal's work with Vedic ritual. Critics and historians are continually integrating formal and interpretive viewpoints, to the degree that the reader primarily receives a polemical position. Moreover, students of architecture rarely are given the opportunity to *study* buildings through a series of carefully constructed exercises aimed at unravelling their formal structure and then comparing their results to previously established lexicons. But more on this point later.

The Architecture Studio

There is, in addition, the issue of style. Style as a semantic system is most often the single item that is most easily grasped by students and by practitioners as well. At least from a superficial or fashionable standpoint, students of architecture are very capable of quickly learning to create formal cliches without examining the syntactic aspects of the work that they are copying. Most of this "learning" goes on in the architectural studio, the center of the curriculum and the center of life in most architectural schools. Thomas A. Dutton, an architecture teacher at Miami University, begins his study of the architecture studio by saying: "There is no doubt the design studio occupies the premier position in most architectural programs across the nation. Evidenced by the commitment and intensity given to it by students and professors, the tendency to place other coursework at the curriculum's margin and its potential for integrating skills, values, and architectural literacy, the design studio has become the 'heart and head of architectural education'...."[12] Architecture students are committed to a minimum of nine classroom hours a week in the studio. Studio work outside of these nine hours normally requires at least another eighteen hours. Normally students spend more time on studio projects than all their other requirements combined. No wonder then that an emphasis on form development continues into the present day. And it is primarily in the studio where this emphasis takes place. Although the secrets of ancient geometry are no longer the focus of the studio, there is an implicit curriculum. And that curriculum is about composition.

How, then, is it possible to understand design and composition and their relationship to meaning without the burden of the interpretation of style or currently fashionable trends? Staal's research into ritual again provides guidance. As a heuristic device, I have substituted "architecture" for "ritual" in order to transform his three recommendations into pertinent guidelines for architecture. First, we should detach the study of architecture from the area that we have placed it: in the realm of culture and society. Second, we must study architecture in much greater depth than is normally required of students of architecture, especially focusing on the design studio. And third, we should conceive of architecture in more abstract and syntactic terms. Let us examine each point.

Three Recommendations

Detaching the study of architecture from culture sounds heretical in a series of essays devoted to popular culture. But this criticism misses the point. The opening lecture to students in my second-year Theory of Architecture class is entitled "To Know Architecture You Must Know Culture." The central theme of this lecture is that culture is an underlying, stable structure and a dominant order. Architecture is a part of culture and exists within its boundaries. Culture provides frames of interpretation for the diverse forms of architecture that are constructed within it. The purpose of detaching the study of architecture from the particular demands of culture is that it forces us to look straight into the eyes of architecture itself. This artificial division also requires that we develop a methodology of *architectural* analysis which concentrates on the object itself. Cultural forces, by their very complexity and specificity, belong to a deep structure which is out of the reach and control of the architect. Moreover, such a concern for cultural forces draws the architect's attention away from the demands of composition and towards a reading of or interpretation of the object based on some one or some other understanding of culture. Clifford Geertz has shown that there are many "orders of interpretation," none of which are true in and of themselves.[13] For instance, Chester Liebs notes the low, flat mansard roofs (Figure. 2) that were added to many of the drive-ins built during the '60s and '70s sent the message: "We're for the environment; we don't pollute; we fit in; buy here."[14] Of course, this is the interpretation that Liebs makes; but is it an authoritative one? There surely must be other interpretations which are just as plausible. And how will those mansard roofs be interpreted in the future when pollution or context are not important design issues? Neither architectural students, architectural faculty, nor practicing architects are equipped to make such interpretations, now or in the future. And even if they were, I doubt if that ability would do them much good. As I have pointed out earlier, interpretations are volatile. This is not meant to disaffirm the architect's responsibility for understanding the current field of interpretations but how can he predict future interpretations? But form, like the structure of ritual, always remains relatively constant. When form does change, it is altered intentionally by somebody and for some expressed purpose. If there

Figure 2 Noble Roman's Pizza, Cincinnati, Ohio.

is a language of architecture, then it exists within the common realm of syntax rather than the wide field of meaning.

At an elemental level, the terms *axis, center, and domain* used by Christian Norberg-Schulz touch on this common language.[15] Each of these elements transcends culture; each is manifest in all cultures at many scales; each can be found in vernacular, popular or monumental architecture. When made abstract, *axis* becomes line; *center* becomes point; and *domain* becomes area. When tied to a cultural language, *axis* is transformed into street; *center* is transformed into square or piazza; and *domain* becomes a neighborhood or village. As street, piazza or village, they now are permitted to gather the cultural baggage that rightfully belongs to them. At this stage as architects we must accept this baggage. In other words, it is at the point of transformation that they take on meaning. As axis, center and domain, they are syntactic elements that belong to architecture alone.

Two other examples which illustrate the value of detaching architecture from culture are Klaus Herdeg's study of *Formal Structure in Indian Architecture*[16] (Figure. 3) and Witold Rybczynski's *How the Other Half Builds.*[17] Herdeg's work examines the components of the formal structure of monumental and historical Indian architecture, while Rybczynski has set about to study the physical structure of informal housing in the vernacular and popular architecture of the same country. Both studies suspend judgment and focus on what is there: the objects themselves, the spaces that the objects define, and the structure of the relationships between objects and space. One comment of Herdeg's as a result of his study of Surkhej, a pleasure, religious and mortuary complex near Ahmedabad, is worth noting. To quote:

Proportions:
The layout of the entire complex was generated by a system of proportions and axes which is based on a square whose sides have length 3a, and a rectangle whose sides are related according to the ratio of a/b equals 21/13.[18]

This is a language which is understandable but abstract enough that it could apply to any building constructed at any time and in any place. Like Tones Brunes, an architect can study the compositional order that lies behind the Temple of Ceres, the Theseum, the Temple of Poseidon or the Parthenon and come to the same conclusions: that ancient geometric principles were followed religiously by those who were charged with the building task. By detaching the study of architecture from culture, we clear the air, so to speak, and discover the elements over which architects have complete control.

Second, we must learn to study architecture in greater depth. This seems rather obvious on the surface. But there are only a handful of good sources available to students who wish to examine the theories of composition that underlie the design of buildings. Some few books scratch the surface. Francis D.K. Ching's *Architecture: Form, Space, & Order*[19] is on the right track. The book itself is organized into chapters titled: Primary Elements, Form, Form & Space, Organizations, Circulation, Proportion and Scale and Principles. The chapter on Principles has the subheadings: Ordering Principles, Axis, Symmetry,

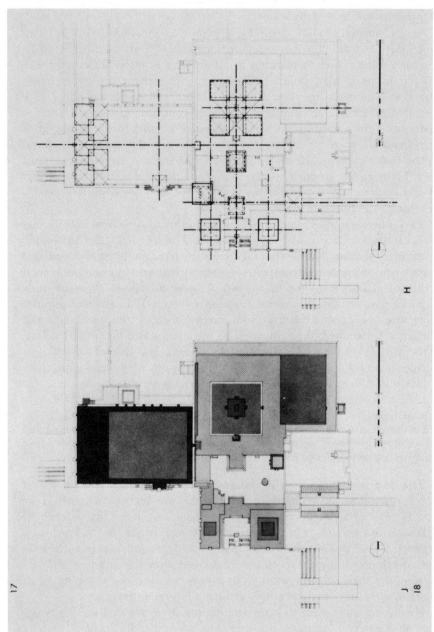

Figure 3 Syntactic studies of the plan of Surkhej
Source: *Formal Structure in Indian Architecture*

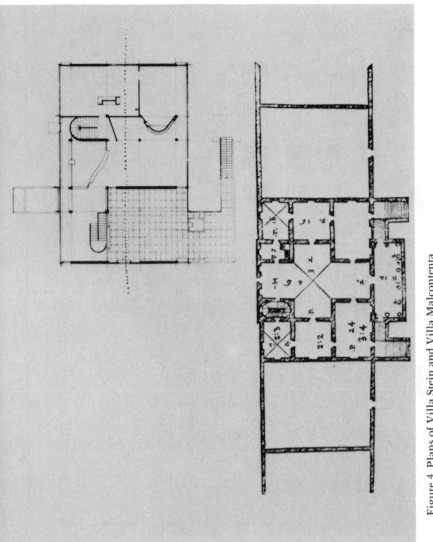

Figure 4 Plans of Villa Stein and Villa Malcontenta
Source: *The Mathematics of the Ideal Villa.*
Colin Rowe, p. 21.

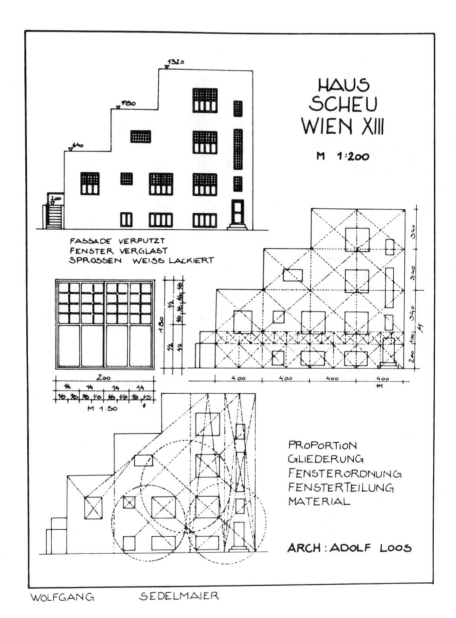

Figure 5 Syntactic study of elevation of Haus Scheu Wien XIII
Architect, Adolf Loos; Study by Wolfgang Sedelmaier
Source: *Elements of Architecture.*
Rob Krier, p. 59.

Hierarchy, Datum, Rhythm & Repetition, and Transformation. Ching's entire book of 385 pages is devoted to exploring the syntactic elements of architecture. Ching does not dismiss meaning though, for on the last page he recognizes that architecture has "...associative values and symbolic content that is subject to personal and cultural interpretation and can change with time."[20] But Ching's book is sophomoric in its depth and development; fine for beginning students but too pictorial and not analytical enough. Blaser's *Drawings of Great Buildings*[21] and Stierlin's *Encyclopedia of World Architecture*[22] only provide the raw material and not enough of it in any depth to be usefully decomposed.

Closer to the second point is Colin Rowe's essay entitled "The Mathematics of the Ideal Villa."[23] Although this essay is purely conjectural, Rowe's studies of the Villa Stein in Garches, France, by the architect Le Corbusier, built during the early stages of the Modern Movement, and the Villa Foscari in Malcontenta di Mira in northern Italy by the architect Palladio, built towards the end of the Renaissance, reveal a world beyond the material surface of both buildings. Rowe chooses these two buildings (Figure. 4) because they are both single blocks; they are similar in volume "each measuring 8 units in length, by 5 1/2 in breadth, by 5 in height." He continues, "Then, further to this, there is a comparable bay structure to be observed. Each house exhibits an alternating rhythm of double and single spatial intervals;...."[24] The entire essay unfolds these two buildings as if one were peeling layers away from a onion, each layer revealing only what is visible. Or in other words, focusing on the structure of the object and, I might add, in a great degree of detail. In this essay Rowe is not interested in references outside of the buildings themselves. Rowe's work further suggests that what is needed is a morphological branch of architectural studies which suspends judgment and focuses on the object itself. Morphological studies are analytical and concentrate on the form and structure of an object without regard to the object's function or meaning. They are not about designing but provide the building blocks for design (Figure. 5). *They make design possible.* This kind of knowledge made up the secrets of ancient geometry which were once the common knowledge of those entrusted with building. This is what the hidden agenda is in the design studios of most architectural schools. While Staal's exhaustive study, *Agni—The Vedic Ritual of the Fire Altar,*[25] encompasses two fully illustrated and completely diagrammed volumes explaining in the finest detail the structure of this ritual, there are no such comparable works in architecture.

Third, we should conceive of architecture in more abstract and syntactic terms. This recommendation again sounds simple on the surface but is complex below the surface. For instance, as I sit in my office composing this piece, I look up from my work to the open door beyond. Near the bottom of the door is a 15" by 24" ventilation grille painted red to match the door. The door is connected to a black steel frame by three hinges. At the line on the floor where the door closes are 8" by 8" vinyl tiles which change from a black marbleized pattern to a grey marbleized pattern at the doorline. Profound? Remarkable? Ordinary? Hardly so! In and of itself that detail has no meaning. It is abstract, one small piece in a large, abstract world of similar pieces. Alone, it is untranslatable. They are just sitting there being a red door, hinged to a black frame, swinging over some multicolored tile patterns. They are nonrepresentational objects which, as I have explained earlier, are given a variety of meanings over time by those who bring meanings to the occasion. The architect may have meant the red color to signify the door of architectural faculty members in order to distinguish it from the blue door of interior design faculty members and, in addition, make an association to the red square found on the bottom of Frank Lloyd Wright drawings and the dominance of red as a primary color in much modern movement art and architecture. The change in the floor color could have signified a change from a circulation space to an office space, using the color change to signify functional differentiations. But no one that I asked seemed to have a definitive answer. They all volunteered interpretations though. "Perhaps," thought one social science faculty member, "it was the Marxists who were sequestered behind the red doors." It is human nature to find a meaning even in the most banal of objects but, again, beside the point.

The point is that in the end the architect *must compose!* And the elements of composition, the building blocks themselves, are abstract. Somebody had to decide on the size of the door, the proportions and the location of the grille, the colors of the door and its frame, the color, size, pattern and pattern placement of the tile, and so on and so on. Since it should be obvious that many colors, patterns and arrangements are possible, the decision ultimately becomes one of composition. Therefore it is the compositional demands, the syntax of architecture, which is perhaps the only true responsibility of the architect. Interpretations should be left to others.

Conclusions

All three recommendations are not meant to suggest a return of architecture to form-making separated from the demands of culture. Quite the contrary. Any cursory study of architecture and culture clearly shows that syntactic elements have meaning and very powerful meanings at that. Any architect who does not understand those meanings would be culturally irresponsible. On the other hand, an obsession with meaning can lead to architectural constipation— that is, the inability to compose anything. Still, architecture cannot be separated from culture any more than ritual can be separated from culture. Rituals are one way that culture is made visible. Architecture is another way.

The psychologist Wolfgang Kohler has pointed out that where a whole form is given first, meaning "creeps into it." That meaning can automatically produce a form where none existed before has, to his experience, never been shown.[26]

If students of both architecture and popular culture are to be grounded in the fundamentals, if they are to fully understand architecture and fully understand culture, then they must not only learn where these two disciplines overlap but they must also learn where they are distinct. For students of architecture that knowledge is about composition; for students of popular culture that knowledge is about meaning.

Notes

[1]Brunes, Tones, *The Secrets of Ancient Geometry—And Its Use*, Vol. I, Rhodos, International Science Publishers, Copenhagen, 1967.

[2]Eco, Umberto, "Function and Sign: Semiotics of Architecture", *VIA 2: Structures Implicit and Explicit*, Graduate School of Fine-Arts, University of Pennsylvania, Philadelphia, 1973, pp. 131-153.

[3]*Ibid*, p. 140.

[4]Staal, Frits, "The Search for Meaning: Mathematics, Music and Ritual", *American Journal of Semiotics*, Vol. 2, No. 4 (1984), pp. 1-57.

[5]*Ibid*, p. 4.

[6]*Ibid*, p. 46.

[7]*Ibid*, p. 46.

[8]Bonta, Juan Pablo, *Architecture and its Interpretation*, Rizzoli, New York, 1979.

[9]*Ibid*, p. 225.

[10]*Ibid*, p. 225.

[11]See *Rituals and Ceremonies in Popular Culture*, edited by Ray B. Browne, Popular Press, Bowling Green, 1980, especially "Rituals in Architecture: The Celebration of Life", pp. 61-80, by Dennis Alan Mann.

[12]Dutton, Thomas A., "Design and Studio Pedagogy", *Journal of Architectural Education*, Vol. 41, No. 1, Fall 1987, p. 16.

[13]Geertz, Clifford, *The Interpretation of Cultures*, Basic Books, 1973.

[14]Charm, Rob., "Passing Fancies", *Autoweek*, Jan. 11, 1988, p. 27, quoting Chester Liebs from his book *Main Street to Miracle Mile*.

[15]Norberg-Schulz, Christian, *Existence, Space and Architecture*, Praeger, New York, 1971; also in the *Concept of Dwelling*, Electra/Rizzoli, New York, 1985.

[16]Herdeg, Klaus, *Formal Structure in Indian Architecture*, a series of Plates from an exhibit sponsored by Cornell University in 1967.

[17]Rybczynski, Witold, *How the Other Half Builds*, Research Paper No. 9, Dec. 1984 from the Centre for Minimum Cost Housing, McGill-University, Montreal.

[18]Op. Cit. Herdeg, p. 18.

[19]Ching, Francis D.K., *Architecture: Form, Space & Order*, Van Nostrand Reinhold Co., New York, 1979.

[20]Ibid, p. 386.

[21]Blaser, Werner (editor), *Drawings of Great Buildings*, Birkhauser Verlag, Basel, 1983.

[22]Stierlin, Henri, *Encyclopedia of World Architecture*, Van Nostrand Reinhold, New York, 1983.

[23]Rowe, Colin. *The Mathematics of the Ideal Villa and Other Essays*, MIT Press, Cambridge, 1976.

[24]*Ibid*, p. 3-4.

[25]Staal, Frits, *Agni: The Vedic Ritual of the Fire Altar*, Vol, I & II, Berkeley, 1983.

[26]Kohler, Wolfgang, *Gestalt Psychology*, 1929; found in Susanne Langer's *Philosophy in a New Key*, Mentor, New York, 1942, p. 64.

On Teaching Law
and
Popular Culture

Anthony Chase

The Deluge

Whose memory will ever be able to separate the Summer of '87 from images of Oliver North and Fawn Hall, Arthur Lyman and Admiral Poindexter? Lawyers for the investigating committee, for witnesses, and for future defendants starred on television and in countless editorial cartoons in the national press. But the sometimes histrionic, if not historically commanding, summer of Washington wackiness was just the tip of the iceberg—like prominence recently achieved by American attorneys. To be sure, lawyers have played a visible role in every important period of American history. But the glacial emergence of law and lawyers as quintessential proscenium and accompanying troupe of actors dominating the theatre of American popular culture seemed, by the middle of the decade, to have reached unprecedented proportion.

Consider other signs and symbols from the repertoire of public art, the movies, for example. A string of films in the mid-1980s drew top Hollywood stars to the camera and huge crowds to the movie houses: *Jagged Edge, Legal Eagles, From the Hip, The Big Easy, Suspect, Nuts,* to name just a few of the pictures featuring lawyers—indeed, often women lawyers. A novel about a lawyer, written by a lawyer [*Presumed Innocent,* Scott Turow] topped the bestseller list for weeks and would soon become, itself, "major motion picture." *L.A. Law* was but one of several prime-time television series that gave focus to lawyers and legal practice. But the saga of a blue-chip Los Angeles private firm was in many ways unique. Not even in the early-1960s series, *The Defenders,* had legal issues been more directly and didactically translated into critical social issues.

Returning to the barely distinguishable world of legal fact, a series of controversial Supreme Court nominations brought what once were regarded as abstract questions of the role of the judiciary in a democracy from the tiered lecture halls of university law schools into the living rooms of millions of Americans via public, then cable, and finally network television news coverage. The "Big Story of the Week" could be a *legal* story fifty-two weeks a year.

Reprinted from *Focus on Law Studies,* Spring 1988, Vol. III, No. 2. Copyright 1988 American Bar Association. Reprinted with permission.

The Conjuncture

In spite of the escalating cultural importance of our being able to come to grips with the meaning of law in our society, and with the public understanding of, and need for, a legal profession, our interpretive institutions seemed overwhelmed by the task. Journalists often seemed to have little technical facility with legal process and rule; the teaching of basic law and legal consumerism had penetrated only a handful of public school districts, or at least not enough of them for us to say that our secondary pupils were receiving the essential information they need. And the law schools continued to focus upon the narrow teaching of doctrine and perpetuation of forms of scholarship which disdained the kind of research done by other university professors, a research which systematically reached out to other academic disciplines and sought to contextualize central subject matter critique. Fortunately, the law and society movement at all levels of education and public policy, as well as the teaching of law in its broadest social context through centers of undergraduate legal education, provided not only bright spots in an otherwise dark and worrisome portrait of legal interpretation, but also a gesture in the direction of a way out, toward solid models for interrogating the relation between law and society, between lawyers and popular culture in the U.S.

The Method

I am not sure that there is a "method" for teaching law and popular culture, or at least not just *one* method for approaching the subject; it is much too soon for that. But I do believe there are several interesting ways of attempting to organize a critique of law and popular culture, of getting a handle on what seems like a great mess, a hopelessly disparate and conflicting ensemble of images, intuitions, sensibilities, prejudices, and dreams. One approach I have tried is to see lawyers and popular culture in terms of a shifting series of opposites in a range of discrete areas of legal and lawyer experience partitioned off from the whole. For example, we might consider the positive and negative images of lawyers in their general relation to categories like virtue, money, power and order, with the potential for situating actual trajectories for each set of shifting relations in historical time and geographical space.

The positive conception of a lawyer's relation to virtue seems best expressed in public art through the characterization of ardent defenders of the isolated individual, with his or her back to the wall. *To Kill a Mockingbird* and *Anatomy of a Murder* are just two wonderful illustrations of this canonization of the attorney unwilling to sell out a difficult client. The opposite notion, within the lawyer/virtue context, is perfectly revealed in *The Fortune Cookie*, where an ambulance-chasing lawyer manufactures phony personal injury cases only to get his fingers burned by rugged American integrity before the check is cashed. There are dramatically contradictory images of lawyers in their relation to money, power, and order which parallel American attitudes toward attorneys and virtue, and which seem to reflect the split image of the law that Americans carry around with them (so well described by historian Willard Hurst, among others).

Another approach is to begin to catalog the conflicting images and perceptions of the legal system within a range of specific cultural forms, with the forms themselves each having their own aesthetic criteria and specific relation to the elaboration of lawyer roles projected over time. Consider as separate these cultural forms within popular art: Fiction and Non-Fiction Television, Advertisements, Soap Operas, Bestselling Novels, Pop Music, Radio and Music TV, Motion Pictures, Comedy, Animation and Comic Books, Public Celebrations and Rituals—the list can certainly be extended.

Some cultural forms seem capable of generating more substantial "critical realism" or depth analysis than others. An advertisement shown during a commercial break in the December 17, 1987, network broadcast of *L.A. Law*, for example, revealed how important it was to a young Hispanic attorney, struggling to prepare a case and burning the midnight oil in the hope of "making partner," that he not only have a (very attractive) "significant other" to tolerate his late hours but, just as valuable in the general scheme of things, have access to wholesome *fast food* (she brings him a feast—a Big Mac and fries!): the cuisine symbolic of an economy racked by underemployment, declining real wages, several-wage earner families, de-skilling of work, and destruction of real jobs. But with the soft pastel lighting of the attorney's workspace and crisp McDonald's serving cartons, the Southern California fast lane momentarily seems uncrowded. Though quite revealing, advertising is not likely to develop the insight possible within, say, the novel. But who would confidently foreclose to pop music or new wave comic books the chance to really understand the legal system and what it means, to become the genuine oracles of tomorrow's mass culture?

Additionally, there are particular categories of focus, of inquiry, which transcend the boundaries of single formats of popular culture. For example, is there such a thing as a "law" or "lawyer" *genre* in American popular culture? What is that form's history in mass entertainment as a whole? What are the constituent elements of the legal genre which may overlap with, yet still differentiate it from, other genre forms and categories? We are speaking here of art and sociology as a single figure of analysis, joined in a special kind of critique. Law and popular culture is a discipline "under construction."

This openness of the discipline—the possibility of every scholar who investigates this area and every teacher who puts together a syllabus or turns out the lights and turns on the projector contributing to the very form and shape of the field—makes law and popular culture a very attractive intellectual work-place. Students not only bring with them the specialized knowledge that they have extracted from undergraduate courses in constitutional history, sociology of law or criminology, or professional courses in legal ethics, specific doctrinal fields like torts and criminal law, or courses in civil rights and liberties, but (as important) years of engagement in the popular culture of their time and their national as well as subcultural communities. Although it takes hard work to bring to the surface the imprint of everyday life on our fundamental conceptions of the world, that work becomes a central form of activity in the law and popular culture classroom. These classrooms are the animated construction sites of law and popular culture research.

International Approaches to Popular Culture: Possibilities, Problems, and an American/ Canadian Example

Bruce C. Daniels

Possibilities

In the years since World War Two, humanist scholars have forsaken grandiose accounts of subjects such as the novel, western civilization, and Christianity. Recent literary critics, historians, and theologians tend to cast their nets much less widely than their predecessors. Case studies of narrowly-defined specific topics have replaced the more general studies of earlier eras. Writers who have the temerity to skip through centuries, disciplines, and comprehensive subjects are often dismissed as amateurs, journalists, sophomores or—worst of all—popularizers.

Those who have created this system of research and scholarship, as well as those who enjoy its benefits or suffer its shortcomings, have a name for it—specialization. At one time a person was an *expert* on history or art; now he or she is a *specialist* in a sub-field of history or art. Finding a general practitioner in the humanities is as hard as finding one in a medical clinic; and finding one in the forefront of research is nearly impossible.

Almost everyone decries the effects of excessive specialization. Among the loudest to complain are those at the center of the problem—the specialists themselves. They complain, and rightly so, that the large picture has disappeared and been replaced by an ever-growing number of microscopic slides. Disciplines are Balkanized into fragments of the whole; fragments shatter into shards; conflicting ideologies and methodologies segregate the shards. In essence, specialization has meant atomization. Some degree of specialization has always existed in all disciplines; but, specialization once meant emphasizing one aspect of a discipline without excluding a substantial knowledge of the other aspects. Today, specialization implies compartmentalization and it tends to promote research techniques and results that are not widely known outside of each particular compartment.

Despite widespread agreement that the present system of specialization creates problems, solutions are elusive. Obviously, specialist studies will continue and they will probably grow even more particularistic. Too many people are generating too much knowledge for generalists to be able to keep abreast of more than a small fraction of all the detail. The answer seems to

198

be not to do away with specialization but to develop other types of scholarship that will integrate specialist studies into larger, more comprehensive units. To some degree, textbooks put Humpty Dumpty back together again as do well-taught survey courses in a university. Interpretive syntheses also do and they are increasing in number.

One very important means of resisting Balkanization is inherent in the very methodology of most specialists. Invariably, good scholars who limit their topic to a small subject, try to squeeze significance from their research that extends far beyond the immediate data. Thus, a sociologist studying the courtship patterns of one-hundred couples in Ohio, might formulate a hypothesis about marriage that could be tested for validity in Florida, Montana or England. A religious scholar examining the creation of thirty new church parishes in Massachusetts might try to identify some underlying social conditions that characterized religious dissent in many disparate societies. As scholars limit their research to a small locale, they often draw conclusions of national, international, or universal applicability. This has been the standard method of the social sciences since their inception. Social scientists have been interested in general laws; humanists have been interested in specific events, individuals, and works of literature. But as the degree of specialization has increased among humanists, so also has the tendency for their research to rely more on hard empirical data and less on subjective evaluations. Quantitative research has become an equal partner with qualitative research in the arts, and humanists are becoming more like social scientists. Thus, at the same time that they are turning more inward through specialization, humanists are looking more outward through their connections to the social sciences. At one time historians and literary scholars tended to study the past and the language of one nation. Today they usually specialize in one small part of that nation's experience but are more likely than they would have been previously to place that small part in an international context. For example, an historian writing about the American Federation of Labor might be more familiar with the work of labor historians in France and England than with the work of American Civil War specialists. Similarly, subjects such as vernacular architecture or myth in literature tie students of art or language into international networks of greater importance to them than a network based on the art or language of one country.

As much as any area of the humanities, the field of popular culture holds rich possibilities for international analyses and comparisons. Prior to the twentieth century, high culture in western civilization tended to have international standards and popular culture tended to have national or even regional ones. Although the ballet and classical music of Russia, France, England and the United States differed, enough features were held in common to enable performers and audiences from each to appreciate and readily understand the work of all four countries. This was much less true for popular culture: vernacular music and dance, sports, rituals, celebrations and so forth differed greatly among nations and were less appreciated and understood by those outside of the nation's borders. Alterations in technology, however, have dramatically changed the locus of popular culture. Far more than high culture, popular culture depends on prevailing modes of technology for its dissemination. High culture is by definition elitist and speaks primarily to a well-educated minority. Lines of communication always existed among the elites of the western world and for them an increase in the efficiency of transporting sights, sounds, and words did not mean a radical change. For vernacular culture, however, the spectacular increase in communications efficiency had an equally spectacular substantive effect. The natural, organic, spontaneous part of vernacular culture continued to be local in orientation and became known primarily as folk culture. But, artists and entrepreneurs who consciously created cultural products in order to meet a market demand, found themselves faced with extraordinary opportunities. Railroads, telegraphs, automobiles, telephones, record players, radios, movies, television, and airplanes increasingly made it a relatively simple matter to market and sell mass entertainment on an international level. Thus, popular culture became distinct from folk culture as the former became an international phenomenon that transcended the nation-state.

At the end of World War Two, the United States vaulted into a position of power in politics and economics greater than that of any other nation in world history. The other super-power, The Soviet Union, challenged American might but did not equal it. No similar power accrued to American high culture nor, of course, did folk cultures around the world become Americanized. But, the United States did achieve a power in popular culture equal to or perhaps greater than its political and economic power. American music—first jazz, then Rock and Roll, and most recently Country; American television shows—"I Love Lucy," "Bonanza," and "Dallas;" American youth dress—blue jeans, sweatshirts, and printed T-shirts; American food and drink—hamburgers, cola, and wine coolers; have become ubiquitous in most parts of the world. Only a few isolated enclaves have resisted this onslaught. In the Soviet Union, teenagers offer tourists large sums of money to buy the jeans they are wearing. A Disneyland amusement park opened recently in Japan. The Indian film industry makes hundreds of movies in Hindi with Indian actors and actresses who are placed in boy-girl scenarios appropriate to American courtship patterns but totally removed from traditional Asian ones. Popular culture has developed far more of an international market than has high culture. Ballet and classical music were restricted primarily to western civilization: they made few inroads in Asia and Africa which maintained their own forms of elite art. The popular culture which originated in the United States probably has had more of an effect on western civilization than on other parts of the world, but, nevertheless, its effects on non-Christian, non-western societies have been profound.

Thus one might hope that scholars specializing in aspects of American popular culture would compare and contrast their conclusions with those of scholars examining similar phenomena in other societies. Alas, this has seldom been the case. Students of popular culture have, by and large, not situated their work in an internationalist milieu and have not embraced the generalist approach of the social sciences. Despite extraordinary and successful efforts by the *Journal of Popular Culture* to be a forum for international study, most of its essays are based on the culture of individual nations. In the last four years (vols. 17-20), it has had in-depth sections on India, New Zealand, Bulgaria, the German Democratic Republic, Latin America and Japan.[1] Yet, essays here or elsewhere seldom make explicit comparisons among nations. This is understandable since an internationalist perspective requires more thought, more reading in secondary sources, and more research; but it is also a pity. Scholars will be able to appreciate more fully the meaning of specific heroes, icons, popular art and rituals in one culture when they analyze explicitly their meaning in other ones. Inasmuch as the manifestations of popular culture intersect with the underlying belief and value structures of society, one would expect that the same artifacts and activities might have differing meaning in differing societies. For example, American youth may wear blue jeans to indicate their distaste for the regimented jacket, tie, business suit, or skirts of their parents. Soviet youth may wear them to defy the social standards desired by the government. And, Asian youth may wear them to show that they are westernized and modern. If the popularity among Americans of westerns on television and in the movies is explained as a function of the recent frontier experience, what explains their popularity in Italy? A macho Mediterranean culture? Why have dozens of European and Asian countries fallen in love with American basketball but only a few with baseball? Asking and answering questions such as these will help students of popular culture separate the particular from the general and will help them identify more precisely the relationships between surface behavior and underlying meaning.

Problems

Some of the gains from an internationalist approach will be hard won. Problems in research and interpretation are many. The greatest difficulty will arise from the need to know some elements of the history, demography, economics, geography and so forth of other countries. Much of this can be gathered from a few general secondary sources but researchers will have to guard against superficial and facile explanations. One will also have to be aware of and sensitive to political concerns and cultural legislation past and present. In the United States, free-market forces determine the creation and distribution of popular culture more than they do in any other major country. Even in the United States, tax regulations, licensing requirements, anti-monopoly laws, and a wide variety of other governmental restrictions affect the flow of cultural goods. The political leaders of most countries, however, intervene more directly in the cultural market through such devices as government-funded television networks, radio stations, and newspapers. Most countries also have defensive legislation that places roadblocks in the path of foreign popular culture, and provides bounties and incentives to promote their own. In some countries, television and radio stations are required by law to provide a certain amount of programming that originates within the country itself.[2] Much of the defensive legislation is passed to lessen American influence and to prevent American values and subtle messages from being bootlegged into the country. All of these regulations, however, mean that the popular culture of any given country is a function to some degree of public policy. Scholars therefore must be aware of these policies or else run the risk of badly misreading the cultural map.

Problems of distribution pose even more serious difficulties. The dimensions of popular culture in the United States are shaped around a social structure that is overwhelmingly middle-class. The great majority of Americans are literate, own radios and televisions, and have access to movies, books, records, and information about rituals, holiday gatherings, and celebrations. The American middle-class is such a large percentage of the population and has such a strong buying power that it is safe to assume that only a few Americans do not have the opportunity to avail themselves of most expressions of local and national popular culture. Such is not the case worldwide: some countries have a relatively small middle-class and a much larger class of poor people who cannot afford the price of international popular culture. Even in those countries with social structures like the United States's, such as England and France, subtle differences in the class structure are reflected in the distribution of popular culture. Moreover, what Americans perceive as elite culture often extends beyond the upper classes and into the broad strata of the middle-class in Europe. In effect, elite culture has a greater market share outside of the United States. Opera, for example, is regarded as elite culture in the United States but is part of the popular culture of Italy. Conversely, in countries such as India with a social structure oriented around rural village life, the folk culture is stronger relative to the popular culture than it is in western societies.

Technological differences among societies also create differences in the system of distribution as do size, population and language. The United States has an efficient communications system that serves over 230 million people spread over a large physical area and, until the recent increase in Hispanic culture, functioned almost entirely in English. Most parts of Asia, Africa, Latin America, and Eastern Europe have a less sophisticated and less electronic system. Western Europe's communications may be as sophisticated as that of the United States, but they are built around a different set of physical and linguistic circumstances. Any comparisons among popular cultures must take account of these differences.

An American/Canadian Example

Both physically and culturally, Canada is the United State's closest neighbor. Many aspects of the popular culture of the two countries are similar to the point of being nearly identical.[3] Yet, differences in the popular culture exist that manifest profound differences in the underlying value structures of the two societies. Consider the following examples in the three most commonly-used categories of analysis: (1) images of artifacts and people; (2) popular rituals or events; and (3) themes in popular arts.[4]

(1) The Beaver of Canada and the Eagle of the United States are the animals most often used to symbolize the two countries. The Beaver projects a cautious, conservative image of an animal that husbands its resources and carefully plans for the future. The Beaver is entrepreneurial rather than imperial. The Eagle, on the other hand, is always described in the patriotic literature as "soaring:"—

a majestic hunter that swoops out of the sky, strikes with deadly force, and then returns to its own nest. Beavers live in colonies; Eagles fly alone. Little imagination is required to see why the Beaver is the appropriate symbol for the tory culture of English Canada and the Eagle is the appropriate symbol for the liberal culture of Revolutionary America.[5] The fur trade was relatively more important in Canadian than in American history but this economic fact can only partially explain the choice of animal symbols. Benjamin Franklin's suggestion of the turkey as a symbol for the United States was certainly grounded in more economic reality than the Eagle; so was the other plausible suggestion, the Codfish. Contrast also the Maple Leaf of Canada with the trees most associated with the United States: the White Pine, the Hickory, the Redwood, and the Giant Sequoia. The Maple Leaf evokes a pastoral image, the American trees an image of martial strength.

The conservatism of Canada and the relative lack of an assertive patriotism can be seen in a variety of ways. Canada has few native-born heroes whose names are reflected on the geographical landscape. Most Canadian towns, villages, and counties named after people celebrate English heroes or administrators in the old colonial system. Nothing in Canada begins to approach the pride in one's past revealed by the thousands of places named after Washington, Jefferson, Jackson, Lincoln, and Roosevelt in the United States. Prime ministers in Canada usually pass quietly into history books without becoming part of a mythical culture of greatness. Presidents, on the other hand, with but a few exceptions, assume a non-partisan heroic mantle as soon as they leave office. The prime minister most revered by Canadians, Sir John A. McDonald, is remembered primarily because he brought the transcontinental railroad to fruition thereby guaranteeing that Canada would be a unified two-ocean country. America's heroes—Washington, Jefferson, Jackson, Lincoln, Wilson, Roosevelt and Kennedy—are not only much more numerous, they are also usually associated with liberal values or military might. None have the conservative, entrepreneurial image of a MacDonald.

(2) Comparisons of many of the popular rituals of the two countries reflect differences in their origins. The United States fought a bloody war to leave the British Empire, Canada left peacefully through negotiation. Independence day in the United States usually brings with it parades of fifers and drummers, mock battles, and tributes to military heroes. Independence day in Canada was known as Dominion Day until recently and is largely devoid of martial trappings. Both countries celebrate Christmas in a similar fashion, but in Canada, Boxing Day on December 26th is also celebrated as a holiday as is the British tradition. In general, one does not find in Canadian holidays the rejection of British tradition that is found in the United States. American Thanksgiving focuses on the Pilgrims and their voyage to the New World to escape English persecution. Canadian Thanksgiving is not tied to any similar incident but is simply a day of thanks and gratitude for the blessings of Canadian life. In both countries, of course, people give thanks by gorging themselves.

The rituals of campus life for young people reflect the socially liberal and socially conservative ethos of the two countries. A cult of the ideal campus life exists in the American mind. Young people go away to college where junior proms and senior balls, fraternity and sorority parties, football and basketball games, homecoming queens and winter carnival kings, provide the staff of a traditional education that is interrupted occasionally by the nuisance of classes and final exams. The reality obviously is quite different than the mythology would suggest. But almost no such culture or mythology of such a culture exists on any Canadian campus. Fraternities in Canada are few and relatively unimportant; ritualistic dances exist on only a few campuses; sports games are lightly attended and most schools have no cheerleaders. Canadian students are much more inclined to commute to classes and attend the university nearest their home instead of going away. Canadian university students do, of course, have beer bashes and indulge in rowdy behavior from time to time, but in general there never has been a "panty raid" atmosphere on Canadian campuses. The underlying reasons for these differences have yet to be explored in depth but, on the surface, American campuses seem to reflect a more self-indulgent attitude toward youth and Canadian ones a more sober attitude of restraint. These differences in the popular culture of student life take place in university systems that often look alike, teach a similar curriculum, and have the same standards of training for faculty.

(3) The popular arts of Canada and the United States also reflect surface similarities and underlying differences. Canada is the most vulnerable of any country in the world to the invasion of American popular art.[6] English culture is protected by an ocean, a sizeable population, and the self-confidence bred by a long and rich tradition; Mexico, France and Germany are protected by language barriers. English Canada, however, has little to throw in the way of American television, romance novels, rock music, and so forth. Neither language nor distance protect a relatively small country struggling to maintain a separate identity from the extraordinary power of the United States's entertainment industry. Yet, amidst all of the American popular art that saturates Canada, one finds persistent strands of Canadian-generated popular art whose formulae and themes contrast meaningfully with American ones. Ironically many of these themes are anti-American and stress the Babbitry of American popular culture. See for example, the award-winning film, "My American Cousin"; one of Canada's best-known novels, Margaret Atwood's *Surfacing*; and the play presently being staged in western Canada, *Bordertown Cafe* which all contrast the civility of Canada with the crassness of the United States. A pastoral formula widely used in Canadian popular art makes the same point implicitly. *Anne of Green Gables*, Canada's most popular and well-known play; "The Beachcombers," the oldest surviving Canadian television situation comedy; and "Why Shoot the Teacher", one of Canada's first internationally distributed films are soft, gentle affirmations of the superiority and charm of life in rural Canada.[7]

The relationship between American and Canadian country music illustrates some differences that are far less meaningful—in fact for the greater part, these differences are contrived. Although American in origin, country music is as popular in Canada as it is in the United States. The broad themes of country music—poverty, marital problems, traditional morality, temptations to sin, and anti-elite bias—are not difficult to apply to the Canadian social structure. The specific American setting of country music and many of its icons, however, cannot be located in Canadian culture. Appalachia, the American South, and Texas provide the locale for many country songs which often feature sharecropping, "Mexican girls," and patriotic expressions of love of the American way of life. None of these, of course, can comfortably be fit into songs that would in any way be regarded as having Canadian content. Instead, the broad American themes are either developed in songs free from any identifying landmarks or are simply fit into places and situations that could be Canadian: the Rocky Mountains, the prairies, mine disasters, the trans-Canada highway and so forth.[8] The resulting hybrid songs are American to the bone but cosmetically made to appear Canadian.

The fact, however, that only slight changes are made in Canada to American country music, suggests that the same underlying cultural forces sustain this popular art in both countries. Probably this is true to an even greater degree for Rock music: few, if any, differences exist between Rock songs written or produced in English Canada and the United States. Yet, as we have seen, in some areas of popular culture such as campus life, the differences between the two countries are sufficient to affect day-to-day living patterns. And, in other instances, such as the selection of national symbols and the celebration of a ritual such as independence day, the differences bespeak a sharp contrast between some of the basic values held by the two countries. Herein lies the beauty and utility of an international and comparative view of popular culture. In the present case it can begin to help sort out which differences between American and Canadian culture are meaningful and which ones are not. This perspective can also begin to help supply some reasons why these differences exist and how they manifest themselves. These sorts of comparisons are the things that all tourists do every time they travel: and no one who travels and makes these comparisons thinks they are not important and revealing. Popular culturists should simply add some precision and sophistication to this tourist type of analysis. The above comparisons made between the United States and Canada are somewhat glib and offered more as an example of the usefulness of the comparative approach than as a solid piece of finished research. International comparisons will have to be specialized and rely on empirical data to be convincing. Yet, the results of the research will appeal to more than narrow specialists and address matters that range beyond the immediate data. When specialists within popular culture dare to pursue their topics and data across international borders, they will often find themselves in possession of material richer by far in interpretive value than anything they may have imagined in their wildest scholarly daydreams.

Notes

[1]"India," *Journal of Popular Culture*, 20 (Fall, 1986), pp. 124-192; "New Zealand Literature and Culture", *JPC*, 19 (Fall, 1985), pp. 63-189; "Bulgarian Popular and Folk Culture," *JPC*, 19 (Summer, 1985), pp. 114-170; "Essays from the German Democratic Republic," *JPC*, 18 (Winter, 1984), pp. 49-184; "Latin American Popular Culture," *JPC* 18 (Summer, 1984), pp. 58-183; "Japanese Popular Culture," *JPC*, 17 (Summer, 1983), pp. 99-164.

[2]For an example see Canada's legislation. In 1968 the Canadian Radio-Television Commission was created and charged with being a watchdog of the Canadian media. Radio Stations (A.M.) must play thirty per cent Canadian material. See *Radio (A.M.) Broadcasting Regulations* (Ottawa: Supply and Services Canada, 1979), pp. 10-11.

[3]All references to Canada in the following pages pertain to English Canada. Obviously, French-Canadian culture is more distinct from the United States's.

[4]I have used the categories described in a widely used introductory text for the study of popular culture, Christopher Geist and Jack Nachbar (eds.), *The Popular Culture Reader* (Bowling Green, Ohio: The Popular Press, 3rd ed., 1983), pp. 6-7.

[5]For the influence of the American Revolution on popular art and literature see Michael Kammen, *The American Revolution and the Historical Imagination* (New York: Alfred Knopf, 1978), Chap. III. For the importance of a revolutionary tradition or its absence in other countries see Richard Morris, *The Emerging Nations and the American Revolution* (New York, Evanston, and London: Harper and Row Pubs., 1970), *passim*.

[6]For a discussion of the problems of creating and maintaining a distinctive Canadian culture see Northrup Frye, *Division on a Ground: Essays on Canadian Culture* (Toronto: Anansi, 1982), *passim*; George Grant, *Lament for a Nation* (Toronto: McClelland and Stewart, 1965), *passim*.

[7]"My American Cousin," (Toronto: Peter O'Brien Independent Pictures, Inc., 1984); Atwood, *Surfacing* (Toronto: McClelland and Stewart, 1972); Kelly Reban, "Bordertown Cafe" (Gas Station Theatre, Winnipeg, 1987); Lucy Maud Montgomery, *Anne of Green Gables* (Toronto: Ryerson Press, 1942); "The Beachcombers" (Toronto: The Canadian Broadcasting Company, 1972-present); "Why Shoot the Teacher" (Edmonton: Fraser Films; Toronto: Lancer Teleproductions, 1976).

This paragraph is based on John C. Lehr, " 'Texas (When I Die):' National Identity and Images of Place in Canadian Country Music," *Canadian Geographer*, XXVII (1983), pp. 361-369.

Popularity:
The *Sine Qua Non* of Popular Culture

Harold E. Hinds, Jr.

Popular culture studies are thriving—and yet they disappoint. The Popular Culture Association's annual conventions thrive on ever larger numbers of participants and ever greater diversity. So many new monographs devoted to some aspect of popular culture appear each year that it has become impossible to delve into them all. And the flagship journal, the *Journal of Popular Culture*, has been joined by a number of other scholarly journals devoted at least partially to examination of the field. Popular culture studies are "in" and increasingly respected.

Why, then, the disappointment? Because there is still no widely accepted, basic definition of "popular culture"; and therefore no focus for theoretical considerations. Ray Browne's early suggestion that definitional inclusiveness is preferable to exclusiveness[1] has been taken so literally that popular culture's umbrella now shelters an extremely disparate group of subjects and borrowed methodologies. Indeed, the development of a general theory or set of theories of popular culture and a methodology or methodological approach unique to it may have become impossible without a sharper focus. In 1972 even Browne noted that early, broad definitions might need to be pared a bit.[2] This essay, after reviewing a number of current, competing definitions of popular culture, will suggest a considerably pared-down definition, which should allow for the development of popular culture theories and methodologies.

A recent (1987) flyer from Cambridge University Press illustrates just how inclusive the term "popular culture" has become. Among the "Recent Books in Modern European and British History" that the Press advertised were the following: (1) *Power in the Blood: Popular Culture and Village Discourse in Early Modern Germany*, by David Warren Sabean, which reveals "peasant life" though the examination of a series of episodes in village life, such as "a peasant's refusal to celebrate church ritual, a prophet who encountered an angel in his vineyard..."; (2) *Lay Theology in the Reformation: Popular Pamphleteers in Southwest Germany, 1521-1525*, by Paul A. Russell, which examines the case made in printed Protestant tracts, a by-product of the invention of movable type, for a lay theology and greater lay piety; (3) *Fascism in Popular Memory: The Cultural Experience of the Turin Working Class*, by Luisa Passerini, which uses the oral recollections of workers to recall the fascist period and their resistance and/or acquiescence to *Il Duce*. Clearly, to Cambridge University Press, the phrase "popular culture" and the adjective "popular" are readily accepted and salable commodities, and can be applied indiscriminately to folk culture, mass culture, and working-class culture.

These three very different cultures are often the subject of popular culture investigations. Raymond Williams noted in 1976, in an etymology of the word "popular," that its most recent connotation is "culture actually made by people for themselves" and is largely synonymous with the term folk culture.[3] And indeed, folk culture has increasingly been incorporated into the academic discipline of popular culture. In reviewing the state of the discipline and the *Journal of Popular Culture* in 1980, Christopher Geist advocated further broadening of the field, and added that whatever broadening had occurred was due in large part to Ray Browne's vigorous solicitation for the *Journal* of In-Depth Sections which broke new ground.[4] Some of these sections devoted to such new turf as Bulgaria[5] have indeed included significant articles clearly labeled "folk" culture. Other areas of expansion which have carved out a more comfortable niche for folk culture within the field include: (1) Alvar Carlson's In-Depth Section on Cultural Geography, a field which devotes considerable attention to the origin and diffusion of folk cultural artifacts and traits; (2) Fred E.H. Schroeder's In-Depth Section on "Popular Culture Before Printing," which focused attention on a largely folk world, a world characterized by traditional oral culture, performer-audience interaction, direct communication, and isolated and self-sufficient small cultural groups.

The discovery by historians of ordinary people has also contributed to a greater incorporation of the folk. In particular the *Annales* school of French historians set out to rewrite pre-nineteenth-century European history from the point of view, not of the literate elite, but of the illiterate, subordinate classes, of the folk.[6] The best summary in English, to date, with an *Annales*-type emphasis, Peter Burke's *Popular Culture in Early Modern Europe*, makes it clear that he considers popular culture to be culture of the non-elite, the folk.[7]

Internationalization of the popular culture field has also, largely through semantic confusion, aided in the incorporation of folk culture studies into popular culture. In the foreign culture with which I am most familiar, Spanish-speaking Latin America, the English-language term "popular culture" is often translated as *"cultura popular,"* which in Spanish literally means folk culture. And as an editor of the annual journal *Studies in Latin American Popular Culture*, I frequently receive submissions from Latinos on some aspect of folk culture, and far less frequently manuscripts on mass culture. Books with *" cultura popular"* in the title almost always treat folk, not mass, culture.

If folk culture has gained increased incorporation into popular culture, the prominent role of mass culture has never been in doubt. Initially, the *Journal of Popular Culture* was largely devoted to popular culture transmitted by the mass media, i.e., mass culture.[8] And Geist found that in the late 1970s mass culture still predominated, especially popular literature, although some other mass media, notably television, were represented.[9] Despite Ray Browne's efforts to plow new ground with In-Depth Sections, both the *Journal* and most works published with the phrase "popular culture" somewhere in their title still are overwhelmingly devoted to mass culture.

Popular culture as working-class culture is not well represented in the *Journal* and owes its development largely to European and Latin American scholars. Basically these scholars argue that the hegemonic sectors who own or control mass culture industries attempt to impose their capitalist world view through media products; and that this mass culture is not true popular culture because it does not reflect the people's culture and values. Rather, popular culture is that which springs directly (unmediated by elite culture) from the people, the working class, or combines this proletarian culture with mass-mediated culture which is creatively subverted by the working class for its own uses. Numerous Third World media scholars and pundits take the former view,[10] and British scholars, being less inclined to see the people as passive consumers of media and culture, have increasingly adopted the latter point of view.[11]

At times one or more, even all, of these types of popular (folk, mass, working-class) culture are combined in popular culture studies. Ray Browne argues for an inclusive approach, excluding only the "narrowly intellectual or creatively elitist."[12] Recently he states in "Popular Culture as the New Humanities" that by popular culture "we generally mean all aspects of the world we inhabit.... It is the everyday world around us...[it] is the voice of the people."[13] Arthur Asa Berger states "As far as I'm concerned, it is everything that is not high or 'unpopular' culture."[14] Marshall Fishwick posits that any " 'intellectual or imaginative work' " that is "not narrowly elitist or aimed at special audiences" constitutes popular culture.[15] Michael Schudson, in two recent surveys of the growth of popular culture studies, defines popular culture as including both mass and folk culture, but excluding elite culture.[16] And finally, in a provocative new study Peter Narváez and Martin Laba argue that there is a folklore-popular culture continuum, and that at times either contains elements of the other; e.g., folk songs can be transmitted via modern media.[17]

What is offered then is a hodgepodge of definitions of popular culture. It may be as broadly defined as everything but elite culture, and as narrowly as a culture created by the mass media. Given this vagueness it is not surprising that popular culture studies have not spawned a unique set of theories and/ or methodologies. In fact, those theories and methodologies which have been associated with the field are derived from other disciplines and are not specific to popular culture studies. The Fall 1975 special issue of the *Journal of Popular Culture* devoted to "Theories and Methodologies in Popular Culture" mentions content analysis, structuralism, formalism, and myth-symbol-image types of analysis, among others. Michael Schudson's recent surveys of new approaches to popular culture offer an extensive listing: for example, studies which stress the role of markets and organizations; Clifford Geertz and Victor Turner's anthropology of performance and the idea that virtually anything is a "text" that can be read; Claude Levi-Strauss' notion that the human mind reorders reality into binary oppositions; Roland Barthes' semiotics; and Janice Radway's focus on the act of reading. Now that the "concept of textuality has been applied to materials not previously regarded as textual at all,"[18] especially commonplace, non-literary objects, what these approaches have in common is that they can be applied to any text, whether elite, folk, popular, working-class, or whatever. For example, Levi-Strauss' binary oppositions can be applied not only to folk totems and myths, but to Shakespeare, or fashions, or horror films. Therefore, while these theories and methodologies have deepened our understanding of culture, they have not helped distinguish popular culture from culture in general.

One definition, however, does offer some promise of providing a basis for the development of theories and methodologies unique to popular culture studies. Gary Fine has observed that the *sine qua non* of popular culture is popularity.[19] This notion is at least partially echoed by others. Jack Nachbar, et al., in *The Popular Culture Reader*, write: "In general...the definition of popular culture as mainstream or mass culture is a useful one.... There is, after all, a logical pattern established by assuming a kind of formula for the study of popular culture in which the more popular a thing is, the more culturally significant it is likely to be."[20] For Leslie Fiedler, popular culture is simply " 'Majority' Culture."[21] Fred Schroeder, in *Outlaw Aesthetics*, observes that the popular arts are subject to competition in the market place and it is the vote of the consumer that makes them popular.[22]

I believe, then, that the definition of popular culture ought to be: those aspects of culture, whether ideological, social, or material, which are widely spread and believed in and/or consumed by significant numbers of people, i.e., those aspects which are popular.[23] Why has this common-sense definition, while agreed to by some, failed to gain acceptance and why does it offer a possibility of spawning a theoretical and methodological base when other definitions have failed this test?

The failure of adoption, I believe, relates to the history and sociology of the popular culture movement. Ray Browne's call for inclusiveness, not exclusiveness, has both nurtured exciting growth and led to a reluctance to do any pruning. Indeed, many, if not most, candidates standing for election to an Executive-level office in the Popular Culture Association have taken a stand for diversity, plurality, and inclusiveness. None, if memory serves, have run on a platform of stepping back and assessing where the movement is headed or have argued for the development of theories and methodologies especially appropriate to popular culture studies.

The membership of the Popular Culture Association and the authors of articles in the *Journal of Popular Culture* are predominantly from the humanities, especially English and history.[24] Popularity, to be demonstrated, demands a willingness to use, at a minimum, crude statistical and quantitative techniques and measures. Unfortunately, most academicians in the humanities are poorly trained in such analytical tools, even hostile to them, and schooled in valuing the uniqueness of each cultural idea and artifact more than in measuring them in quantity. Indeed, when Gary Fine, a sociologist, edited a special issue of the *Journal* devoted to "Sociology," he assured the journal's largely humanities readers that "For this interdisciplinary journal, an attempt was made to refrain from incorporating tables and statistics."[25] And a perusal of the *Journal*'s contents over the years will quickly demonstrate that not only are numbers avoided, but that an overwhelming percentage of articles do not bother to offer any proof of popularity other than a simple assertion; or the implication that since, for example, films are a mass medium, then the film under discussion must be popular. The reader has no idea whether the idea or product under discussion is consumed by 1 or 5 or 50 or 95 percent of a regional, national, or international culture.

If popularity is the key factor in popular culture, it is surprising that the concept has not been systematically analyzed and debated, especially within the *Journal of Popular Culture*.[26] Even if we can agree that to qualify as popular an idea or artifact or product must be accepted or consumed by lots of people, we still must ask, how many is lots? Should the geographical distribution be greater than just one local culture or subculture, or the demographic distribution extend beyond a single narrowly defined socio-economic group? Should the basic geographical unit of measure be the modern nation state or at least a complex society? Discovering a threshold, even an elastic one, for popularity will demand the careful collection of data and examples. But I would argue that popularity at a minimum demands adoption/consumption in more than one regional culture and by more than one narrow socio-economic group.

Popularity demands numerical data. In the first, and even in the second world, such data is often available.[27] It may not be as complete as one would like, or free from errors and inconsistencies of collection or recording. For the most part contemporary data is more complete, more reliable than that for earlier periods. Careful attention to such issues and problems can still produce meaningful statements about an idea's or product's extent of acceptance. If one works in the third or fourth world, or on periods which are largely free of numerical data, then, of course, even qualified statements as to popularity are extremely difficult. In such cases, scholars should at least note that a meaningful statement cannot be made, and state why, despite the absence of statistical data, they believe their subject to merit the label of popular. But above all, whether because of math anxiety or imperfect data, we must not throw the baby out with the bath water. Given the centrality of popularity, it must always be demonstrated, even if imperfectly.

If popularity is the *sine qua non* of popular culture, notwithstanding that very little systematic thought has been given to just what popularity means and entails, why might this central concept spawn theories and methodologies unique to popular culture? First, inclusiveness has not produced the hoped-for theories. Evidently, sweeping so many disparate elements into the popular culture grab bag has made this task well-nigh impossible. And even those approaches which do manage to embrace everything within the broadest of popular culture definitions, can be applied just as well to elite culture, which even the broadest definitions exclude.

Second, those areas in popular culture studies which have been the subject of considerable theoretical development and debate, aesthetics and formula, have not led to the generation of general theories or methodologies of popular culture and/or are seriously flawed. Can there be a philosophy of taste, an aesthetics, of popular culture? John Cawelti, Leslie Fiedler, David Madden, and especially Fred Schroeder, in *Outlaw Aesthetics*, have proposed such an aesthetics. Roger Rollin has countered with a devastating critique, that it is "an impossible mission—to devise an aesthetics of Popular Culture which will incorporate a value-theory." For in popular culture, the only authority on beauty, excellence, or value is the people, those who elect to accept or consume something. "In popular culture, the rule is 'one person-one vote'."[28]

John Cawelti's seminal "The Concept of Formula in the Study of Popular Literature" is perhaps the most important article ever published in the *Journal of Popular Culture* which attempted to provide a basic theoretical perspective on the discipline.[29] Cawelti states that "In general, a literary formula is a structure of narrative or dramatic conventions employed in a great number of individual works."[30] The concept of formula has been extended to incorporate nearly all of popular culture. In the most recent edition of *The Popular Culture Reader*, Christopher Geist and Jack Nachbar write: "Whatever approach you choose to take toward the study of the popular arts and culture...the concept of formula will be an essential part of your study. For in almost all of the popular culture, repetition, imitation and familiarity are key principles of understanding."[31] Regrettably, there is a major flaw in the notion of formula being nearly synonymous with popular culture. The concept is too inclusive. It includes every member of a set (genre, formula), *even* if a member of that set is a failure, that is, even if no one or a mere handful of people consumes it. We have not argued for a given percentage of adoption by the public being equivalent to a significant threshold of popularity, for this will necessitate much research and may well differ for different cultures, for different ideas, products, etc.; but to include failures within popular culture just because they attempt to imitate successful ideas or works in a particular popular genre, as Geist and Nachbar argue, would subvert the notion that popularity is the key concept in popular culture, an idea which Geist and Nachbar accept.[32] It may be worth asserting that failures, rarely the subject of popular culture analysis, should be studied. Such analysis would perhaps give us greater insight into why others in a similar group or genre succeeded.[33]

Third, even though popular culture studies have very rarely used the criteria of popularity carefully and systematically, such an effort can be very productive for theory building. Will Wright's *Sixguns & Society: A Structural Study of the Western* is an excellent example of this. Wright found that including films in his study that the public failed to respond to means that "few clear patterns will emerge;" but if only the films which were box office hits are analyzed, then patterns of narrative and symbolic structure are discernable. Selecting only popular western films for analysis, Wright is able to "develop a cognitive theory of myth structure," which in turn allows "the structure of the Western...[to] be formally analyzed with respect to how its social meanings are communicated by its symbolism."[34] Regrettably, this model study which treats popularity as the *sine qua non* of one type of popular culture has had little impact on other popular culture studies.

Fourth, if popularity is the *sine qua non* of popular culture, then ideas, products, or whatever of similar popularity can be compared, those of different popularity contrasted. How are ideas and items of similar levels of popularity alike? What do they have in common in terms of creation, content, dissemination, and consumption? How do they differ? At what threshold level, if any, does popularity become a distinguishing, dominant factor? How do different economic, industrial, cultural, and social systems correlate with various levels of popularity? Are similar types of products and ideas adopted at comparable levels of popularity in such disparate countries as the US, USSR, and Mexico? In short, by a systematic examination of the essential variable, popularity, we will be able to build a theoretical base and adopt or create appropriate methodologies. By holding popularity relatively constant and discovering patterns, or the lack of them, we should unveil just what is unique about popular culture.

Fifth, by selecting one key variable, popularity, as the essence of our discipline, we can delete older analytic conceptualizations which have mystified, not aided, in discerning the basic elements and characteristics of popular culture. Popular culture commentators have subdivided culture into folk, elite, and mass;[35] or into high, folk, mid, and mass;[36] or high and popular;[37] and so on. Popularity demands that it alone be considered as a criterion, not categories imposed by some extraneous value or social system. Popular culture studies have been unable to deal with the anomaly of "why certain creative texts can and do become popular,"[38] or why the popular becomes elite, or the folk popular. By not prelabeling ideas or products, we avoid forcing the popular into conceptual straight-jackets which may have little to do with popularity. Only that which is demonstrably popular will be categorized, and then only in terms of levels of popularity. Whether elite, folk, or mass in origin, its adoption by a certain level of the population will determine its association with popular culture. Ridding the discipline of categories which have obstructed theory building and methodological creativity should allow for a fresh beginning, one which holds promise of being more fruitful.

Sixth, periodization has been a major problem. Russel Nye, in his classic of 1970, *The Unembarrassed Muse*, argued that

The term 'the popular arts' cannot be used accurately to describe a cultural situation in Western civilization prior to the late eighteenth century. Certainly large numbers of people before that time found pleasant and rewarding ways of cultural diversion, but not until the emergence of mass society in the eighteenth century—that is, until the incorporation of the majority of the population into society—could either popular culture or popular art be said to exist.[39]

This view has been explicitly criticized, although not mentioning Nye by name, in Fred Schroeder's In-Depth Section on "Popular Culture Before Printing" and by Joise Campbell's Section on "Popular Culture in the Middle Ages," both in the *Journal of Popular Culture*.[40] Personally, I remain skeptical of Nye's critics. But the jury is definitely out on the question of just when popular culture began, precisely because, despite provocative essays in the *Journal*, no general test, such as popularity, has been systematically applied.

Lastly, a large number of general assertions have been made over the years about popular culture which are based only on an episodic examination of data which may or may not be relevant. If they were critically examined by a uniform across-the-board test, popularity, those which survived might well provide fundamental building blocks for popular culture theories and methodologies. Examples of such assertions are far too numerous to be listed, but a few selected examples will be given.

(1) Wilma Clark: "popular art *protects* the audience from what may be a painful exploration of the nature of reality."[41]

(2) Russel Nye: "popular culture is the most visible level of culture."[42]

(3) Tom Kando: popular culture is "the study of everyday life."[43]

(4) Fred Schroeder: "Popular works are not self-sustaining, because their meanings are thinly layered and tied to the moment."[44]

(5) Peter Prescott: "the novels most widely read tend to be innocent of just those qualities that make novels worth reading."[45]

(6) Jack Nachbar, et al.: "the more popular a thing is, the more culturally significant it is likely to be."[46]

This essay has argued that popularity is the *sine qua non* of popular culture, and that cultural elements which cannot demonstrate a sufficient level of popularity should be excluded from popular culture. It is acknowledged that the central concept of popularity needs to be further examined and refined, and that a threshold level for popularity may well differ in different societies and time periods. Indeed, developing a sufficiently sophisticated analytic tool will test traditional humanists. This effort should provide the field with a better theoretical and methodological grounding, something that has eluded popular culture studies to date.

Notes

[1]Ray B. Browne, "Popular Culture: Notes Toward a Definition," in *Popular Culture and Curricula*, eds. Ray B. Browne and Ronald J. Ambrosetti, rev. ed. (Bowling Green, Ohio: Bowling Green University Popular Press, 1972), pp. 1-12. The first edition, which also contained Browne's essay, appeared in 1970.

[2]Ibid.

[3]Raymond Williams, *Keywords: A Vocabulary of Culture and Society* (New York: Oxford University Press, 1976), p. 199.

[4]Christopher D. Geist, "Popular Culture, the *Journal* and the State of the Study: A Sequel," *Journal of Popular Culture*, Vol. 13, No. 3 (Spring 1980), pp. 391-393.

[5]*Journal of Popular Culture*, Vol. 19, No. 1 (Summer 1985).

[6]Chandra Mukerji and Michael Schudson, "Popular Culture," *Annual Review of Sociology*, Vol. 12 (1986), pp. 51-53.

[7]Peter Burke, *Popular Culture in Early Modern Europe* (London: Maurice Temple Smith Ltd., 1978).

[8]Norman L. Friedman, "Mass Communications and Popular Culture: Convergent Fields in the Study of Mass Media" *Mass Comm Review*, Vol. 4, No. 1 (Winter 1976-1977), p. 22.

[9]Geist, pp. 391, 400.

[10]For example, see Guillermo Bonfil Batalla, et al., *Culturas populares y política cultural* (México: Museo de Culturas Populares, SEP, 1982); Herbert Schiller, et al., *Foro internacional de comunicación social* (México: El Día, 1982); and Ludovico Silva, et al., *Medios de comunicación, ideología y estrategia imperialista*, Cuadernos del Centro de Estudios de la Comunicación, 5 (México: UNAM, 1979); Luís Ramiro Beltrán and Elizabeth Fox de Cardona, *Comunicación dominada: Estados Unidos en los medios de América Latina* (México: Editorial Nueva Imagen, 1980).

[11]John Fiske, "Television and Popular Culture: Reflections on British and Australian Critical Practice," paper presented at the Iowa Symposium and Conference on Television Criticism, The University of Iowa, April 1985. Fiske ably reviews recent research by students of British television and its audience.

[12]Browne, "Popular Culture: Notes Toward a Definition," p. 11.

[13]Ray B. Browne, "Popular Culture as the New Humanities," *Journal of Popular Culture*, Vol. 17, No. 4 (Spring 1984), p. 1.

[14]Arthur Asa Berger, "The Poop on Pop Pedagogy," in Browne and Ambrosetti, eds., p. 75.

[15]Russel B. Nye, "Notes on Popular Culture," quotes Fishwick. See excerpts from Nye's key essay in George H. Lewis, *Side-Saddle on the Golden Calf: Social Structure and Popular Culture in America* (Pacific Palisades, California: Goodyear Publishing Co., Inc., 1972), p. 18. See also Marshall W. Fishwick, *Seven Pillars of Popular Culture* (Westport, Connecticut: Greenwood Press, 1985).

[16]Michael Schudson, "The Validation of Popular Culture: Sense and Sentimentality in Academia," *Critical Studies in Mass Communication*, Vol. 4 (1987), pp. 51-52; and Mukerji and Schudson.

[17]Peter Narváez and Martin Laba, *Media Sense: The Folklore-Popular Culture Continuum* (Bowling Green, Ohio: Bowling Green State University Popular Press, n.d.).

[18]Schudson, p. 56.

[19]Gary Alan Fine, "Popular Culture and Social Interaction: Production, Consumption, and Usage," *Journal of Popular Culture*, Vol. 11, No. 2 (Fall 1977), p. 453.

[20]Jack Nachbar, Deborah Weiser, and John L. Wright, eds., *The Popular Culture Reader* (Bowling Green, Ohio: Bowling Green University Popular Press, 1978), p. 5.

[21]Leslie Fiedler, "Giving the Devil His Due," *Journal of Popular Culture*, Vol. 12, No. 2 (Fall 1979), p. 197.

[22]Fred E. H. Schroeder, *Outlaw Aesthetics: Arts and the Public Mind* (Bowling Green, Ohio: Bowling Green University Popular Press, 1977), pp. 8, 13-14.

[23]A somewhat similar definition is used by the editors of *Studies in Latin American Popular Culture*. See "Editors' Letter to Future Contributors," contained in each volume's front matter.

[24]Friedman, p. 22; Geist, pp. 390-391, 395, 398-399.

[25]Gary Alan Fine, "POPULAR...CULTURE: Sociological Issues and Explorations" *Journal of Popular Culture*, Vol. 11, No. 2 (Fall 1977), p. 382.

[26]Promising beginnings are found in Richard A. Peterson, "Where the Two Cultures Meet: Popular Culture," *Journal of Popular Culture*, Vol. 11, No. 2 (Fall 1977), pp. 388-390; Peter Nagourney, "Elite, Popular and Mass Literature: What People Really Read," *Journal of Popular Culture*, Vol. 16, No. 1 (Summer 1982), pp. 99-107.

[27]For a partial listing of data sources, see the "Appendix" to David Byron McMillen and Marilyn M. McMillen, "The Analysis of Popular Culture Through Social Indicators," *Journal of Popular Culture*, Vol. 11, No. 2 (Fall 1977), pp. 506-526.

[28]Roger B. Rollin, "Against Evaluation: The Role of the Critic of Popular Culture," *Journal of Popular Culture*, Vol. 9, No. 2 (Fall 1975), pp. 355-365; and Roger B. Rollin, "Son of 'Against Evaluation': A Reply to John Shelton Lawrence," *Journal of Popular Culture*, Vol. 12, No. 1 (Summer 1978), pp. 113-117.

[29]Cawelti's article appeared in Vol. 3, No. 3 (Winter 1969) issue, pp. 381-390. See also his *Adventure, Mystery, and Romance: Formula Stories as Art and Popular Culture* (Chicago: The University of Chicago Press, 1976).

[30]Cawelti, *Adventure, Mystery, and Romance*, p. 5.

[31]Christopher D. Geist and Jack Nachbar, eds., *The Popular Culture Reader*, 3rd ed. (Bowling Green, Ohio: Bowling Green University Popular Press, 1983), p. 304.

[32]Ibid, p. 4. For another critique of the concept of formula, see David N. Feldman, "Formalism and Popular Culture,"*Journal of Popular Culture*, Vol. 9, No. 2 (Fall 1975), pp. 384-402.

[33]For two recent studies of failures, see Steven Bach, *Final Cut: Dreams and Disaster in the Making of "Heaven's Gate"* (New York: New American Library, 1987); Christopher M. Byron, *The Fanciest Dive* (New York: New American Library, 1987).

[34]Will Wright, *Six Guns and Society: A Structural Study of the Western* (Berkeley: University of California Press, 1977), pp. 12-13, 15.

[35]Browne in Browne and Ambrosetti, eds., p. 10.

[36]Dwight MacDonald, *Against the Grain: Essays on the Effects of Mass Culture* (New York: DaCapo Press, Inc., 1983), pp. 3-78.

[37]Herbert J. Gans, *Popular Culture and High Culture: An Analysis and Evaluation of Taste* (New York: Basic Books, Inc., Harper Colophon Books, 1975), p. 14.

[38]See Janice Radway, "Phenomenology, Linguistics, and Popular Literature," *Journal of Popular Culture*, Vol. 12, No. 1 (Summer 1978), p. 98, n.20.

[39]Russel Nye, *The Unembarrassed Muse: The Popular Arts in America* (New York: The Dial Press, 1970), p. 1.

[40]These In-Depth Sections of the *Journal of Popular Culture* are found in Vol. 11, No. 3 (Winter 1977), pp. 627-753; and Vol. 14, No. 1 (Summer 1980), pp. 33-154.

[41]Wilma Clark, "Four Popular Poets: A Century of Taste," in *New Dimensions in Popular Culture*, ed. Russel B. Nye (Bowling Green, Ohio: Bowling Green University Popular Press, 1972), p. 209.

[42]Nye in Lewis, ed., p. 19.

[43]Tom Kundo, "Popular Culture and Its Sociology: Two Controversies," *Journal of Popular Culture*, Vol. 9, No. 2 (Fall 1975), p. 440. See also flyer for 1988 PCA national meeting, where popular culture is "the culture most people enjoy...and all...phenomena of everyday life."

[44]Schroeder, *Outlaw Aesthetics*, p. 40.

[45]Peter S. Prescott, "The Making of a Best Seller," *Newsweek* (May 25, 1961), p. 77.

[46]Nachbar, Weiser, and Wright, eds., p. 5.

Contributors

Ray B. Browne is editor of the *Journal of Popular Culture*, the *Journal of American Culture*, the Chair of the Department of Popular Culture at Bowling Green State University and author and editor of more than three dozen books on various aspects of popular culture.

Anthony Chase is Professor of Law at Nova Law Center, Ft. Lauderdale, FL.

James Combs is Professor of Political Science, Valparaiso University. He is author, among other things, of *Polpop: Politics and Popular Culture in America.* (Popular Press, 1984).

Bruce C. Daniels is a Professor of History, University of Winnipeg, Manitoba, Canada.

George N. Dove is author of, among other things, *The Boys from Grover Avenue: Ed McBain's 87th Precinct Novels* (Popular Press, 1985) and *The Police Procedural* (Popular Press, 1982). He is a retired Dean.

Gary Edgerton is Associate Professor and Chairperson of the Communication Department at Goucher College. He is also an Associate Editor of *The Journal of Popular Film and Television.*

Marshall W. Fishwick, Professor in the Department of Theater and Communications, VA TECH University, is author and editor of some three dozen books, including *The God-Pumpers: Religion in the Electronic Age* (Popular Press, 1987) and *Springlore in Virginia* (Popular Press, 1985).

Linda Fuller is on the faculty of Mass Communication, Worcester College.

Beverly Gordon, is on the faculty of the School of Family Resources and Consumer Sciences, University of Wisconsin-Madison.

Theodore Groat is Professor of Sociology, Bowling Green State University, and the author of numerous studies in Sociology and allied fields.

Harold E. Hinds, Jr. is co-editor of *Studies in Latin American Popular Culture*, and is Professor in the Division of the Social Sciences, Univ. of Minn., Morris.

Peter Homans teaches the psychology and sociology of religion in the Divinity School, and social science in the College, at the University of Chicago. He is also a member of the Committee on the History of Culture there. His books and articles have centered upon the history and theory of psychoanalysis, and theories of contemporary culture, social change and religious traditions.

Carlton Jackson is the author of several books, among which are *Hounds of the Road: A History of the Greyhound Bus* (Popular Press, 1986), and *The Dreadful Month* (Popular Press, 1982). He is Professor of History, Western Kentucky University.

George H. Lewis, author of numerous studies in sociology and popular culture, is Professor of Sociology, University of the Pacific.

Paul Loukides is a member of the English Department, Albion College.

Dennis Alan Mann is Professor of Architecture, University of Cincinnati.

Arthur Neal is Distinguished Professor of Sociology, Bowling Green State University, and author of numerous books and articles.

Diane Raymond is Professor of Philosophy, Simmons College.

Michael R. Real is Chair of the Department of Telecommunications and Film, San Diego State University. He is author of several books on popular culture.

David Shumway is a member of the English Department, Carnegie-Mellon University.